Human Rights and the
Negotiation of American Power

PENNSYLVANIA STUDIES IN HUMAN RIGHTS

Bert B. Lockwood, Jr., Series Editor

A complete list of books in the series is available from the publisher.

Human Rights and the Negotiation of American Power

Glenn Mitoma

PENN

UNIVERSITY OF PENNSYLVANIA PRESS

PHILADELPHIA

Published by
University of Pennsylvania Press
Philadelphia, Pennsylvania 19104-4112
www.upenn.edu/pennpress

Printed in the United States of America on acid-free paper
10 9 8 7 6 5 4 3 2 1

Library of Congress Cataloging-in-Publication Data
Mitoma, Glenn Tatsuya.
  Human Rights and the negotiation of American power / Glenn Mitoma. — 1st ed.
    p.   cm. — (Pennsylvania studies in human rights)
  Includes bibliographical references and index.
  ISBN 978-0-8122-4506-6 (hardcover : alk. paper)
  1. Human rights—History—20th century. 2. United Nations. General Assembly.
Universal Declaration of Human Rights. 3. Hegemony—United States. 4. United
States—Foreign relations—20th century. I. Title. II. Series.
JC571.M585   2013
341.4'8—dc23   2012038312

For Mia Angela

Contents

Human Rights and the
Negotiation of American Power

Introduction: Human Rights Hegemony in the American Century

> America resembles a huge giant who is just beginning to wake up to the
> fact that he is not alone nor can be left alone in the world, that he must try
> to get along with others who have been there all the time and who in fact
> are now pressing on him, and that in this necessary and sudden association
> something, perhaps something big, is expected of him. He is just beginning
> to rub his eyes and wake up to these expectations. In the daze of the
> moment, he half believes what his eyes are just beginning to see, half wishes
> it were not true, half hopes things will work out that all will go back to
> normal, namely to a state of affairs where he is again left alone, without
> bother, without headache, without responsibility, without danger. . . . The
> foot is not sure, the heart is not whole: the giant is still in the process of
> awakening.
>
> —Charles H. Malik, "A Foreigner Looks at the United States" (1951)

Shortly before noon on March 15, 2006, the United Nations General Assembly voted by the overwhelming margin of 170 to 4 to dissolve the storied Commission on Human Rights, once one of the UN's most prominent and prestigious bodies. The move concluded a long fall from grace for the commission, which, over the past several years had been accused by governments and leading human rights nongovernmental organizations (NGOs) of both coddling repressive regimes and repeatedly singling out one state, Israel, for hyperbolic condemnation.[1] Deemed irreparably compromised in a March 2005 report by the office of secretary-general Kofi Annan,[2] the commission was to be scrapped and replaced by a new Human Rights Council that intended, according to the adopted resolution, to both promote "universal respect for all human rights and fundamental freedoms" and, going beyond the old commission mandate, "address situations of violations of human rights." It was, said General Assembly president Jan Eliasson, "a fresh start for human rights," and perhaps even for the UN itself.[3]

But among the four nations that voted against the formation of the council was the United States of America. Joined by perennial UN pariah Israel and the less than inspiring coalition of former U.S. territories Palau and the Marshall Islands, the United States had argued that the rules governing election to the new council were not stringent enough to prevent gross abusers of human rights—Sudan, Cuba, Iran, Zimbabwe, Belarus, and Burma were all cited—from gaining seats on the council. Warning that the proposed replacement for the Human Rights Commission would likely be no better than its predecessor, U.S. ambassador John Bolton took the high road, proclaiming that the long and exemplary tradition of American support for universal human rights made it impossible to compromise on an issue of such moral import. "The United States," he said, "has been one of the strongest proponents for . . . meaningful engagement on human rights issues." A council that was "a compromise and merely the best that we could do" was unacceptable to a nation that had for decades been "at the forefront of human rights and democracy promotion, both in our own nation and around the world."

The rest of the General Assembly were not impressed with Bolton's rationale, but the ambassador was correct that the U.S. position on the formation of the Human Rights Council was in keeping with American tradition—just not the way the famously anti-UN neoconservative suggested. Indeed the refusal by the Bush administration to endorse or even take part in the new Council extended the complex and contradictory relationship, first established in the early 1940s, between the United States and international human rights. This relationship, sardonically described as "exceptional" by Michael Ignatieff, is characterized by a central paradox: while American global leadership was the essential condition for the ascendancy of human rights as an international discourse, American policy has consistently both restrained broader interpretations of human rights and held international enforcement mechanisms at arm's length.[4]

This paradox is often dismissed as simple hypocrisy, evidence of the cynical nature of U.S. foreign policy—that it has a double, or even triple, standard on human rights because, well, it can. Speaking in 2001 as part of Oxford University's Amnesty Lectures series, Tzvetan Todorov lamented the U.S. refusal to intervene in human rights abuses in states like Israel or Turkey. "Human rights abuses will be prevented [by the U.S.], but only in countries with which [it is] not allied. . . . The lesson is," concluded Todorov, "that you do well to side with the mighty."[5] Others have offered a more nuanced explanation. Andrew Moravcsik argues that the ambivalent U.S. position on human rights is rooted in a domestic political calculus that favors a conservative commitment to absolute national sovereignty.[6] Whatever its good intentions abroad, the American political establishment is structurally predisposed to protecting its national prerogatives. Simple or complex, these explanations emphasize the problem international human rights presents to U.S. policy makers and the extent to which U.S. policy was designed to mitigate that problem. Missing is an account of how this problem emerged in the first place, and why twelve successive U.S. administrations have felt compelled to declare not just their allegiance to, but their leadership of the struggle for, human rights worldwide. Indeed, more puzzling than why the United States fails to live up to its rhetoric on human rights is why it engages in that rhetoric at all.

What follows suggests that part of the answer to this question lies in the period during and immediately after the Second World War, wherein both the current (if precarious) U.S. global predominance and the ongoing "Age of Rights" find their origins. This coincidence is no mere accident, and understanding the link between the rise of the United States as the most important world power and the emergence of human rights as the most compelling discourse of global morality requires an appreciation of the U.S. role in the formation of the UN human rights system. Franklin Roosevelt is routinely credited with propelling human rights to the forefront of American foreign policy, but his "Four Freedoms" speech was less important for the future of U.S. human rights policy than was the work done by a small, long forgotten NGO, the Commission to Study the Organization of Peace (CSOP). Led by a core group of cosmopolitan internationalists dedicated to the rational organization of international society, the CSOP incubated a postwar plan that included the international protection of human rights, an idea that was adopted by the U.S. government in the interests of securing both national and global public support for the Allied cause. Once enshrined as an official Allied war aim, human rights became part of an international conversation in which the American government ambivalently engaged, but which ultimately resulted in a prominent place for human rights in the 1945 UN Charter.

The growing importance of the United States and the emergence of human rights as an organizing principle of the Second World War opened up a space for a new kind of transnational politics aimed at cultivating and channeling U.S. influence in the world. Two of its earliest and most sophisticated practitioners were Charles H. Malik of Lebanon and Carlos P. Romulo of the Philippines. Both participated in founding the United Nations Organization in 1945, served as charter members of the Commission on Human Rights, and worked for an expansive, explicit, and enforceable international human rights regime. Each man pursued his human rights work as a conscious effort to spread American influence around the globe. At the same time, however, their understandings of how that influence should be manifest were often at odds with the policies pursued by American officials. Romulo insisted that U.S. human rights traditions were essentially anticolonial and included balancing rights and responsibilities. Malik continuously called on the United States to shoulder its responsibility in the field of human rights, framing the stakes in terms of the irreducible worth of the human person and, as the Cold War heated up, the survival of Western civilization. Each made essential contributions to the development of the UN human rights program, and examining this history from their perspectives reveals the way in which international human rights became one of the fields in which post-war American power was contested and negotiated.

Both Romulo and Malik were ultimately frustrated in their efforts to secure American support for international human rights laws, in large part because the U.S. government became increasingly obsessed with containment. Certainly, the precipitous collapse of the Grand Alliance into the Cold War meant that the ideals of human rights would find little place in the new realist orthodoxy. And yet, it was not a foregone conclusion that human rights would be sacrificed rather than enlisted, and the brief U.S.-led crusade to hold the governments of Hungary, Rumania, and Bulgaria accountable for violating the rights of their citizens demonstrated the potential use of human rights as an ideological weapon. But for American officials, containment applied not only to the Soviet Union but to human rights as well, and as with the wartime origins of the U.S. human rights commitment (such as it was), postwar U.S. human rights policies were driven largely by the efforts of domestic civil society organizations. On the one side, U.S. officials began to craft their positions in order to contain a push by the National Association for the Advancement of Colored People (NAACP) to petition the UN in protest of U.S. violations of African American human rights. On the other side, policy makers found themselves accommodating rising criticism from the American Bar Association (ABA) that the UN human rights program was contaminating American legal and political institutions with foreign values and practices—accommodations that eventually resulted in U.S. abandonment of the International Bill of Rights. In both cases, the impulse was to contain and quarantine the emerging international human rights system to ensure it had no domestic effects.

Among the conclusions to be drawn from this history is that despite recent revisionist claims that the founding of the UN and the drafting of the Universal Declaration of Human Rights are stories of a "catastrophic failure" to inaugurate a new era of universal human rights,[7] in fact, the work done in the 1940s laid the critical foundation on which the later renaissance of human rights could be built. In his important book, *The Last Utopia: Human Rights in History*, Samuel Moyn argues that the mid-1970s, rather than the 1940s, was the critical moment in modern human rights history. Only with the failure of more totalizing ideologies—most significantly communism and Third World nationalism—to deliver on the promise of global liberation did human rights inspire a true social and political movement. Even then, Moyn insists, the human rights movement was not centered in the UN, and was less concerned with international law than with more modest political projects led by NGOs that did not aspire to statehood, such as Amnesty International's campaigns on behalf of individual political prisoners.[8] Moyn positions his work as a corrective to the "church history" that imagines the history of human rights as a story of a linear "rise and rise" of morality over power from 1945 to the present,[9] and while there's little doubt that some degree of revisionism is needed, dismissing the 1940s as an irrelevant failure is to toss the baby out with the bathwater. The period surrounding the Second World War remains vitally important to the history of human rights not because it marked the triumph of right over might, nor because that generation of leaders were prophets of a world to come, but because it provides insight into the nature of the U.S. relationship to international human rights, establishes the essential connection between human rights and civil society, and suggests a more complicated intellectual history for the UN human rights program than previously assumed.

Human Rights and American International Life

Variously characterized as ambivalent, paradoxical, ambiguous, reluctant, and hypocritical, the American attitude toward international human rights has long fascinated scholars and frustrated activists. Both Oxford University's

Rothermere American Institute and Harvard's Carr Center for Human Rights Policy have invited academics from around the globe to discuss this troubled and troubling relationship, with results that reflect many of the trends in scholarship over the past thirty years. At these gatherings as well as in the literature, the most prominent contributions have come from political scientists and legal scholars, who have in the main sought explanations in domestic political culture and legal institutions or in the machinations of realist international diplomacy. Whether the issue is capital punishment or the International Criminal Court, much of this work is critical of U.S. human rights policy, and while it is hardly among the worst offenders, the preponderance of power the United States enjoys makes its abuses and failures particularly lamentable.[10]

Michael Ignatieff, former director of the Carr Center and keynote speaker at the Rothermere conference, has summarized these trends with typical concision. In the introduction to his edited volume, *American Exceptionalism and Human Rights*, Ignatieff describes the three dimensions of this exceptionalism as (1) exempting itself from the provisions of human rights treaties, (2) excusing its allies' abuses while highlighting and condemning those of its enemies, and (3) insulating its domestic legal institutions and practices from contamination by international human rights norms. By way of explaining this behavior, Ignatieff and his contributors explore a number of possibilities, including "realism" (the U.S. doesn't play by the rules because it doesn't have to), "culture" (the U.S. mission in the world is to spread enlightenment, not to be enlightened), and "institutions" (the federal structure of the U.S. government and the "advise and consent" powers of the Senate effectively tie the hands of the executive on treaty law).[11] Ignatieff, political scientist cum politician, concludes, however, that the best explanation lies in the domestic political dynamic: "American commitment to international human rights has always depended on the political fortunes of a liberal political constituency," writes the would-be leader of Canada's Liberal Party, "and as these fortunes have waxed and waned, so has American policy toward international law."[12]

Although most often articulated by legal scholars or political scientists, virtually all discussions of the "paradox" of the American relationship with rights rely on claims about the historical role the United States has played in supporting the development of international human rights standards. And while a few valuable studies have appeared describing the origins and nature of a specifically American culture of rights in the eighteenth century,[13] the consensus among scholars appears to be that the high-water mark for U.S.

leadership in the field of human rights occurred during and immediately following the Second World War, and culminated with the drafting and adoption of the Universal Declaration of Human Rights (UDHR) by the United Nations. Ignatieff is typical then when he notes in his second paragraph that "thanks to Eleanor and Franklin Roosevelt, the United States took a leading role in the creation and drafting of the United Nations and the drafting of the Universal Declaration of Human Rights in 1948," and nearly all contributors to his volume genuflect before the alter of the Roosevelts.[14]

But if the "political fortunes" of American liberalism have never been higher than they were under Roosevelt and Truman, the histories of that period reveal a surprisingly high degree of ambivalence from policy makers about human rights. Even in her rather Whiggish account of Eleanor Roosevelt's leadership in the drafting of the Universal Declaration, Harvard University jurist Mary Ann Glendon concedes that Roosevelt was hardly the most enthusiastic member of the UNCHR when it came to creating a robust and effective international human rights system.[15] Elizabeth Borgwardt situates Eleanor Roosevelt's efforts in the context of the broader Roosevelt legacy of the New Deal, linking the postwar international institutions of the UN, the International Monetary Fund, and the World Bank as expressions of "America's vision for human rights." Even so, it was a vision often advanced half-heartedly, at least as it was pursued by the U.S. government. Borgwardt sums up the American predicament with a quote from Roosevelt speechwriter Robert Sherwood: "When you state a moral principle, you are stuck with it, no matter how many fingers you have kept crossed at the moment."[16] Whether in Eleanor's stewardship of the Commission on Human Rights or Franklin's New Deal for the world, the Roosevelts' human rights sainthood relies on the hagiographic effect of distance and comparison to even more tentative administrations.

Rowland Brucken's history of the rise and fall of the "uncertain crusade" of American policy makers makes clear some of the sources of the ambivalence of the Roosevelt, Truman, and Eisenhower administrations. Brucken has closely examined the internal foreign policy debates and concludes that the progressive cosmopolitanism of the U.S. State Department was contained by American public opinion, at least as it was represented by the ABA.[17] As Brucken's study demonstrates, ABA pressure undoubtedly led to diminished U.S. engagement with the UN human rights program—but the enthusiasm for human rights within the State Department is easy to overstate. Even before the ABA began their campaign against international human rights, the

U.S. government began pushing for a weaker system in response to initiatives by another organization that sought more rather than less U.S. accountability under international law. Carol Anderson's history of the NAACP pursuit of redress for racial injustice by invoking international human rights is a damning indictment of U.S. claims to leadership in this field. "Although the United States was willing to use the rhetoric of human rights to bludgeon the Soviet Union and play the politics of moral outrage that the Holocaust engendered," Anderson heretically offers, "the federal government, even the liberals, steadfastly refused to make human rights a viable force in the United States or in international practice."[18] Anderson, and to a lesser extent Brucken, make plain that U.S. leadership on human rights was as much about ensuring an anemic international system as it was about crusading for a new postwar order.

This book approaches the paradox of reluctant American leadership as a function of both the determinative role of American NGOs, including the CSOP, NAACP, and ABA, as well as the revealing work of the two prominent non-American diplomats Malik and Romulo. Decentering the American government reveals the extent to which the UN human rights regime was the result of a simultaneously collaborative and contentious effort on the part of a variety of actors, most of whom were not named Roosevelt. The mantle of leadership was pressed upon rather than willingly embraced by the American government, and if U.S. representatives were often ambivalent about this role, it was because the stakes of these debates were the scope and nature not only of international human rights law, but also of American global leadership itself. This struggle over the meaning of America, far from being constrained by the political boundaries of the United States, spilled out across both the Atlantic and the Pacific oceans as the world attempted to come to terms with the new American ascendancy.[19]

Human Rights and NGOs

The pivotal role played by the CSOP, NAACP, and ABA in shaping U.S. human rights policy points to another reason why the 1940s remains a critical period for understanding the modern history of human rights. Within the scholarship of human rights, the role of NGOs has hardly been overlooked. With a few exceptions, most studies of human rights NGOs focus on the period beginning in the mid-1970s, when organizations like Amnesty International and Geneva Watch (later Human Rights Watch) gained widespread notoriety.[20] Without doubt, the last four decades have witnessed a blossoming of human rights NGOs at all levels, but this rich harvest needs to be understood in the context of the seeds sown during the Second World War. Over the course of the late 1940s and early 1950s, the potency of civil society was clearly demonstrated as the NAACP and the ABA—working from different directions and with opposing intensions to be sure—forced changes in the specific provisions of the International Bill of Rights and a diminished American engagement with human rights generally. But even before these interventions, the CSOP turned the slogan of human rights into an instrumental reality. From the outbreak of war in Europe in 1939 through the San Francisco conference in 1945, no group did more to ensure that human rights were a core value of both the Allies' war objectives and any postwar international organization. By lobbying the U.S. government and by cultivating public support, the CSOP placed human rights on the international agenda, pioneering the central role NGOs have played in the postwar development of international human rights. [21]

The importance of the "consultant group" of representatives from American civil society organizations at the UN founding conference has been more widely appreciated than the early efforts of the CSOP.[22] Samuel Moyn is dismissive of the human rights provisions written into the UN Charter at the behest of this consultant group, calling them purely "symbolic," but this assessment fails to grasp how both the provisions and the process by which they ended up in the charter represented important innovations in international politics—innovations that enabled the future human rights politics he is so keen to highlight.[23] True enough, these provisions were crafted and ultimately endorsed by the U.S. government as a public relations gesture, intended to solidify broad domestic and international support for the new United Nations. But as the influential work of Jürgen Habermas has long contended, the principle of "publicity" and the discursive politics of the "public sphere" are not merely epiphenomena created as either propaganda or a mask for the "real" political power wielded by states.[24] The process of public deliberation, negotiation, and consensus formation—which the CSOP deliberately tried to introduce into international politics through the medium of human rights—constituted a real and important (if hardly dominant or especially effective) component of the UN system.

The history described in this book locates the origins of the UN commitment to human rights in the research, lobbying, and education efforts of the CSOP. This organization exemplified the commitment among a broad swath of U.S. NGOs to pursuing the norms of publicity at the international level. By combining public pressure with private advice, the CSOP articulated human rights into the core of the postwar global ethos in ways that fostered—both intentionally and unintentionally—the emergence of a more global civil society. The principles of universal human rights—which the NAACP sought to exploit and the ABA sought to resist—drew individuals into an unprecedented relationship with international institutions, such as the UN, in a way that posited a transnational "imagined community," humanity, with common interests at stake. Even more so than at the national level, many of these global interests could not be adequately represented by the state, and either existing national organizations took on transnational agendas—as in the case of the NAACP—or new transnational organizations emerged in response. Ironically, even the ABA's challenge to the legitimacy of the UN human rights regime only confirmed the increasing relevance and authority of civil society in international life. Ultimately, the most significant result was the opening of a new global public sphere where a broad mix of international, national, and local NGOs could imagine they were comrades in—and indeed cultivate nonimaginary ties with—a worldwide community of human rights organizations.

The work of the CSOP, NAACP, and ABA each demonstrate the way international human rights were subjected to an early and essential public sphere deliberation by an active and relatively autonomous civil society. What is less apparent, but no less significant, is the extent to which the UN human rights regime was intended, at least by some of its proponents, to extend and deepen the global relevance of civil society institutions. Indeed the CSOP's original argument for the development of an international bill of rights, first articulated by Quincy Wright, was as a defense of a growing international public sphere that could mitigate the growth of expansionist authoritarian nationalism. Thus, not only would international guarantees of human rights bring individuals into an unprecedented, direct relationship with international institutions, but the protection of rights—particularly freedom of thought, freedom of the press, and free association—on a worldwide basis would allow for development of a broad range of transnational, nongovernmental connections. This emphasis was picked up and rearticulated in the UN by others, particularly Charles Malik and Carlos Romulo, who saw in the charter's commitment to international human rights opportunities to expand the global public sphere to include colonial peoples, and protect the autonomy of civil society from encroachment by the state.

Human Rights, the West, and the Rest

The third reason the 1940s remain central to the history of human rights is that the transcultural legitimacy of the International Bill of Rights (made up of the UDHR and the two international covenants) has frequently been asserted or contested based on particular readings of its drafting history. Among those that maintain the universality of human rights values across all cultural differences, the UDHR and the covenants offer a coherent, if imperfect, set of standards negotiated in good faith by a relatively broad swath of representative governments. Mary Ann Glendon and Susan Waltz have been at pains to point out the contributions that small and non-Western countries made during these deliberations.[25] Others, including Michael Ignatieff, note that whatever limitations in inclusiveness marked the negotiations of the 1940s, '50s, and '60s, they have been progressively overcome by the dissemination, adoption, and reformulation of the UDHR articles by more and more governments and groups throughout the world.[26] Paul Gordon Lauren, author of a widely read and hagiographic history of international human rights, notes that whatever the philosophical or political origins of the human rights tradition, the most compelling story over fifty years has been the unprecedented speed with which the rhetoric of rights has been adopted all over the world by individuals and organizations at all levels of society.[27] In this regard, the universality of the UDHR is a potential to be fulfilled through global action, rather than a premise to be defended through theoretic analysis.[28]

For those who find the contemporary human rights system to be, in the (in)famous words of Adamantia Pollis and Peter Schwab, "a Western construct with limited applicability," the International Bill of Rights bears the telltale signs of Western ethnocentrism in its uncanny resemblance to such works as the French Declaration of the Rights of Man and the Citizen and the U.S. Declaration of Independence and Bill of Rights.[29] Both in form and content, the UN human rights system reflects the influence of those eighteenth-century precedents, neither of which are part of the legal, political, or cultural patrimony of most of the world's societies. Beyond this narrow heritage, the UN was itself a creation of the Western powers, most notably the United States, and, at least for the first dozen years or so, largely mirrored the values and interests of its most powerful member.[30] Thus, the Universal Declaration is, according to Makau Mutua, "a telling testament to the conceptual, cultural, economic, military, and philosophical domination of the European West over non-European peoples and traditions."[31] Any usefulness of human rights instruments or discourse for the oppressed is ultimately mitigated by the more insidious and therefore critical danger of cultural imperialism.

The polemics of the "cultural relativism versus universalism" debate have waxed and waned since the UDHR was drafted, and this book is focused less on establishing the cultural paternity of human rights ideals or institutions than on examining the way in which the questions of universality, cultural difference, and the consequences of imperialism were a part of the original organization of the UN human rights regime.[32] Particularly significant in this respect are the contributions of two participants in the development of that system, Malik and Romulo. Their work has not gone unnoticed. Malik was second only to Eleanor Roosevelt as the public face of the Commission on Human Rights during the late 1940s and early 1950s, and Romulo was perhaps the most recognizable Asian diplomat in the United States during this period. In the historiography, both men, alongside Peng-Chun Chang of China, are perennial Asian characters in any account of the drafting of the Universal Declaration. Such accounts often seek to recruit the two, presenting Malik and Romulo as either proof of the multicultural foundation of the UDHR or, alternatively, as victims of a colonial false-consciousness, more Western than their Western counterparts.[33]

In contrast, this study assumes a more nuanced and less essentialist theory of cultural identity that precludes the possibility of designating Romulo or Malik as authentic Third Worlders or dark-skinned Westerners. Rather, by placing their contributions to the discourse and practice of international human rights in the context of their negotiation of various aspects of American empire, this history suggests that the postwar human rights system was one of the arenas in which the struggle for a post-*colonial* international order was engaged. For their parts, Malik and Romulo self-consciously assumed identities of cultural hybrids, personally and geographically situated between East and West and uniquely prepared to shoulder the burden of reconciling what two hundred years of imperialism had torn asunder. Their nationalisms, as much as their identities, were such that they allowed for—even required— the cross-cultural fertilization of colonialism and sought not a return to a primordial, precolonial past, but progress toward a fully modern, postcolonial future. In this context, the fact that human rights instruments, and indeed the human rights discourse itself, were shot through and through with the language of the colonizer inspired neither surprise nor despair. For it was precisely because the discourse of human rights resonated with the heritage of the European Enlightenment at the same time that it projected a future of global justice, that individuals like Malik and Romulo found it particularly potent in their struggle to remake the global order.

Particularly important in this regard is the fact that both Malik and Romulo were educated in American schools in their home countries and in the United States. There, they learned the language of rights from American tutors, cultivated a broad and deep sympathy for the political ideals and culture of the United States, and established reputations as young Western-oriented leaders. Despite U.S. officials eventually considering them among their closest allies in Asia, neither Malik nor Romulo was uncritical of U.S. foreign policy—the thrust of their activism directed at ensuring both the democratic participation of non-Western people in international life, and the progressive engagement of the U.S. in world affairs. While hardly anti-Western, Romulo cultivated a pan-Asian identity whose values explicitly included human rights and whose solidarity would help to begin to rectify the long global preeminence of Europe. Malik, meanwhile, sought a closer identification with the West for both himself and his country of Lebanon, hoping that an international bill of human rights might foster liberal reforms the world over. Deploying arguments now being revived under the banners of discourse ethics and procedural inclusiveness, both Malik and Romulo emphasized the need not only to include a range of voices in human rights discussions, but also to deliberate continuously and carefully toward consensus.[34] The contributions of Malik and Romulo—along with the broader context in which the discourse of human rights was articulated to the process of decolonization under the rubric of the "right to self-determination" —indicate a need to reappraise the relationship between human rights, imperialism, and cultural legitimacy.[35]

In spring 1951, ten months after the outbreak of war on the Korean peninsula, the State University of New York organized a symposium in Rochester at which both Clark Eichelberger and Charles Malik spoke. As much as any other individuals, these two were key architects of the UN human rights system. As co-founder of the CSOP, Eichelberger helped lay the foundation of an international organization dedicated to promoting human rights and Malik, as a member of the UN Commission on Human Rights, was at that moment working toward completion of the International Bill of Rights. Both their talks focused on the U.S. role in the world, and while neither was centered directly on the emerging international human rights system, each speech held open the possibility that defining the moral obligations of American global leadership was among the most critical tasks of that particular moment.

As he had been for over a quarter century, Eichelberger was keen to reconcile American nationalism with cosmopolitan internationalism. Flush with hope that the United States—"today a leader in the United Nations with several hundred thousand young men serving with soldiers of the United Nations under a supreme commander and a United Nation's flag"—had finally overcome the long tradition of isolationism, he predicted that as "far into the future as you and I can see" there would not be "any conflict between our loyalties to the United States and our loyalties to the United Nations."[36] Ultimately a prayer rather than a prophecy, Eichelberger's vision of the future proved a mirage not only because the precedent of collective "peace enforcement" through the UN would not be repeated until the 1991 Gulf War, but also because "loyalty" was increasingly defined in exclusively nationalist terms.

Eichelberger was likely aware he was swimming against the tide of public attitudes toward internationalism in general and the UN in particular, as his talk noted the "strange shock" many Americans felt when a court ruling the previous year made clear that American participation in international institutions had consequences for domestic life as well. Citing the U.S. obligations under the UN Charter to promote human rights and fundamental freedoms "without distinction as to race, sex, language, or religion," a California appellate court invalidated that state's Alien Land Law, which deprived Asian immigrants the right to own land. The ruling, whose basis was soon overturned, "shocked" indeed and fueled the momentum of voices—such as that of Frank Holman of the ABA—calling for a withdrawal from UN activities. For Eichelberger, the ruling represented one of the "more difficult obligations" that came with U.S. leadership, and he chose to celebrate rather than lament the "sacrifice of sovereignty" that was part and parcel of a more just and stable world.[37] Americans need not fear participation in and obligations under the UN, Eichelberger reassured, so long as "the highest expression of the United States [goes] into the United Nations."

Eichelberger's short talk reiterated many of the themes he and other members of the CSOP had advanced during the Second World War as they established the foundation of the postwar international organization. As the war laid waste to the lives, homes, and countries of millions of human beings in all corners of the globe, visions of a radically different kind of international society were welcomed as desirable, if not absolutely essential. The far less creative destruction of the Cold War, however, was quickly retrenching old attitudes about sovereignty and isolationism, and the political influence of groups like the CSOP declined in favor of those like the ABA. And yet, even with diametrically opposed agendas, both the CSOP and the ABA recognized that human rights were among the "more difficult obligations" for the United States to fulfill, and what was at stake was no more or less than the meaning of America itself.

That meaning was at the heart of Charles Malik's address. The Lebanese minister to the United States and the UN declared that "the meaning of America, what America is in herself and what therefore she should not be ashamed of before the whole world" was "hidden and rare" but something that nevertheless needed to be shared.[38] Although his talk was titled "A Foreigner Looks at the United States," Malik had a long and intimate relationship with American institutions and life, beginning with his experiences as a student in an American missionary school. Dutifully playing the role of new arrival, Malik marveled at the "tremendous industrial and inventive capacity" of the United States and heaped praise on the country's scientific and technological achievements. These, he said, could and should be shared with the world, not simply, as in Korea, in the service of military defense, but also "in the interests of human welfare and of the arts of peace." But the real question, Malik insisted, was whether the United States was willing "to share not only the machine," but also "your supremest [sic] values."[39]

Since his graduation from Harvard University in 1938, Malik had been articulating those "supremest values" in universal terms of a "Greco-Roman-Hebrew-Christian-Western-European-humane outlook" and a conception of the human being as "the subject of basic and inalienable and universal rights."[40] As a member of the Commission on Human Rights, Malik was still struggling to see that outlook and conception enshrined in positive international law. A month after speaking in Rochester, Malik was elected chair of the commission, succeeding Eleanor Roosevelt as the body prepared the final drafts of the international human rights covenants. In some ways, that moment signaled the beginning of the end of U.S. leadership on human rights, and that Malik took over is an indication of his commitment to seeing the International Bill of Rights completed regardless of U.S. policy. And yet as his SUNY talk made clear, and I hope the following study explains, the advent of American global leadership provided the necessary conditions for the emergence of the international human rights system in part because it opened up a new multisided discussion about what that leadership would mean.

The United States, Malik said, resembled "a huge giant who is just beginning to wake up." Blessed with tremendous material resources, the giant could simply dominate the world through strength and power—as other

giants had done or aspired to do. Alternatively, the giant, with "wistful nos-
talgia" for "the good old days of isolation and self-sufficiency," could try to
go back to sleep and avoid the responsibility, danger, and challenge of his
potential. It was, Malik said, up to "friends from within and from without,"
to constantly "remind our giant . . . by patient persuasion and suffering love,"
that it was possible to navigate between the Charybdis of isolationism and
the Scylla of imperialism only by allowing the Declaration of Independence
to be "superseded by a declaration of interdependence." Whether this was
possible, whether the United States could present an adequate "moral and
spiritual message" at the same time it recognized its "essential partnership"
with the rest of the world was the essential question of moment for Malik.
"The foot is not sure, the heart is not whole: the giant is still in the process of
awakening."[41]

Chapter 1

The Study of Peace, Human Rights, and International Organization

Signed by representatives from fifty-one nations on June 26, 1945, the UN Charter placed a commitment to international human rights at the core of the organization's raison d'être. The second stanza of the preamble proclaims an abiding "faith in fundamental human rights, in the dignity and worth of the human person, in the equal rights of men and women and of nations large and small." Among its four main purposes, the charter holds that the UN seeks to "achieve international cooperation in . . . promoting and encouraging respect for human rights and for fundamental freedom without distinction as to race, sex, language, or religion." Toward this end, the charter specifically delegates responsibility for human rights to three of its five principal organs. It authorizes the General Assembly to "initiate studies and make recommendations" for "assisting in the realization of human rights and fundamental freedoms." A more explicit mandate is given to the Economic and Social Council, which is required to set up a commission "for the promotion of human rights." Finally, the Trusteeship Council, in its oversight of the system to administer certain colonial territories, is obliged "to encourage respect for human rights and for fundamental freedoms" in those territories. Both the frequency and imprecision with which human rights were invoked in the charter ensured that the United Nations would become the principal site of human rights discourse and politics over the next decade and beyond.

These provisions, along with the more robust peace enforcement powers (and more limited democracy) of the Security Council, were key to distinguishing the new United Nations Organization from its interwar predecessor, the League of Nations. The League's covenant contained not a single mention of human rights, and while some of its efforts on behalf of minorities in Eastern Europe were significant in elaborating specific practices and precedents in international human rights protection, the League staunchly rejected human rights promotion as a general principle applicable around the world. As Mark Mazower has demonstrated, the UN Charter was designed by the "Big Three" powers, U.S., UK, and USSR, to ratify and protect, rather than undermine, their status as Great Powers with special prerogatives on the world stage.[1] As such, there is significant continuity between the prewar international system centered on imperialism and the postwar international system based on national sovereignty.[2] But if it is true that the UN "became an even fiercer defender of national sovereignty than the League had been," it was both because the Charter raised the possibility that human rights might be a legitimate object of international concern and because the waning of empire produced more and more small states for whom scrupulous observance of national sovereignty was one of the few ways of promoting a more democratic world order.[3]

What remains impressive about the UN Charter from a human rights perspective, then, is not that it signaled an end to power politics or the dawning of a new era of justice in international affairs—as we shall see, few at the time were under such illusions. Rather, the significance of the charter's human rights provisions lay in the political dynamic for which they were both the result and the basis. This chapter describes the origins of these provisions in the research, lobbying, and public relations work of a small group of elite American internationalists on the Commission to Study the Organization of Peace (CSOP). Elaborated and insisted upon by this organization, the commitment to international human rights in the charter demonstrated the extent to which the U.S. government in particular was open to pressure from the public sphere in framing its participation in organized international life. The limitations of that openness were evident throughout the charter, from the veto power of the five permanent members of the Security Council to the weak and truncated trusteeship system. And yet, the seminal human rights provisions of the charter were sufficiently novel, prominent, and open-ended to inaugurate a new era in international politics and life—one in which the discourse of rights became the lingua franca of global morality, the structures of international law became the fora of individual rights, and the practices of social movements became the politics of global justice.

With the exception of Dorothy Robins's pioneering study, most histories of the charter neglect the role of NGOs, focusing instead on the U.S.

government as the primary force behind the development of the UN. Ruth B. Russell's classic history of the charter focuses almost exclusively on U.S. officials, not surprising given her close relationship with Leo Pasvolsky, the State Department official most responsible for negotiating and drafting the charter.[4] Stephen C. Schlesinger's study of the San Francisco conference likewise emphasizes how much of the document was dictated by Washington—in part to dispel the contemporary criticism that the UN is inherently un-American.[5] Published in 1971, Robins's book came well before the current interest in NGOs and politics, and while it foregrounds the work of "U.S. citizen organizations," she emphasizes the period immediately prior to the San Francisco conference and fails to identify the origins and intent of the charter's human rights provisions.[6] This chapter fills in some of these gaps, making the case for the centrality of the CSOP as the single most important organization in this regard.

In the human rights historiography, the importance of NGOs in drafting the charter's human rights provisions has not gone unnoticed, but the focus has tended to be on the lobbying work by the so-called "consultant group" of U.S. civil society organizations at the San Francisco conference. Paul Gordon Lauren and William Korey have described the pressure this group put on the U.S. delegation to sponsor and advocate for broader human rights commitments in the charter, as an inauguration of the increasingly sophisticated NGO activism that would have such a dramatic impact on human rights politics in the last decades of the twentieth century.[7] Others, including M. Glen Johnson and more recently Elizabeth Borgwardt, have read the charter's human rights provisions as a tribute to and institutional embodiment of Franklin D. Roosevelt's "Four Freedoms," originally enunciated in his 1941 address to Congress.[8] This chapter places Roosevelt's contribution in the context of his exposure to the ideas and advocacy of the CSOP. And while it is hardly the case that the president needed the commission's help in formulating the rhetorical masterpiece of the "Four Freedoms," the idea that U.S. support for, as the president's speech put it, "the supremacy of human rights everywhere," meant that the propagation of an international bill of rights within the context of a larger international organization was rooted in the particular proposals of this civil society organization.

The CSOP, Postwar Planning, and Human Rights

The origins of the Charter's human rights provisions lie largely in a group of progressive American internationalists who, over the course of the Second World War, articulated an intellectual rationale for a global human rights regime, lobbied and advised U.S. policy makers, and conducted a broad public advocacy campaign on behalf of international organization in general and human rights in particular. Inheritors of the uncertain victory of Progressive and Social Democratic reform, this group sought to engineer an international order where peace would be predicated on the systematic and organized elimination of the economic, social, and cultural root causes of war. In this, they were quite explicitly continuing the Wilsonian efforts that had resulted in the establishment of the League of Nations after the First World War. But having watched the failure of the League up close—as a political issue in the United States and then as a peace organization in Asia, Africa, and Europe—this group hit on an international human rights system as a critical corrective to the League that would both promote justice and give individuals an interest in global governance. Their proposals inspired, extended, and specified the rhetoric of human rights that emerged from various quarters—not the least of which was the president of the United States—as a way of describing the stakes of the war against Germany. In the work of the CSOP, human rights went from inspirational war aim to concrete postwar plan.

The need for a new approach became apparent in 1938—a full year before German forces surged into Poland and World War II began—when the deepening crises in Europe and Asia signaled to many the collapse of the interwar international order. Having failed to stop Japanese aggression in Manchuria in 1931, and then even to condemn the Italian invasion of Ethiopia in 1935, the League of Nations had become irrelevant as a peacemaking body; so much so that by the time Germany moved to annex the Sudetenland from Czechoslovakia, no one even bothered to bring the issue before the assembly.[9] Figures as distinct as Soviet foreign minister Maxim Litvinov and former South African prime minister Jan Christian Smuts found themselves in perhaps grudging agreement with the pro-Mussolini editors of *Tribuna*, who concluded that 1938 marked "the end of the whole diplomatic construction and international political system based on . . . the League of Nations."[10] So too was the man professionally predisposed toward optimism about the League, U.S. national director of the League of Nations Association (LNA) Clark M. Eichelberger. After attending the ruinous 1938 assembly in Geneva, Eichelberger returned to the United States condemning the "mutilation" of Czechoslovakia as "one of the greatest betrayals" in history and convinced that, while the ideals of the League were sound, only a more strident and thoroughgoing revision of international politics could "deflect humanity from the road to disaster."[11]

Eichelberger had served as director of the LNA since 1933 and was a veteran of both the First World War and the effort to draw the United States out of the isolationist shell into which it had withdrawn after that conflict. The son of a shoe salesman in Freeport, Illinois, Eichelberger developed an early interest in progressive politics that, after serving as an Army corporal in France during the war, brought him into association with the "militant internationalists" for whom Woodrow Wilson's vision of a more just and rational world order inspired an unprecedented lay engagement in international affairs. After the war, Eichelberger made a name for himself speaking about international topics on the Radcliffe Chautauqua lecture circuit before being hired by Raymond Fosdick to lead the Chicago office of what was still called the League of Nations Non-Partisan Association. Set up in early 1923 by former Supreme Court justice John H. Clarke and Taft attorney general George W. Wickersham, the LNA was dedicated from the beginning to cultivating grassroots public support for American entry into the League. Although hired on the strength of his speaking abilities, Eichelberger soon demonstrated an unexpected organizational enthusiasm and initiative that made the Chicago office the center of an empire of local chapters throughout the Midwest and the home of the LNA journal, the *League of Nations Chronicle*. On becoming national director, Eichelberger expanded on the LNA traditional focus on education, and began a more systematic effort to directly influence policy makers in government and opinion makers in the media.[12] This organizational structure failed to deliver on its stated goal of American membership in, let alone leadership of, the League of Nations, but Eichelberger's experiences with the LNA would prove most important to the CSOP's later success in delivering a UN Charter with provisions for human rights.

At Eichelberger's initiative, the LNA board approved the creation of an "Unofficial Enquiry" in April 1939, dedicated not only to the study of "the bases of a lasting peace and the organization of international society," but also to public education and advocacy on behalf of the principles of internationalism.[13] The group's awkward and seemingly vague name, which would be changed to the equally ponderous Commission to Study the Organization of Peace, is perhaps more revealing than it appears at first blush. The Unofficial Enquiry was formed in conscious imitation of President Wilson's "Enquiry," established in 1917 to research and make recommendations regarding peace settlements.[14] The Enquiry—whose members included Colonel Edward M. House, Walter Lippmann, and the man who would serve as the chairman of the CSOP, James T. Shotwell—had helped devise the League of Nations system and had provided the intellectual basis for Wilson's peacemaking and postwar plans. That Enquiry had been, of course, "official"—a state-authorized commission, albeit with an intentionally broad civilian membership. Eichelberger's Unofficial Enquiry revived this model of a relatively high-profile commission of experts, but did so fully within civil society. This shift from state to civil society was critical to the emphasis on human rights by this new organization.

At the first meeting on November 5, the Unofficial Enquiry rechristened itself the Committee for the Study of the Organization of Peace, later edited to the Commission to Study the Organization of Peace, and elected Shotwell chairman.[15] Shotwell was professor of history and international relations at Columbia University and one of the most prominent public intellectuals on the subject of international affairs. Shotwell was born and raised in rural Strathroy, Ontario, but his family settled in the Great Lakes region of North America with what he proudly regarded as a studious disregard for national borders and nationalist sentiments.[16] Although a medievalist by training, his academic career was dedicated to demonstrating the humanitarian impact of rational, scientific thought on Western civilization. As Charles Benedetti has described, by the First World War Shotwell shared the optimistic, Progressive faith of his friends John Dewey and Herbert Croly, and sought to extend the principles of rational organization to the one area of modern life in which an archaic anarchy persisted unabated: the international sphere.[17] A friend and advisor to Wilson, Shotwell was deeply chastened and disappointed by the president's doomed attempt to achieve Senate ratification of the Treaty of Versailles. Nevertheless, he continued to advocate U.S. entry into the League of Nations long after it had become politically anathema, and was a consistent voice for an internationalist U.S. foreign policy during the interwar period.

Shotwell served in an official government capacity from time to time throughout his career, but his most dramatic impact on U.S. foreign policy came through his efforts as a private citizen. In 1927, while working with the Carnegie Endowment for International Peace in Paris, Shotwell met with French foreign minister Aristide Briand and suggested that he seek a treaty between the United States and France forswearing war between the two nations. For Shotwell, this appeared an excellent way to leverage what he saw as one ascendant strain of American opinion, pacifism, against another, iso-lationism. Briand was perhaps less interested in securing a perpetual peace than in solidifying American support for French continental predominance and, less than a month later, he proposed just such a treaty to his Ameri-can counterpart, Secretary of State Frank B. Kellogg. Neither government, however, could control the public enthusiasm ignited by the idea of "outlaw-ing" war, and the eventual shape of the Kellogg-Briand Pact, also known as the Pact of Paris, which was opened for signature on August 27, 1928, to all nations interested in renouncing war, owed more to this international pub-lic outcry than to the geopolitical machinations of either Kellogg or Briand. Shotwell was a critical figure in what he characterized as a "quasi-evangelical crusade" to enlist public support for the idea of the pact and, while he was ultimately ambivalent about the treaty's final form, he nonetheless saw the potential of unofficial diplomacy and public opinion in the development of American foreign policy.[18]

As chairman, Shotwell brought his commitment to systematic inquiry, his political connections, and his progressivist—and paternalist—belief in the importance of cultivating and channeling public opinion to the work of the CSOP. Eichelberger served as director of the commission and, while lack-ing the prestige and academic credentials of Shotwell, provided the adminis-trative backbone that sustained the organization even beyond its relevance. The official membership of the commission was intended to demonstrate a wide spectrum of opinion on international affairs and thus included such ideologically diverse members as Charles P. Taft, scion of the great Republi-can dynasty, and Max Lerner, Marxian liberal columnist and scholar.[19] While many of the commissioners would make little contribution to the research or lobbying work of the CSOP, Eichelberger's intention was to establish a promi-nent public alliance of internationalists capable of countering the voices of isolationist nationalism who had coalesced around famed aviator Charles Lindbergh and fascist sympathizer Father Charles Coughlin.[20] Whatever the apparent political heterogeneity of the seventy official "commissioners," the leadership of the CSOP was ideologically homogeneous, committed to an elite and technocratic internationalism that sought the rational and con-trolled evolution of the global order toward some form of world government.

From the very beginning, human rights were a central feature that distin-guished the commission's plan from the League system, and were the lynch-pin of the CSOP's multipronged approach, which included research, lobbying, and public relations. The first report, published in November 1940, outlined the basic principles the CSOP considered "fundamental to the organization of peace." Peace, the CSOP contended, must be understood not simply as a static renunciation of war in the mode of the Kellogg-Briand Pact, but as "a dynamic and continuous process for the achievement of freedom, justice, progress and security on a world-wide scale." This sort of peace required the deliberate planning for and creation of a new postwar organization to replace the failed League system. The new organization, the report suggested, should be a more robust "federation" of nations capable of curtailing what it referred to as "exaggerated developments in the idea of sovereignty." Unconstrained sovereignty made for a chaotic and dangerous international environment— a Hobbesian state of nature—and the report listed five areas in which the sovereign prerogatives of nation-states must be limited if a progressive and dynamic peace was to be possible. The first three were classic constraints on war-making powers: the submission of disputes to international arbitration, the renunciation of force, and the control of armaments. The fourth, coordination of economic activity, was aimed at removing an underlying cause of conflict and had, in fact, been pioneered by the League and especially the International Labor Organization. The final limit on sovereignty suggested by the CSOP in 1940 was more novel. Noting that the "destruction of civil liberties anywhere creates the danger of war," the report went on: "Nations must accept certain human and cultural rights in their constitutions and in international covenants."[21]

This short phrase was not elaborated on in this "preliminary" report, but its appearance suggests how early the idea of international human rights protection was included in the CSOP's postwar planning. Equally vague invocations of human rights had already begun to appear in connection with the European war. On both sides of the Atlantic, a few people were suggesting that human rights were at stake in the fight against Nazism, including writer H. G. Wells and feminist Carrie Chapman Catt. After the British entry into the war, Wells was quick to declare, as the title of his October 1939 *Times* column put it, "War Aims: The Rights of Man." More significantly, Wells was a longtime supporter of world government who had for years worked through the literary organization PEN International to establish a sort of global republic of letters; he published a popular pamphlet in early 1940 entitled *The Rights of Man or What Are We Fighting For?*, and managed even to draft his own "Declaration of Rights."[22] Over a year before Wells published his first call to make the war a human rights crusade, Catt told the National Committee on the Cause and Cure of War that to defeat the rising dictatorships needed the "biggest, breeziest, cheeriest campaign for the rights of man the world ever knew." Among those in the audience listening to Catt was Clark Eichelberger.[23]

Quincy Wright and the Theory of International Human Rights

Wells and Catt trumpeted human rights as a call to arms and demonstrated the growing purchase of "human rights talk" in the public sphere, but the organization and institutionalization of this rights discourse as a prominent feature of the *post*war order would require the sustained efforts, expertise, and political access of the CSOP. The intellectual basis of much of the commission's work came from Quincy Wright, the man responsible for the call for universal human rights standards in the CSOP's first report.[24] Along with Eichelberger and Shotwell, Wright was one of the original organizers of the commission.[25] From a prominent academic family with a penchant for social reform, Wright earned his doctorate at the University of Illinois where he studied with James W. Garner, one of the few early twentieth-century scholars of international law in the United States. By the time of his appointment as a full professor at the University of Chicago in 1923, thirty-two-year-old Wright had already established a reputation as one of the most innovative and productive minds in the field. From 1927 to 1941, he directed the university's Causes of War Project, which included faculty and graduate students in the political science, anthropology, psychology, and sociology departments, and produced the pioneering two-volume *A Study of War*, widely hailed as a masterpiece.[26] Published in 1942, *A Study of War* would have come as a surprise to those expecting a presentation of battlefield tactics and analysis of the strategic deployment of organized force. Instead, readers found a close examination of war as an institution in world history, and, more importantly, an outline of the conditions necessary for establishing and maintaining peace. *A Study of War* is, as one former student put it, a testimony to Wright's "faith in mankind's capacity to cope with its most terrible affliction." [27] In the final stages of this ambitious project, just as the CSOP was beginning its work, he was well positioned to provide the intellectual framework for much of the commission's work during the war.

Human rights figured into Wright's vision of peace in two ways. First, an international human rights system would be a critical device in the management of global reforms intended to remediate the social, economic, and political causes of war. Wright shared Shotwell's Progressive faith in scientific rationality, and his earlier analysis of some of the League's activities pointed toward his later proposals on human rights. Wright's early views in this regard are evident in his assessment of the League of Nations Mandates, the system by which the victors of the Great War agreed to apportion and oversee governance of territories taken away from the Ottoman and German empires but "not yet able to stand by themselves under the strenuous conditions of the modern world."[28] With both technocratic optimism and elitist paternalism, Wright had argued that the League of Nations Mandatory system could, with sufficient international oversight and a genuine commitment to preparing "backward" peoples for independence, provide the kind of orderly reforms to imperialism necessary to avoid violent conflict.[29] Of course, the mandates covered only a very small portion of the colonial world (no colonies of France, the United Kingdom, and the Netherlands, for instance, were subject to League supervision) and, while it was intended to facilitate the progress of the Arab and African inhabitants of these territories toward self-government, the system just as often worked in practice to frustrate and defer their aspirations to independence. But in principle Mandatory powers acknowledged both the legitimacy of international regulation of "internal" affairs as well as the importance of minimum rights standards in a way that suggested to Wright the possibility of a more ambitious program.[30] The eruption of a Second World War demonstrated the need and provided the opportunity to propose wider and more substantial changes, especially but not exclusively in the colonial world, and Wright moved to develop a general human rights system in an effort to universalize this principle of international progressive reform.

Second, human rights were key to redefining state sovereignty and constituting the individual as a subject of international law. Wright's plan for a perpetual peace relied on the construction of a global federation of states involving the reconceptualization of the principle of sovereignty away from one of "sovereignty above the law" to one of "sovereignty under the law."[31] Self-interested states—particularly powerful ones—would be reluctant to subordinate themselves to the rule of law, but Wright thought that pressure to do so might come from their public constituencies, particularly if those publics recognized that their interests could be better protected by a global federalism. "To secure these changes," he wrote in *A Study of War*, "it seems necessary that certain human rights be incorporated in international law."[32] In this way, Wright argued, individuals as well as states would become subjects of international law, giving citizens of various states "direct access to international procedures for protecting the rights guaranteed by that law."[33] International human rights institutions and mechanisms, Wright hoped, would undermine traditional state sovereignty and be the foundation of a new kind of international citizenship.

Wright made explicit the connection between Progressive reform and the development of global citizenship on the one hand, and world peace on the other, in a thirty-two-page CSOP pamphlet published as *Human Rights and World Order* in fall 1942. Wright's hypothetical example, clearly based on Nazi Germany, weaves together both Progressive fears of the vulnerability of publics to demagogic appeals and liberal fears of an authoritarian state, and presents internationally protected human rights as the way to foster a moderating global public sphere and stifle the rise of "fanatical nationalism." Noting that one of the first steps of a potential tyrant is to abolish civil rights domestically in order to "isolate the public from outside influences," Wright contended that such isolation led to a "vicious circle" of growing national neurosis. Eventually resulting in a form of social insanity, the abrogation of individual human rights produces a national public that virtually demands internal persecutions as well as external aggression. "A government which isolates its public from external influences in order to augment national solidarity," Wright warned, "finds itself compelled to embark upon dangerous policies in response to the desire of a public uninhibited by the chastening criticism of foreign and world opinion."[34] Wright's vision was one in which internationally guaranteed human rights checked the dangerous irrationality of isolated populations, limited the influence of tyrannical demagogues, and sustained global solidarity.[35]

Wright's thinking was not typical of everyone involved with the CSOP or with later supporters of the charter's human rights provisions. Nevertheless, his intellectual work, along with that of James Shotwell, demonstrates a certain degree of continuity between the Progressive reform efforts pursued earlier in the century on a largely national basis and the program of international reform, inclusive of human rights protections, pursued by the CSOP. It also suggests the tension—which was never resolved despite the efforts of many governments to do so—between traditional notions of state sovereignty and international human rights. Certainly, as Mark Mazower and Samuel Moyn argue, those state powers involved in the construction of the UN system, including the United States, did everything they could to preserve and protect their sovereign authority, including shaping a distinctly state-centered human rights regime. Nevertheless, as Quincy Wright understood, by giving a place to the individual in international law, human rights opened up the possibility of new kinds of legal personhood and political practice that transcended and challenged such sovereignty.

The CSOP and Roosevelt Administration Policy

For the CSOP, international human rights were intended to constrain state sovereignty and lay the foundation for more cosmopolitan forms of governance and citizenship. Unsurprisingly, such a view was never embraced by the Roosevelt administration. CSOP access to and influence on official postwar planning, however, helped to ensure that the discourse of human rights remained a part of administration rhetoric and that the question of how to institutionalize such rights was not ignored. Shotwell, Eichelberger, and Wright all received appointments at one point or another as official advisors to the State Department. Wright corresponded with Secretary of State Cordell Hull through the duration of the war on matters of international law, and Eichelberger enjoyed no fewer than eight face-to-face meetings with the president between 1936 and 1944, the bulk of which were dedicated to discussions of the CSOP's work.[36] Two months after the establishment of the CSOP, in December 1939, the State Department briefly created its first postwar planning unit, only to scuttle the effort as the war itself loomed. Under the circumstances, both Cordell Hull and undersecretary of state Sumner Welles were happy to encourage the CSOP to continue their efforts, effectively outsourcing postwar planning for the better part of two years. [37]

Ceding policy research and planning to think-tank wonks was different from abandoning the resonant power of human rights talk, which the administration certainly did not do. Instead, President Roosevelt articulated what was arguably the most dramatic and significant "vision" of human rights of the wartime period: the Four Freedoms. Near the end of his annual message to Congress in January 1941, he proclaimed "four essential human freedoms"—freedom of thought and expression, freedom of religion, freedom from want, and freedom from fear—that the United States would seek to promote not just at home but "everywhere in the world." "Freedom," Roosevelt concluded, "means the supremacy of human rights everywhere. Our support goes to those who struggle to gain those rights and keep them. Our strength is our unity of purpose. To that high concept there can be no end save victory."[38] With remarkable economy, Roosevelt managed to articulate together principles embodied in the U.S. Bill of Rights, his own New Deal policies, and the struggle against fascism under the rubric of freedom and human rights.[39] Whatever its significance as a watershed moment for how Americans understood their role in the world, Roosevelt's Four Freedoms offered no guidance as to how "the supremacy of human rights" was to be achieved or even how such supremacy might be gauged. If the discourse of human rights was becoming more hegemonic, the structures and practices of human rights were still inchoate.

In the short term, the promotion of human rights equated to more aid for the beleaguered British, but what a long-term human rights system might encompass only began to come into focus after the United States was a full-fledged belligerent. In particular, the possibility of an international bill of rights emerged in the context of the introduction of "human rights" as an official war aim of the Allies in the January 1942 Declaration by United Nations. Drafted during Churchill's first wartime visit to Washington, the one-page statement characterized the war as one "to defend life, liberty, independence and religious freedom, and to preserve human rights and justice in their own lands as well as in other lands."[40] The earliest draft of the Declaration by United Nations, written at the State Department, mentioned "human freedom and justice" but not human rights. Paul Gordon Lauren has suggested that the term was written into the declaration by Roosevelt himself,[41] and its inclusion may have been instigated by a fortuitous coincidence of timing. As drafts passed back and forth between the White House and the State Department, the country celebrated, on December 15, the sesquicentennial of the first ten amendments to the U.S. Constitution, commonly known as the Bill of Rights. That evening, in a radio address to the nation, Roosevelt recalled how "a new nation, through an elected Congress, adopted a declaration of human rights which has influenced the thinking of all mankind from one end of the world to the other." Referring to "the American bill of human rights," the president warned that the "political and moral tigers" of Germany, Italy, and Japan would return the world to the darkness of "absolute authority and despotic rule" if the principles embodied in the Bill of Rights were not defended the world over.[42] Less than two weeks later, the president returned the draft declaration to Secretary Hull with the phrase "human freedoms" replaced by "human rights."[43]

That Roosevelt seeded the postwar human rights system with the Four

Freedoms speech and the Declaration by United Nations is widely known and acknowledged, to the point that he is often lauded as the father of the modern human rights movement. Less well known and appreciated is the fact that Roosevelt's rhetorical championing of human rights was more the result of political than moral genius. and that his efforts were themselves seeded by less prominent voices, particularly the CSOP. Two days before the president's anniversary speech, James T. Shotwell, speaking on the CBS network, went further than Roosevelt was willing to go, not just placing the principles of the Bill of Rights at the moral center of the Allied war effort, but placing the instrument of *a* bill of rights at the center of an ongoing system of organized peace. "Our Bill of Rights, which we will celebrate next Monday, should be made the basis of an International Bill of Rights safeguarding not only personal liberty but freedom of thought, of religion, and of expression." While the details of such a document, covering a diverse range of nations and peoples, would no doubt require careful and deliberate study, such an effort was necessary. "Here then is one of our chief war aims which must be clarified by the work of jurists and historians," adding the warning, "so that in the peace settlement it will not prove a source of disillusionment." Thinking of the ongoing work of the CSOP, Shotwell concluded, "Fortunately, the specialists are already hard at work, and a good beginning has been made."[44]

Shotwell and Eichelberger brought the CSOP proposal for an international bill of rights directly to the State Department when Sumner Welles restarted the official postwar planning process in mid-1942. Both men were appointed to the Advisory Committee on Postwar Foreign Policy, which took as its working draft—for a possible permanent international organization—a plan presented by Shotwell that had been developed by the CSOP.[45] The State Department's first "Draft Constitution of the International Organization" took its preamble, including a dedication to "a common program of human rights," directly from the Shotwell proposal.[46] By the end of the year, the Advisory Committee had produced the first State Department draft of an international bill of rights—completed on December 10, 1942, six years to the day before the adoption of the Universal Declaration of Human Rights—containing some sixteen articles guaranteeing such rights as freedom of speech and religion and providing for due process and equality before the law.[47] Rowland Brucken has examined the State Department human rights planning during the war in detail and describes how officials, as opposed to the outside consultants, sought from the very beginning to limit international human rights to those already embodied in American tradition and practice.[48] The 1942 Draft International Bill of Rights certainly leaves this impression as it excludes enforceable economic and social rights, as might have been implied in the idea of a "freedom from want," and studiously avoids any mention of racial discrimination.

The fact that an international bill of rights, whatever its shortcomings, was being drafted and considered by the U.S. State Department was clear evidence of what Clark Eichelberger regarded as the "remarkable" influence of "private citizens" on the early stages of official postwar planning.[49] This connection between the participation of the CSOP and official U.S. support for an international bill of rights was even more apparent after the Roosevelt administration moved from discussions with civil society to negotiations with the governments of Great Britain and the Soviet Union. The October 1943 Moscow Declaration committed the three powers to "establishing at the earliest practicable date a general international organization" and set the stage for further negotiations of a joint plan. Yet while he was busy securing agreement among Washington, London, and Moscow, Secretary Hull effectively ended participation by outside groups and congressional representatives in the postwar planning process. and with it the development of a specific human rights policy.[50] Beginning in fall 1943, Hull would maintain tighter control over a process that would now take place without "the systematic infusion of ideas from the public." Human rights would be but one of the "more liberal ideas" given short shrift.[51]

Dumbarton Oaks and the Return of National Sovereignty

The 1944 conversations between American, Soviet, and British officials at Dumbarton Oaks demonstrated the reluctance of the major powers to cede the prerogatives of state sovereignty to the extent implied by the system of international human rights envisioned by the CSOP. The U.S. State Department, in preparations for the conference, toyed with including a forceful commitment to human rights—perhaps even an international bill of rights—in the organization's charter.[52] But during the late summer talks, U.S. representatives were more concerned with securing Soviet and British support for a new, strengthened international security organization. For their part, the Soviet and British foreign ministries were as yet unconvinced of the necessity for a broad international security system and had spent much less time on preparations for the talks.[53] What proposals they did bring to the table at Dumbarton Oaks indicated that human rights promotion was not to be an outstanding part of the organization they envisioned. The negotiations focused primarily on the ways the new international organization could preserve the preeminent power of the Big Three without proving absolutely unacceptable to smaller states and global opinion.[54] For these reasons, the product of the talks, so anticipated by the world, deferred resolution of what would prove to be the most contentious aspects of the Big Three's plan for postwar organization: the structure and voting of the Security Council and the handling of colonial territories.[55]

Human rights were not entirely absent. Some four weeks into the negotiations, at a meeting of the Joint Steering Committee, head of the U.S. delegation acting secretary of state Edward Stettinius suggested insertion of a new general principle for the future international organization.[56] Written by State Department legal counsel Benjamin V. Cohen, the draft paragraph pledged member states to the promotion and protection of human rights. This commitment, however, came within a larger paragraph that expressed the preeminence of the principle of noninterference in the internal affairs of other states:

> The International Organization should refrain from intervention in the internal affairs of any state, it being the responsibility of each state to see that conditions prevailing within its jurisdiction do not endanger international peace and security and, to this end, to respect the human rights and fundamental freedoms of its people and to govern in accordance with the principle of humanity and justice.[57]

Formulated in this way, human rights were universal in principle, but in practice any guarantees or protections for those rights would be kept solidly on the national level. Rather than challenging state sovereignty and fostering the development of new institutions of global governance, the U.S. proposal officially inscribed human rights in the traditional boundaries of domestic jurisdiction. The template of U.S. advocacy for human rights was being cut: assertions of universal principles coupled with the reinforcement of strictly national institutions.

This attempt to harmonize human rights with national sovereignty was not particularly convincing to the British and Soviet delegations, both of whom sensed in human rights an inherent challenge to the principle of noninterference. Sir Alexander Cadogan, chairman of the British delegation, was sympathetic with the spirit behind the proposal, but worried that even though the article expressly precluded international interference in domestic affairs, it nonetheless seemed to invite open debate and criticism of "the internal organization of member states."[58] Such "internal organization" presumably would include both metropolitan and colonial government, and Cadogan correctly assessed that British rule in her expansive and increasingly troubled empire would not be judged by any future international organization as living up to any human rights standard it would set.[59] Soviet ambassador to the United States Andrei Gromyko, announced that in his opinion human rights were simply "not germane to the main tasks of an international security organization."[60] For their part, the Soviets were the least interested in establishing an international organization with a mandate beyond peace enforcement, narrowly conceived. The entire economic and social program, including anything dealing with human rights, gave the Soviets pause, less because they did not regard such matters as of international concern than out of a suspicion that the future organization would be dominated by noncommunist, if not openly anticommunist, states.[61] Together, the British and Soviet delegations blocked a principle committing states to respect human rights, but agreed, after being reminded by the Americans that public support for the plan would be essential for its realization, to go along with a mention of human rights deep inside the body of the document.[62] Thus some eight pages into the ten-page document, the General Assembly was charged with helping the new international organization "promote respect for human rights and fundamental freedoms."[63]

Revising Dumbarton Oaks:
The Human Rights Commission

Such a vague and marginal mention of human rights failed to inspire broad public support, instead provoking criticisms indicating the extent to which the wartime human rights rhetoric had raised expectations of a more progressive postwar organization. Socialist Party presidential candidate Norman Thomas described the international organization outlined in the Dumbarton Oaks Proposals as a "perfect device for the maintenance of the status quo."[64] Others who had high hopes for the reorganization of the global order in the wake of the Second World War would have agreed with New Zealand's ambassador to the United States, Carl Berendsen, who said simply: "It aims too low."[65] Manley O. Hudson, Harvard professor and judge to the Permanent Court of International Justice, described the single mention of human rights in the Dumbarton Oaks Proposals as "a slighting of the subject."[66]

As disappointment over the Dumbarton Oaks Proposals spread, the U.S. State Department turned to the CSOP to help rally public support—a decision that gave the organization one more opportunity to shape the postwar international human rights system. Eichelberger, Shotwell, and the other commissioners, stung as they may have been by their marginalization before the Dumbarton Oaks conversations, recognized that outright opposition to the proposals might lead to a tragic replay of the American rejection of the League of Nations, this time with much more dire consequences. Dutifully, the group agreed to stump for the plan. In the months between the release of the Dumbarton Oaks Proposals and the convening of the San Francisco conference, the CSOP, as well as a host of other American NGOs, embarked on a two-pronged strategy: rally American public opinion in support of the proposals as a draft outline for a permanent international organization, and lobby for inclusion of more progressive provisions in the final charter, particularly in the area of human rights.[67]

Support for the plan did not mean uncritical acceptance of all its provisions, and the importance of CSOP advocacy for the proposals presented a limited opportunity to press for revisions publically and in private consultations with officials. Prior to the Dumbarton Oaks conference, the CSOP had, of course, developed a number of proposals for a postwar international human rights system. In a confidential outline prepared in October 1943, Eichelberger suggested that the CSOP recommend that the UN set up a "permanent international commission . . . consisting of jurists and experienced students of public affairs" dedicated specifically to protecting "the basic rights of the individual."[68] This suggestion was carried out in late May 1944 with the publication of the final section of the CSOP Fourth Report. Entitled "International Safeguards of Human Rights," the section called for the Allies to convene "an immediate United Nations Conference on Human Rights" to "promulgate an international bill of rights and establish a Permanent United Nations Commission, vested with powers of investigation and advice and charged with the function of further developing standards of human rights and methods for their protection."[69] After the Dumbarton Oaks Proposals, the CSOP sent a delegation to the State Department to press their recommendations. The leader of the delegation, William Neilson, reported to Eichelberger at his October meeting, noting that while the administration appeared unwilling to pursue a general conference on human rights or draft an international bill of rights, there was willingness to consider "the possibility of an organization dealing with Human Rights" being established under the Economic and Social Council.[70]

In the weeks after this meeting, the CSOP developed a strategy to put public pressure on the administration to formally propose a human rights commission at the upcoming United Nations Conference on International Organization (UNCIO) in San Francisco. Working in conjunction with John W. Davis, former U.S. ambassador to London, Clark Eichelberger drafted a two-page statement outlining the ways the Four Powers had committed the proposed international organization to defend human rights, and calling on the press and public to ensure that these promises were kept.[71] Davis was perhaps an odd choice given his relatively conservative views and the fact that he had been an outspoken critic of FDR's New Deal. He was a staunch internationalist, however, and Eichelberger was convinced that the broadest possible support was necessary to achieve not just the human rights commission, but the international organization in general. Eichelberger also rounded up some 150 "prominent persons from all walks of life" to endorse the statement that Davis read over the CBS radio network on February 5, 1945.[72] "To this end," the ambassador concluded, "we urge the United Nations to create in the coming World Organization a Commission on Human Rights and Fundamental Freedoms."[73] This was the first public call for what would become the UN Commission on Human Rights. By orchestrating the Davis broadcast, the CSOP made a seminal intervention in the debate over the place of human rights in the coming world organization.

From a twenty-first-century perspective, the historical significance of the Universal Declaration of Human Rights and the covenants has meant that much of the focus of contemporary scholars has gone into understanding the origins of the International Bill of Rights and its particular provisions, and the formation of the UN Commission on Human Rights (UNCHR) is treated as a necessary prelude to the more important work of drafting particular documents. It is therefore worth remembering that the CSOP emphasis on establishing a human rights commission in the charter of the UN was not merely a concession to political reality (although given the Roosevelt administration's refusal to consider a full-fledged international bill of rights, it was certainly that as well). Rather, an international human rights institution was in some ways just as significant as a specific set of international human rights standards. Such a commission laid the structural groundwork for the kind of global governance the CSOP sought to establish in the long run. As a commission dedicated to human rights within an overarching international organization, this institution was uniquely poised to serve as one of the checks on national sovereignty the CSOP had suggested was necessary in their first report. Such a commission would also provide a focal point for individuals to engage with the international system—another of the CSOP's keys to a lasting peace. And finally, because most advocates believed that the Commission on Human Rights would be staffed by independent experts rather than government representatives,[74] Eichelberger, Shotwell, and others might well have imagined a transition from one commission—the CSOP—to another—the UNCHR—as a way of maintaining an ongoing role for civil society in the postwar international order. In fact, few of these hopes for the Commission would be realized, but the UNCHR would nonetheless become the structural center—for better or worse—of the UN human rights system for the next sixty years.

The Davis broadcast kicked off a vast public information program designed to increase awareness of and support for the creation of a new international organization. In addition to coordinating the efforts of some forty-two other civic organizations, the CSOP oversaw production of a regular radio broadcast on CBS, the writing of opinion columns in major newspapers across the country,[75] and even the production of a comic book, in conjunction with *True Comics Magazine*, outlining the perils of global disorganization.[76] These efforts were to culminate in "Dumbarton Oaks Week." Working with its partner organizations, the CSOP sent a telegram on February 20 to the forty-eight state governors asking them to declare April 16–22 Dumbarton Oaks Week and urging them to promote "the greatest number of public discussions" around the issues of world organization and peace.[77] Official proclamations were less important, however, than the work of the sundry local organizations that had been recruited as sponsors, and the heart of Dumbarton Oaks Week lay in the public readings, radio specials, school programs, and dedicated Sunday sermons that focused attention on the impending San Francisco gathering. The week's activities were to mark a new level in popular engagement with international affairs—precisely the kind of engagement that Quincy Wright and other members of the CSOP thought pointed toward the global citizenship implied by human rights.

Unfortunately, Dumbarton Oaks Week was overshadowed by the shock of President Roosevelt's death on the morning of April 12. In poor health for years, the fact that the president's demise took most of the country by complete surprise is indicative not only of his unprecedented four-term ten-ure, but also of the distance between the public and the executive power. That distance makes all the more remarkable one of Roosevelt's last acts before leaving Washington for his final trip to Warm Springs, Georgia. Ever mindful of the fate of Woodrow Wilson, whose doomed attempt to secure domestic support for the League of Nations proved both his political and personal un-doing, Roosevelt approved a plan to designate a number of organizations as "consultants" to the U.S. delegation in a calculated ploy to ensure broad public support for the United Nations project. By conferring official recognition and unprecedented status to civil society organizations at an intergovernmental conference, the consultant arrangement, like the enlisting of the CSOP in the public campaign for the Dumbarton Oaks Proposals, was an attempt to co-opt would-be critics and secure a broad base of "stakeholders" in whatever type of organization emerged from the UNCIO.[78] Certainly, Roosevelt did not intend for the consultants to actively participate in the shaping of U.S. policy in San Francisco, but such intentions mattered less than the political dynamic the arrangement perpetuated.

Civil Society at the United Nations Conference on International Organization

As delegates, consultants, reporters, and others began to pour into Califor-nia, Eichelberger counted some forty-three members of the CSOP who were attending the United Nations Conference on International Organization in some capacity—a remarkable achievement for an organization whose mem-bership during the war had never exceeded 120. The official U.S. delegation was replete with individuals associated with the CSOP. Dean of Barnard College Virginia Gildersleeve, a CSOP member since 1942, served as one of the seven U.S. delegates, and no fewer than nine other CSOP members were among the U.S. advisors, including John Foster Dulles, Benjamin Gerig, Phillip C. Jessup, Walter Kotschnig, and Clyde Eagleton. Members were also prominent among the conference secretariat, with, among others, Malcolm W. Davis, Eugene Stanley, and Huntington Gilchrist serving in various posi-tions.[79] The ubiquity of the CSOP at San Francisco is indicative of the broad and prominent membership of the organization as well as the political strat-egy of co-optation pursued by the U.S. government. By inviting a wide swath of the intellectual, political, and cultural classes to participate in some fashion in the founding of this new international organization, the Roosevelt-now-Truman administration hoped to ensure a solid base of public support for continued postwar internationalism.[80] A charter with human rights commitments at its core was one of the consequences of that participation.

Significantly, as their wartime work reached its culmination, Clark Eichelberger and James Shotwell chose to remain within the "unofficial" sphere of civil society. Both men were consultants, Eichelberger for the League of Nations Association (to be rechristened after the conference as the United Nations Association), Shotwell for the Carnegie Endowment. The two were joined by a host of other consultants including O. Frederick Nolde of the Federal Council of Churches (FCC) and Joseph Proskauer of the American Jewish Committee (AJC), the four of whom together constituted the core of the consultant group advocating for human rights. Many, including the first head of the UN Secretariat Human Rights Division John P. Humphrey, have credited the consultant group with forcing the American delegation to back the expanded human rights provisions of the charter and thereby ensuring their inclusion.[81] Of course, the specific nature of the provisions to be adopted, as well as the groundwork for securing a receptive audience in the administration and the wider public, had been laid out over the preceding five years by the CSOP. Nonetheless, the final push at the San Francisco conference demonstrated the growing clout of the civil society sector more generally in human rights politics, as well as the strategy that the United States and other governments were developing to deal with that clout.

Perhaps the most eloquent and effective advocate for human rights among the consultants was former New York Supreme Court justice Joseph Proskauer. As a leading member of the American Jewish community, he had watched the Nazi rise to power with alarm and spent most of the war raising money for relief efforts on behalf of Jewish refugees. The AJC, of which Proskauer had been elected president in 1943, refrained from advocating a more interventionist U.S. policy prior to Pearl Harbor, and was among the most prominent anti-Zionist Jewish voices as the end of the war approached. In the context of their opposition to establishment of a Jewish state in Palestine, the AJC and Proskauer turned to international human rights as a possible alternative method of protecting Jews from persecution.[82] In December 1944, Proskauer was at the head of a coalition of mainly religious organizations that issued a "Declaration of Human Rights" that called for the promulgation of an international bill of human rights guaranteeing "every man, woman, and child, of every race, creed and in every country, the fundamental rights of life, liberty and the pursuit of happiness."[83] Less than a month before the president's death, Proskauer met with Roosevelt at the White House to press for a stronger human rights commitment at San Francisco. And while he told the president that the AJC had a draft international bill of rights it would like considered at the conference, he specifically sought an endorsement of a commission on human rights—precisely what the CSOP had called for in the Davis broadcast a month earlier.[84]

At the San Francisco conference, Proskauer's moral authority as a representative of a group many people regarded as the primary and most aggrieved victims of the war, coupled with his dignified judicial demeanor, worked to pin down a commitment from the much younger head of the U.S. delegation, secretary of state Edward Stettinius.[85] As related in the Stettinius official diary of the conference, the charming and affable former advertising executive was put on the spot by Proskauer at a critical meeting on May 2. After the consultants had presented their recommendations for elevating human rights to a place of prominence in the charter, Proskauer looked Stettinius in the eye and asked him frankly, "Are your for it?" After the room fell quiet, Stettinius, who had been appointed secretary of state precisely to manage such encounters, responded firmly, "I am, sir."[86] That commitment proved to be a decisive point of leverage for the remainder of the conference as the consultants continued to pressure the American delegation, both during private consultations and in the press, to make good on Stettinius's promise to back their amendments.

Next to Eichelberger and Shotwell, Fred Nolde was perhaps the most informed and engaged member of the consultant group on the issue of human rights. A former Lutheran minister and professor of religious education at the University of Pennsylvania, Nolde was executive secretary of the Joint Committee on Religious Liberty, a group established by the FCC and the Foreign Missions Conference of North America. He was also a member of another important organization whose work focused on postwar "global order" and human rights, the FCC Commission to Study the Bases of a Just and Durable Peace (CJDP). Established by John Foster Dulles and Walter Van Kirk in December 1940, the CJDP was dedicated to the principle that a lasting peace required a "common spirit" of a "brotherhood of man," and also to providing an avenue for Protestant churches to engage in international affairs. Nolde's religious liberty committee had produced a statement, adopted by the FCC in March 1944, calling for international guarantees of freedom of religion (both belief and practice), and Nolde was in regular contact with the CSOP on questions of human rights. His engagement with human rights and the UN would only deepen after the San Francisco conference as he became perhaps the most influential nongovernmental representative during the drafting of the Universal Declaration of Human Rights.[87]

In San Francisco, Nolde was tapped to present the consultants' recommendations on human rights. Prior to Proskauer's direct questioning of Stettinius, Nolde laid out four specific amendments to the Dumbarton Oaks Proposals that the group wanted the U.S. delegation to sponsor. The first was the addition of a new purpose in Chapter I: "To promote respect for human rights and fundamental freedoms." In Chapter II, the consultants inserted a new general principle openly acknowledging that human rights were "a matter of international concern." Also, given that there seemed to be no chance of negotiating a full international bill of rights at San Francisco, the consultants' amendment to Chapter II contained a "mini-bill" of sorts, listing freedom of speech, assembly, religion, and communication along with the right "to a fair trial under just laws" and a nondiscrimination clause as part of the fundamental rights all members of the UN would secure. The third proposed amendment added "developing and safeguarding human rights and fundamental freedoms" to the list of obligations of the General Assembly in Chapter V. The fourth and final proposed amendment added a specific mandate for a human rights commission to the list of responsibilities of the Economic and Social Council.[88] In his diary, Nolde notes that Proskauer had originally drafted a version of the amendments, but that in a meeting of the consultants, led by Shotwell and Eichelberger, the decision was made to substitute the "form worked out by John W. Davis . . . in N Y."[89] The Davis form was of course the proposals written by the CSOP.

Following Nolde and Proskauer, Eichelberger spoke emphasizing the importance of the establishment of a human rights commission in particular, but by and large both he and Shotwell were content to let the other consultants make the case for the CSOP's recommendations.[90] Such a strategy allowed for representatives of groups with large constituencies—whether religious (Nolde for Protestants, Proskauer for Jews, and Father Edward Conway for Catholics), labor (Philip Murray of the Congress of Industrial Organizations), or racial (Walter White of the National Association for the Advancement of Colored People)—to impress on Stettinius the ways human rights were the critical link between international organization and the American public.

As will be discussed in the next chapter, the expansion of the charter's human rights provisions enjoyed broad support among the more numerous "small powers" that were in attendance at San Francisco. But given the fact that, as described in Stephen C. Schlesinger's history of the UNCIO, the United States was organizer, host, and financier of the effort to construct a permanent postwar peace organization, few articles would be included without the express support of the American delegation.[91] Furthermore, the particular issue of human rights was one on which the U.S. was expected to lead—the conference stage was decorated with four Greek columns symbolizing Roosevelt's Four Freedoms—even if that leadership had to be foisted upon it by the consultant group. Thus, despite arriving at San Francisco determined to keep the revisions of the Dumbarton Oaks Proposals to a bare minimum, Stettinius and the other members of the U.S. delegation decided to rethink their position on the human rights commission. Based on their sense that it was critical to maintaining both public support domestically as well as American moral leadership abroad, the U.S. delegation decided to publicly back, with the exceptions of the proposed new general principle and "mini-bill of rights," the amendments written by the CSOP and presented by the consultants.[92]

There was a catch, however. Officially, the United States was co-sponsoring the conference with the other Big Four allied nations, the United Kingdom, Soviet Union, and China. Prior to the conference, the Big Four had agreed to present a united front, offering their opening amendments on a joint basis.[93] Thus, the Americans would need to achieve consensus on these human rights amendments before presenting them to the wider UNCIO. A fuller discussion of the Chinese role will follow in the next chapter; suffice it here to note that they unreservedly endorsed the amendments. In fact, members of the Chinese delegation had received a preview of the amendments when they had met with Fred Nolde for lunch just hours prior to the consultant meeting with Stettinius.[94] As they were at the Dumbarton Oaks talks, the British and Soviets were a harder sell, and while the two delegations accepted addition of a new purpose in Chapter I and expansion of the General Assembly's authority, they both balked at the specific creation of a human rights commission. That provision was defended in an impassioned, last-minute speech by U.S. advisor and president of Johns Hopkins University Isaiah Bowman at a May 4 meeting of Big Four delegations, which seemed to have an impact.[95]

Perhaps more important to the British and Soviet acquiescence was the work of another U.S. advisor, John Foster Dulles. Dulles's role here and in future years demonstrates the degree to which individual support for international human rights protections was less a function of ideology than of position. During the war, Dulles, among the most prominent and respected Republican voices on foreign policy, had been a member of the CSOP and founded and led the CJDP. Early on, his group had endorsed in principle the need for international human rights protections, and his friend and associate Fred Nolde was among the most effective consultants on human rights. Nevertheless, once incorporated into the official delegation, Dulles became an effective guardian of national sovereignty. As a member of a Big Four subcommittee charged with examining a "domestic jurisdiction" clause, Dulles reported at the same May 4 meeting that they had reached a decision to propose including a new principle in Chapter II.[96] Instead of recommending the promotion of human rights as a fundamental principle guiding the policies of member states, as the consultants had wanted, the Big Four proposed the following amendment: "Nothing contained in this Charter shall authorize the organization to intervene in matters which are essentially within the domestic jurisdiction of the state concerned or shall require the members to submit such matter to settlement under this Charter." [97] As had Benjamin Cohen's paragraph on human rights offered at Dumbarton Oaks, Dulles's formulation, which he would later present to the wider UNCIO committee, ensured that the expanded commitment to promote and protect human rights was contained and constrained by a categorical assertion of the principle of absolute national sovereignty.

Agreement on Dulles's proposal was achieved and with it, human rights were assured their place in the charter of the United Nations. When secretary-general of the conference Alger Hiss brought down the gavel on the final plenary session of the San Francisco gathering on June 26, 1945, Clark Eichelberger's sigh of relief may well have been audible over the din of applauding delegates. In many respects the document that representatives from fifty-one nations had just signed was a personal triumph for the self-effacing Eichelberger. No one had done as much over the past six years to make the United Nations Organization a reality, and the work of the CSOP had proved both pioneering and instrumental in the development of official policy. Nowhere was this more true than in the area of universal human rights, where the intellectual, public propaganda, and official lobbying work of the CSOP was decisive in determining both the place and the form of the human rights provisions of the Charter.

That the American crusade for human rights was led not by the United States government but by the CSOP and its allies pointed to the contingent nature of U.S. support for international human rights law, and revealed a newfound and tenuous susceptibility of the executive branch to public pressure in the arena of foreign policy. This susceptibility would continue into the postwar period, but the direction of the pressure would change considerably as the Cold War combined with an emergent legal isolationism to produce a movement, led by the American Bar Association, to disengage the United States from any UN human rights program. For its part, the CSOP would never again wield the kind of influence it had on U.S. policy during the war, despite eventually counting Eleanor Roosevelt among its members. In seeking the establishment of the Commission on Human Rights as a compromise between an international bill of rights and more vague statements of principle, the CSOP helped create the most important forum for human rights politics for the rest of the twentieth century—an achievement of no small measure.

But while the domestic lobbying efforts of American NGOs would continue to have a dramatic impact on the shape of U.S. human rights policy, the end of the war and the establishment of the United Nations demonstrated the degree to which the debate on human rights was increasingly international. The UNCIO may have made plain the rising global hegemony of the United States, but it also revealed an interest on the part of "small nations" in enhancing the social and economic functions of the UN and establishing the organization's moral foundation in the doctrine of universal human rights. Representatives of the semicolonial nations of the Philippines, Lebanon, and India—all of whom were particularly concerned with ensuring that the UN did not become an instrument keyed toward simply maintaining the global status quo antebellum—expressed this interest perhaps most pointedly. The next chapter will consider how human rights figured into the political strategies of certain Asian nations seeking to constrain and direct the emerging influence of an ascendant America.

Chapter 2

A Pacific Charter

A month after the United States entered World War II, a small group of Americans sent President Franklin Roosevelt a private telegram detailing the need for the United States to embrace war aims and policies that were more definitively antiracist and anti-imperialist. The telegram was signed by five longtime supporters of a more egalitarian racial order both domestically and internationally: Rosenwald Fund chairman Edwin R. Embree and Walter White, national secretary for the National Association for the Advancement of Colored People (NAACP), were joined by Pearl S. Buck, noted advocate of the Chinese cause, Ray Lyman Wilber, founder of the Institute for Pacific Relations, and Quincy Wright, University of Chicago professor and research director for the CSOP. Wright was already hard at work making human rights a fundamental part of the CSOP's plans for the postwar international order. In the wake of the San Francisco conference, White, in collaboration with W. E. B. Du Bois, Rayford Logan, and other members of the NAACP, would seize on the UN human rights provisions in an effort to address the abuse of African American rights in the United States. For the time being, Wright and White joined with the others in urging Roosevelt to give as much emphasis to the American partnership with China as with the United Kingdom in order to counter Japanese propaganda that his close relationship to Churchill constituted "evidence of Anglo-Saxon will to world dominance." While Roosevelt never arranged, as the group suggested, a "dramatic conference" with Chiang Kai-shek "and other leaders of yellow, brown and black millions throughout the world," he was to remain adamant in his insistence that China be granted Great Power status in the alliance as one of the "Big Four," alongside the U.S., UK, and Soviet Union. This effort was a small but meaningful intervention in the shaping of U.S. policy and an indication that the increasingly broad and idealistic rhetoric used to characterize the war effort represented, to some, an opportunity to realize more ambitious changes in the global order.[1]

The joint telegram sent to Roosevelt in January 1942 was both an additional example of civil society engagement in foreign affairs advocacy, and a symbol of another important element in the emergence of human rights politics during the Second World War. In the previous chapter, I argued that the CSOP was the central actor in establishing the specific human rights provisions of the UN Charter. The final fate of those provisions was assured once the Big Four powers endorsed them, both because the United States dominated much of the UNCIO, but also because of the widespread popularity of human rights among the "little nations" at San Francisco. If the Human Rights Commission and the dedication of the UN to the specific purpose of human rights promotion was a testament to the efficacy of the CSOP's intellectual, political, and policy work, these aspects of the charter were also viewed as heralds of a changing international political dynamic. For the leaders of small powers, particularly those emerging from colonial rule, the hope was that this new world order would mean a more "just" international system—defined variously to include equitable economic development, an end to racism and colonial exploitation, cooperation in achieving global social advancement, and a normative respect for the self-determination of peoples. That such hopes often proved illusory was due to the resistance of major powers as well as the paradoxes and contradictions of the positions held by small nations themselves. Nevertheless, during much of the 1940s, representatives from these "little nations," as Leo Pasvolsky once called them, proved to be an essential constituency in support of human rights at the UN.

This chapter reconsiders the wartime period from an international perspective in an effort to explain not so much the origins of the specific provisions of the charter, but rather the way those provisions were understood in the context of the trans-Pacific relationship. Beginning with Asian responses to the Atlantic Charter, the chapter then highlights Chinese participation in the Dumbarton Oaks talks before returning to San Francisco to examine the place of human rights in the rhetoric and policy proposals of various smaller powers. The connection drawn by many in Asia between human rights and anticolonialism, as well as the extent to which this connection was established in recognition of U.S. ascendancy as a world power, is made clear.

The Atlantic Charter on Different Shores

The first indication to much of the world that the conflict into which it had descended on September 1, 1939, might produce a global order different from the one envisioned by Adolf Hitler came in the form of an oddly informal statement issued by the president of the United States and the prime minister of the UK. The result of a dramatic secret meeting between Winston Churchill and Franklin Roosevelt in the foggy and frigid waters off the coast of Newfoundland, the equally dramatic, if extremely public "Joint Declaration" was signed by the two leaders on August 12, 1941, aboard the British battleship *Prince of Wales*. Much of the content of the Atlantic Charter, as the London press quickly dubbed it, was dictated by immediate political expediency. As Elizabeth Borgwardt notes, Churchill steamed across the Atlantic, hat in hand, looking to formalize and extend American support for the British fight against Hitler.[2] In preparing the first draft, the British prime minister, who was not without his own rhetorical gifts, borrowed from Roosevelt's "Four Freedoms" and Woodrow Wilson's "right of self-determination" in a not so subtle attempt to co-opt and flatter his American counterpart.[3] For his part, the American president, already convinced of the necessity of assisting the United Kingdom, reviewed and revised the statement with an eye toward the still influential strands of isolationism in Congress and in American public opinion generally. The deliberately broad and inspirational language of the Atlantic Charter was not intended as a statement of actual policy on the part of the British and American governments (although this would not dampen efforts on the part of some to *make* it official policy). Rather the Atlantic Charter was above all a calculated political maneuver, intended to bolster the flagging morale of the British people in the face of Germany's dramatic engulfing of continental Europe, and to shore up Congressional support for the president's escalating assistance to Churchill's beleaguered country.[4]

The Atlantic Charter stretched to the limit the frayed fiction of U.S. neutrality and outlined a set of eight Anglo-American principles that the two leaders promised would guide their efforts to establish, "after the final destruction of the Nazi tyranny," a new global order. Both governments explicitly rejected the possibility that the war would result in their own territorial aggrandizement, and proposed to enhance free trade, preserve existing borders, and place limits on armaments following the end of hostilities. The statement also pledged that the two "respect the right of all peoples to choose the form of government under which they will live; and they wish to see sovereign rights of self-government restored to those who have been forcibly deprived of them." They expressed their desire to collaborate with each other and the rest of the world in order to secure "improved labor standards, economic advancement and social security." In perhaps its most audacious moment, the Atlantic Charter evoked two of Roosevelt's Four Freedoms when it gave voice to the hope that following the war a peace would be established, "which will afford assurance that all the men in all the lands may live out their lives in freedom from fear and want." The final point of the charter called for the complete disarmament of "nations that threaten, or may threaten, aggression outside their frontiers . . . pending the establishment of a wider and permanent system of general security."[5]

Although echoing some of Roosevelt's Four Freedoms speech, the Atlantic Charter did not use the phrase "human rights," or call for anything like a binding international bill of rights. In fact, it was Roosevelt, the patron saint of the human rights movement, who struck out a more definitive commitment to "defend the rights of freedom of thought and speech" that Churchill had originally written into the joint statement.[6] The charter did, however, catch the attention of many beyond the Atlantic world, particularly with its rashly unqualified restatement of the Wilsonian principle of the right to self-determination. Reaction was perhaps strongest among colonial subjects and their sympathizers, many of whom regarded the Atlantic Charter with a mix of hope and skepticism.[7] The skepticism was easy to understand given the fact that Churchill, less than a month after drafting the document, proclaimed it inapplicable outside of Nazi-occupied Europe. "We had in mind," Churchill told nervous fellow imperialists in Parliament, "primarily, the restoration of the sovereignty, self-government and national life of the States and nations of Europe now under the Nazi yoke. . . . So that is quite a separate problem from the progressive evolution of self-governing institutions in the regions and peoples which owe allegiance to the British Crown."[8] As Wendell Willkie would learn over a year later, Churchill saw no point in resisting Nazi aggression only to then willingly dismember the British Empire. "I have not become the king's first minister," Churchill told reporters shortly after the U.S. envoy remarked critically on British colonial policy, "to preside over the liquidation of the British Empire."[9]

The hope sprang from the fact that the Atlantic Charter seemed to open up new political possibilities that, while brought by the exigencies of the war, might well survive into the projected postwar order. Churchill and Roosevelt had drafted the charter with their domestic constituencies in mind, particularly an American public sour to the traditional workings of international politics.[10] For those who hoped that the Atlantic Charter might point to a drastic revision of the guiding principles of international relations, it was not because the charter indicated a change of heart among ruling international powers. Rather, the charter raised the possibility that the United States, particularly to the extent that its foreign policy might be subjected to the influence of the transnational public sphere, could be prevailed upon to support right over might. This dynamic would extend beyond self-determination to the field of human rights more generally by the end of the war.[11]

Among the first to respond to the Atlantic Charter were those who sought a similar arrangement with the United States. The Chinese, whose situation was far more dire than that of the British, wished desperately for a parallel commitment from the U.S. to the destruction of Japanese tyranny in the Pacific. Unnerved by the summer-long negotiations between the Japanese and Americans, Nationalist Chinese officials were now hopeful that the Atlantic Charter indicated a shift toward a less accommodating U.S. policy toward Tokyo. A few days after the publication of the Joint Statement, Foreign Minister Quo Tai-Chi stated that the Chinese government "wholeheartedly" welcomed and endorsed the Atlantic Charter and pledged China to "make full contribution" to the effort to establish "a real new world order" after the successful defeat of the Axis powers, identifying the struggles in both Europe and the Pacific as part of a single "world-wide conflict."[12] Indeed, T. F. Tsiang, secretary general of the Kuomintang Executive Committee, told reporters that it was "unmistakable" that the broad language of the charter was intended to apply to the whole world. He went further in noting that given the fact that the wars now raging in Asia and Europe were parts of the same global war, there needed to be close cooperation between China, Russia, Britain, and the United States to bring about a worldwide peace.[13] From China, the Atlantic Charter appeared as an important opening in a conversation about the future global order, not merely the Atlantic one.

After the Japanese attack on Pearl Harbor, Chinese leaders no longer needed to convince the Americans that Europe was not the only battlefield, but they continued to press Roosevelt to reaffirm that the principles stated in the Atlantic Charter also pertained to the Pacific regardless of Churchill's protests to the contrary. In a January 1942 telegram, sent shortly after the publication of the Declaration by United Nations, President Chiang Kai-shek warned Roosevelt that the "spread of war in colonial areas differs from war elsewhere." Colonial subjects might well prove reluctant to "defend their present rulers against future rulers." More was required, he suggested, than to regale inhabitants of European colonies with accounts of Japanese atrocities—of which the Chinese were all too aware—in hopes of terrifying them into mobilization. Instead, what was needed was for all Asians to feel like their "national interests" were in some way at stake. Chiang asked Roosevelt to "persuade" both the British and the Dutch to "make changes in their attitude clearly indicating future political changes in the spirit of the Atlantic Charter." Stopping short of calling for a separate Pacific Charter, Chiang chose to urge his American allies to exert private pressure on the more reluctant colonial powers.[14]

Much of Chiang's argument had been advanced several months earlier in a series of Pulitzer Prize-winning articles that had appeared in both U.S. and Filipino newspapers. Written by Carlos Peña Romulo, then editor of the *Philippine Herald*, the series was conceived as an attempt to gauge how the Atlantic Charter was being received in the Pacific region. As he traveled through China, Burma, Siam, Malaysia, Indo-China, and the Dutch East Indies, he reported that the "familiar battlecries of democracy have but a distant echo" among the vast majority of Asia's colonial peoples. He was quick to add that he thought it essential that colonial peoples cast their lot with "the democratic front in the Far East" rather than Japan, but Romulo also noted that unless there was a dramatic change in policy on the part of European imperial governments, they could expect little support among the native populations. After meeting in secret with nationalist leaders in Burma, Malaysia, and the Dutch East Indies, Romulo concluded, presciently, that the Japanese were more likely to be welcomed than resisted by the subject peoples of the European colonies.[15]

As a Filipino, Romulo's position was peculiar. An American colony for some four decades, the Philippines had much in common with the rest of colonial Asia. Filipinos, like Malays, Vietnamese, Indonesians, and millions of brown, black, yellow, and red peoples the world over suffered the burden of white men. Romulo had come of age in an American empire that denied Filipinos full citizenship, extracted and exported most of the islands' economic produce, and ensured that the "color line" which had come to separate the races at home on the U.S. mainland was maintained across the Pacific.[16] Romulo's father and uncles had participated in the Filipino resistance to American annexation of the islands after the Spanish-American War of 1898, and Romulo was a member of the nationalist—albeit nonrevolutionary—political party of Manuel Quezon. His sympathies with other Asian subjects of empire were entirely in keeping with the broad sense of solidarity that, while not as prominently articulated as Pan-Africanism, was growing in a number of Asian quarters.[17]

And yet, Romulo's experience of American empire was not simply, or even primarily, one of exploitation. After the American "pacification" of Filipino resistance, Romulo's father quickly began collaborating with American officials, becoming governor of Tarlac province and a member of the Philippine assembly. From a place of privilege, Romulo became a beneficiary of one of the most significant aspects of American rule: a new public education system. Graduating from Manila High School in 1912, Romulo went on to the newly established University of the Philippines and then to study comparative English literature at Columbia University in 1920. This education provided him with a set of rhetorical tools adapted to the discursive nature of colonial politics. Speaking to university students shortly after his return to the Philippines in 1922, Romulo noted that Filipinos were now versed in American values: "Step by step, from the primary grade to the last rung of our student career, we have been constantly in contact with American ideas of freedom and equality, with American principles and modes of thought." The political edge of such an education lay, however, in the application of these ideals. He continued: "But when we would translate these, our spiritual heritage, into forces that make for our deliverance and emancipation, we are opposed by Americans, misunderstood by Americans, traduced by Americans."[18] This process of translation—which is to be understood here as a creative and politically charged endeavor—was essential to advocacy on behalf of Filipino rights and, eventually, Philippine independence.[19] In the postwar years, Romulo would again try to translate the ideals of human rights for the benefit of colonial peoples.

In 1941, however, the main difference between the Philippines and the British, French, and Dutch colonies Romulo toured was that the former had already received a promise of independence from the United States and had even been provided with a specific date: July 4, 1946. From Romulo's perspective, the right of self-determination had already been conceded by the U.S. within its own empire, and thus the Atlantic Charter represented the expansion of—or at least the possibility of expanding—the principle to a more universal policy. Realizing that possibility would require mobilizing the United States as a progressive international force more generally. Toward this end, Romulo's articles, although ostensibly written "as a Filipino for a Philippine reader," pressed at every opportunity for expanded American involvement in the region.[20] He lauded the steady stream of crates and oil drums, almost all of which bore American markings, traveling up the Burma Road to China and pleaded with U.S. officials not to cut off the flow.[21] He drew a sharp distinction between the United States, which he called "the most progressive and magnanimous of all the ruling powers in Asia," and the rest of the imperial field, noting how the name "America" was spoken with reverence by nationalists in other colonies.[22] Well aware of Churchill's recent caveat regarding the reach of the Atlantic Charter, Romulo warned that America "must make certain that her strength and her resources are being placed in the service of principles which are in keeping with her libertarian traditions and democratic institutions." The United States, lest it allow itself to prop up the oppressive European colonial regimes, had to ensure "that her strength is being mustered in the cause of freedom and democracy for the most advanced peoples of Asia and the enlightenment of other benighted millions."[23] Over the next decade, Romulo would return again and again to this theme of an exceptional American colonialism, exemplified by the Philippines experience, as a model for American engagement with the rest of the world.

Governments in other parts of Asia approached the Roosevelt administration in hopes of enlisting support for the application of the Atlantic Charter to the region. In March 1942, Iranian Minister Mohammad Khan Schayesteh met with State Department officials asking if the U.S. government might "make some declaration regarding Iran in accordance with the principles of the Atlantic Charter." The Iranian government worried that the war would bring a resumption of the "Great Game" of the nineteenth century, and that despite its recent treaty with Great Britain and the Soviet Union, the Soviets harbored "certain designs" on Iranian territory.

Acknowledging a "strong dislike" for the Russians among the Iranian people, Schayesteh also admitted to a general "feeling of mistrust" toward the British, suspecting they would not oppose Moscow's incursions. Thus the Iranians were turning to the United States—whom they regarded as an ascendant power in world affairs—for public support of their territorial integrity. Warning that without faith that their independence would be preserved, the Iranian people might not find the motivation to "resist aggression" from the Axis Powers, Schayesteh was confident public support from the United States would be enough to alleviate any such doubts. In his meeting with Schayesteh, Sumner Welles was quick to reject the possibility of the U.S. issuing such a statement, but it is clear that many in Asia saw the Atlantic Charter as a critical opening through which they could pressure the

Great Powers in general and the United States in particular into supporting their autonomy.[24]

The most explosive issue continued to be the applicability of the provisions of the Atlantic Charter to the British Empire. Burmese prime minister U Saw was so displeased with Churchill's implacable attitude on the Atlantic Charter that he braved the menace of both the Japanese and German navies to confront the King's first minister in person. After suggesting that "before [the British] free the countries under Hitler they should free the countries within the British Empire," U Saw was informed that the British government had no intention of discussing the "constitutional progress" of any part of the empire before the successful conclusion of the war. Although he had come with assurances that there would be full cooperation with the British war effort, the Burmese leader nevertheless warned of the danger of failing to make the principles of the Atlantic Charter applicable beyond Europe. "I cannot foresee," U Saw told the London press, "what the attitude of my people will be when I explain the response of the British Government to my request."[25] As fellow nationalist and future secretary-general of the United Nations U Thant recalled, Winston Churchill was a towering figure in many regards, but in his understanding of Asian nationalism "he was a small man."[26]

After his meetings with British officials in London, U Saw traveled to Washington to assess the American position on the applicability of the Atlantic Charter in Asia. Certainly the prime minister was justified in his curiosity, as the American government had given little public indication as to the extent to which they believed the Joint Statement applied across the globe. Privately within the administration, there had been much conversation regarding the importance of the self-determination clause as applied to the British Empire, and there seemed to be a widespread view that the provisions of the Atlantic Charter needed to apply in Bombay as well as Budapest if they were to serve their purpose as rallying points in a global struggle against Nazi and Japanese tyranny. These convictions were not backed with political courage, and at the urging of Sumner Welles, the president agreed to restrain from offering advice to the British, both publicly and privately, on the administration of their colonies or publicly contradicting the British interpretation of the Atlantic Charter.[27]

Even more than in Burma, the deepening crisis in India demonstrated both the difficulty of containing the Atlantic Charter's influence and the peculiar way it could enter into even U.S. domestic politics. Despite cries of hypocrisy from many of its colonial subjects, the Churchill government only increased the obstinacy with which it refused to concede the universality of the Atlantic Charter's principles. Declaring any discussion of independence or even self-government verboten until the end of the war, London collided with the increasingly militant Indian National Congress. By the fall of 1942, some 50,000 Congress Party members, including Gandhi and Jawarhalal Nehru, had been imprisoned, while hundreds of thousands more continued to make India nearly ungovernable and totally indefensible against Japanese invasion. The Indian nationalist movement did not need the Atlantic Charter either for inspiration or justification, and indeed Indians themselves seemed to have little use for the document after Churchill's vocal repudiation of it. Outside observers, however, found in the Atlantic Charter a significant entrepôt into the intra-imperial affair, one that went not through London but through Washington.[28]

On the first anniversary of the charter, Chiang Kai-shek sent yet another message to President Roosevelt, this one expressing his concern over the mass arrests currently underway in India. Chiang pointed out how deeply these actions threatened the war effort, which continued to look grim during summer 1942. If British action were allowed to continue unchecked and unchallenged, "the avowed object of the Allies in waging this war would no longer be taken seriously by the world and the professed principles of the United Nations would lose much of their spiritual significance." Calling Roosevelt "the inspired author of the Atlantic Charter," Chiang implored the American president to give some measure of reality to the rhetoric of the charter and use his considerable influence to modify British policy.[29] In his response, Roosevelt politely declined to admonish Churchill for the Indian situation either publicly or privately, instead admonishing Chiang about Gandhi's shortsightedness and Pollyanna attitude toward the Axis powers. The president nevertheless affirmed the U.S. ongoing sympathy with the aspiration to independence and noted how that sympathy found practical demonstration in the American policy in the Philippines. Regardless, however, neither the U.S. nor China had "the moral right to force ourselves upon the British or the Congress Party" and a unified Allied front needed to be maintained at all costs.[30]

Whatever the position of the Roosevelt administration in private, it was becoming clear that the public gap between the Allies' lofty statements and their less admirable actions, or more precisely nonactions, was turning into a public relations liability. By March 1943, even the president's personal envoy to India, William Phillips, was suggesting that Roosevelt intervene more directly in the Indian situation. There might be little hope of diffusing the mounting tensions, but at least they might deflect criticisms that the United States was not doing enough to make real the promises of the Atlantic Charter. Williams suggested both a conference, under U.S. sponsorship, of Indian political factions as well as an explicit U.S. guarantee of Indian independence after the war as tactics to draw the Congress Party back to the table and offer the British a face-saving means to de-escalate the situation. Through this plan, which Williams admitted was neither particularly innovative nor likely to succeed, "America will have taken a step in furthering the ideals of the Atlantic Charter."[31]

Roosevelt no more adopted Phillips's suggestions than Chiang's, although the administration did take some action to placate Indian opinion. It was not the British that the administration pressed to live up to the principles of the Atlantic Charter, but the California legislature. After a complaint from the Indian agent general, Secretary of State Cordell Hull cabled California governor Earl Warren to express his concerns over a bill then before the state assembly. As written, the bill would have amended the state's already discriminatory Alien Land Law to deprive Asian immigrants—those from India included—of their ability to work their own farms. This blatant and ham-handed attempt to exploit anti-Japanese sentiment to advance a century-long effort to disappropriate Asian farmers lumped enemy (Japanese) with ally (Indian) and threatened to further detract from the carefully cultivated image of racial progressivism the government was endeavoring to project abroad. Rather than denounce the demonstrably racist basis of the law, however, Hull pressed Warren to seek changes in the law, such as the exemption of nationals of Allied nations from the ban, hoping that such a targeted law would not exacerbate the feeling already growing in India, that "the United States is unconcerned with the practical application of the high principles expounded in the Atlantic Charter."[32]

If officials in London did not regard the principles of the Atlantic Charter as universal, and officials in Washington tempered their enthusiasm for those principles to the point of near total inaction, its import lay in the way it authorized a "diplomacy of conscience" in U.S. foreign policy.[33] In particular, the advocates for colonial independence adopted the Atlantic Charter as a normative standard through which they might pressure not the European colonial powers directly, but the United States as an influential "third party." The results were both international and domestic, and hinged on Washington's perception of domestic and foreign public opinion. After the United States entered the war and the special relationship between the U.S. and the

UK became the center of a wider alliance, the Declaration by United Nations inserted human rights into the global lexicon as a marker of what could and should be different after the war. As planning for the postwar began in earnest in late 1944, the political dynamic that had emerged around the Atlantic Charter began to focus on the place of human rights in the future world organization.

China, Dumbarton Oaks, and "Justice"

Human rights were still marginal to Asian concerns at the time of the Dumbarton Oaks conference, but Chinese participation in the talks provided a telling preview of the discussions in San Francisco. "Participation" may be an overstatement. As noted in Chapter 1, the contents of the Dumbarton Oaks Proposals were negotiated between the U.S., UK, and Soviet Union. Since the U.S. entry into the war, however, China had been one of the "Big Four" allies—largely at the insistence of the U.S.—and, as such, was included in the talks at Dumbarton Oaks. Neither the British nor the Soviets had ever considered the Chinese a "Great Power," and both regarded Chiang Kai-shek's Nationalist forces as a minor factor in the overall military equation of the war. Earlier in the war, both Churchill and Stalin had been willing to defer to Roosevelt's wishes in this regard as the price of full American participation in the fight against Nazi Germany. From the president's perspective, inclusion of the Chinese as one of the Big Four had less to do with the current reality of Chinese power and more to do with cultivating China as a U.S.-friendly regional replacement for Japan in the global balance of power. Roosevelt's "Four Policemen" model of peace enforcement, which he never fully developed, required a strengthened China for the Asian beat. If Chiang owed his ascendancy to the United States rather than global rivals Great Britain and the Soviet Union, all the better from Roosevelt's point of view.[34]

With Allied victory looking more and more certain by the summer of 1944, the Soviets were granting fewer and fewer concessions to their American allies and refused outright to meet face to face with Chinese officials.[35] The Soviets claimed that their formal neutrality in the Pacific war left them unable to negotiate with the Chinese representatives, but Stalin's antipathy for Chiang Kai-shek as well as his fear of a new competitor for supremacy in Asia were enough to cause him to shun the Chinese. As a result, the Dumbarton Oaks talks proceeded in two phases: the first was held over six weeks in

August and September where the plan was actually negotiated between the Soviets, British, and Americans; the second—postponed and truncated because of the difficulty in securing agreement during the first phase—occurred during the first week of October during which the American and British delegations presented Chinese officials with what amounted to a fait accompli.[36] The Chinese, while nominally full partners in issuing the Dumbarton Oaks Proposals, had very little to do with their drafting. As historian of the conference Roger Hilderbrand notes, "The Asians were there, after all, to be blessed, not to reform the church."[37]

After a protracted six weeks of intense negotiations between the Big Three, the Chinese were brought in for nine short days of discussions, nominally a second round of negotiations. At the opening session, both the Americans and British explained to the Chinese that the document before them simply could not be altered and that any results from the current talks could only be formulated into a second, separate document.[38] Over the course of the following week, however, the American and British negotiators worked in concert to ensure that no such second document would in fact be released. Instead, incorporating a strategy devised during an October 3 meeting of the American group, it fell to Leo Pasvolsky, the State Department senior advisor on international organization, to "explain away" the majority of the Chinese concerns, "making them appear as they were already dealt with in the proposals as is."[39] The Chinese delegation was under no illusions and V. K. Wellington Koo, ambassador to London and delegation chief, in particular felt that the main goal for China was not to revise the proposals but to maintain its current membership in the Four Powers club.[40] The Chinese ultimately proved amenable to signing on to the Dumbarton Oaks Proposals, without a supplemental attachment, acceding less to the force of Pasvolsky's logic than to the reality of their position as junior partner in this particular endeavor.

Despite the absurdity of an ex post facto negotiation, the Chinese comments and criticisms of the proposals suggest that they had some different aspirations for the coalescing international organization. At the outset, Ambassador Koo expressed disappointment that the proposals did not include a stronger commitment to international law or a more detailed statement of the principles that would guide the organization's work. The Chinese were particularly keen to see an explicit commitment to "justice" in the opening paragraphs of the organization's charter.[41] "Justice" was, and is, a nebulous concept (even more so than human rights), but the Chinese desire to prioritize it alongside peace and security reflects their recognition that peace often meant the preservation of the status quo, regardless of the dictates of justice.[42] In suggesting that the pursuit of justice be a guiding principle (if not an express purpose) of the new international organization, Koo and his associates highlighted the Chinese ambition, shared with numerous other less powerful nations, that the future world order allow for peaceful, progressive change and not just enjoined stability.

U.S. secretary of state Edward Stettinius found such suggestions "extremely idealistic," but in reality they reflected the enlightened self-interest of the Chinese.[43] As the weakest party in this particular quartet, it was easier to be the voice of principle at Dumbarton Oaks, as China would benefit least from an international system predicated on power politics. Wellington Koo had long believed in the potential for international law to serve as a buffer between weaker states and the depredations of stronger ones. A graduate of Columbia University, Koo was an experienced diplomatic hand, having represented China at the Paris Peace Conference of 1919 and negotiated the adjustment of the humiliating, quasi-colonial treaties with European powers established in the wake of the Boxer Rebellion. Well aware of China's relative weakness vis-à-vis the other Great Powers and deeply familiar with the ambitions of both the United States and the United Kingdom, Koo had learned from Chinese experience since the nineteenth century that without some sort of institutional restraint the strong would take what they could while the weak would do what they must. International laws, particularly when based on a commitment to the sovereign equality of nation-states, could serve as such an institutional restraint. From this perspective, sovereign equality could be the basis of a more democratic international system, free of the kinds of unequal treaties and foreign relations that characterized China's international life during the previous century. Sovereign equality also conveyed a more scrupulous observance of the principle of noninterference in domestic affairs. International law, at least in the period prior to the elaboration of the human rights covenants, implied more, not less, state sovereignty, suggesting that the "justice" the Chinese sought from the new international organization was explicitly inter-state justice, rather than individual justice.[44]

Some of the ambiguities of the Chinese emphasis on international law and justice are evident in another proposal advanced without success at Dumbarton Oaks. The Chinese suggested that "equality of all states and all races" be the second general principle for the organization.[45] This coupling of the equality of states with the equality of races gave the principle of sovereign equality a moral dimension that transcended the functioning of the

international system. The development of European imperialism was deeply
entangled with the ideology of racism. Destabilizing the doctrine of white
supremacy both within and between nations was the aim of a long and ongoing struggle—one that would soon intersect with the emergence of the UN
human rights system. At Dumbarton Oaks, the Chinese had planned to advance that struggle by pressing for an explicit commitment to racial equality as a corollary of the commitment to sovereign equality. Koo was familiar
enough with the system of racial segregation in the United States to know that
such a commitment would have domestic as well as international implications. Recognizing the need for continued U.S. patronage of the Nationalists
going forward, Koo decided not to press racial equality for fear of jeopardiz-
ing the "cordial" relationship with the U.S. Given the determinative role racial
ideology had played not only in imperialism, but in both the current European and Pacific wars, the Chinese were not mistaken in foreseeing a need to
address the question of race in the coming international organization.[46]

Although they pursued the moral questions of justice and racial equality,
the Chinese proposals did not articulate these concerns in the language of
human rights. At Dumbarton Oaks, the only initiative on human rights came
from the American delegation. The single reference to human rights that had
made it into the Dumbarton Oaks Proposals piqued Chinese interest, however, and at one of the final sessions of the conversations, Dr. Chang Chung-
fu, an advisor to the Chinese delegation, asked for clarification of the phrase
"promote respect for human rights and fundamental freedoms" contained
in Chapter XI. He asked the authors of the draft what they had in mind and
inquired specifically as to whether "promotion" entailed the drafting of an
international bill of rights. As usual, Pasvolsky gave the definitive interpretation of the draft proposals, informing Dr. Chang that while the proposals
recognized the general importance of human rights, particular lists of rights
as well as the development of any international machinery for their implementation would be left up to the General Assembly. Such work, Pasvolsky
indicated, "would not likely happen for some time" as the future world organization would no doubt have to conduct "appropriate studies" of the subject
and then secure agreement among all the member states.[47] Regardless of the
actual time frame, Pasvolsky's response made it clear that human rights—
while they had made it, perhaps through the back door, into the Dumbarton
Oaks Proposals—were not among the priorities for the Big Three governments. The Chinese could take it or leave it, along with entire document, but
they could not hope to achieve any modifications or further elaboration.

At the final plenary session of the conversations at Dumbarton Oaks, held on October 7, 1944, the Chinese, British, and American delegations made a public show of Four Power unanimity in releasing the proposals for international organization, the absence of the fourth power notwithstanding. Despite more than a week's worth of discussions, the Chinese were signing onto a document that had been completed on September 27, the final day of the Soviet phase of the discussions. Privately, Koo told the other members of the Chinese delegation that the organization outlined in the Dumbarton Oaks Proposals was a dramatic improvement on the old League of Nations, even if some of the provisions were less than adequate. He thought their delegation had performed well, not only highlighting the "moral" dimension of the future organization, but also giving voice to the "small powers" that were not in attendance.[48] The delegation had succeeded in preserving China's status as a Great Power, even if they left little mark on the proposals themselves. To the degree they still wished to see their own ideas about the future international organization realized—or at the very least genuinely considered—they would have to bide their time until the full UN conference, over six months later.

San Francisco Redux: Human Rights and "Little Nations"

As described in the previous chapter, the UNCIO held in San Francisco in the spring of 1945 was where the CSOP achieved its aim of securing a prominent place for human rights in the new international organization. CSOP members along with other consultants pressured the U.S. government into sponsoring amendments to the Dumbarton Oaks Proposals that eventually became the human rights provisions of the UN Charter, including the Human Rights Commission. Once the other "Sponsoring Powers"—the UK, Soviet Union, and China—endorsed these amendments, they were virtually guaranteed to become part of the final document, as the conference approved almost everything of consequence supported by all four nations. Nevertheless, without the votes of the so-called "small powers"—mostly from Asia, Latin America, and the British Commonwealth—the amendments on human rights could not have been adopted, and the discussions around these and other proposed human rights provisions reveal that human rights was fast becoming a global discourse on justice and progressive change. At the time of the Dumbarton Oaks conversations, this connection between international justice and social progress on the one hand, and human rights on the other hand, remained (at least for the Chinese) unarticulated. By the time delegates descended on San Francisco, many, particularly from Asia and Latin America, had come to regard the human rights functions of the emerging international organization as the chief indicators of its potential to serve these interests.

The clearest articulation of this discursive function came in the opening statement of one of the most unlikely delegates to the conference, Charles H. Malik of Lebanon. Malik's appearance on the dais at San Francisco's War Memorial Opera House was improbable for a number of reasons. Lebanon contributed next to nothing to the Allied effort, having declared war on Germany and Japan and signed the UN Declaration only weeks before the conference. The sovereignty of the Lebanese government was tenuous at best—the country had declared its full independence in 1943 only to have the Free French government, which claimed authority over Lebanon and Syria based on the old League of Nations Mandate system, nullify the declaration. While the French had been forced to make concessions to the Lebanese government by the British and Americans on the eve of the San Francisco conference, a small crisis erupted when Free French troops reentered Syria and Lebanon and began a series of maneuvers suggesting they were interested in reestablishing their prewar colonial mandate.[49] As for Malik himself, he had been an untenured professor of philosophy at the American University of Beirut up until six weeks before the conference, when the government of Bishara al'Khoury selected him to serve as the new minister to the United States. Despite a total lack of diplomatic experience or training, Malik had close relations with the American community (mostly Protestant missionaries and educators) in the Levant and a growing reputation as an important Arab religious and philosophical thinker.[50] Over the next seven years, he would become a major intellectual force in the development of the UN human rights system.

In his opening remarks to the San Francisco conference, Malik immediately linked peace with human rights and global justice: "The peace which man believes in and will spontaneously rise up to defend is only that which is grounded in his ultimate rights and freedoms and in the reality of justice." Unconsciously echoing Quincy Wright's vision of a dynamic peace, Malik suggested that a peace that lacks justice "only cloaks terrible inner conflict" and that a security that does not seek to protect human rights "is utterly insecure."[51] The French gambit to quietly reinstate the old colonial order in the Near East was precisely such a chimerical peace, and the Lebanese delegation made headlines during the conference denouncing those ambitions.[52] Other Arab, Asian, and South American delegations expressed solidarity with the Lebanese and Syrian cause, making evident the broader desire to move away from the prewar order.[53] The French actions also reinforced the desire of many smaller states to see that the new international organization included effective mechanisms for change, particularly in the development of self-government and independence for colonial territories. More so than many other representatives, Malik believed that these mechanisms must include individual protections—specifically protections for freedom of thought and conscience—that transcended state sovereignty, setting his formulation of "justice" apart from what the Chinese had proposed at Dumbarton Oaks.

The hope for such mechanisms proved difficult to realize at San Francisco. The Big Three allies of the U.S., UK, and Soviet Union got a Security Council along the lines of what they had negotiated among themselves at Dumbarton Oaks and at the February 1945 Yalta meeting of Roosevelt, Churchill, and Stalin. It was to be a limited body of eleven members, with five permanent seats allocated to the Big Three plus France and China, and six "nonpermanent" members elected to two-year terms by the General Assembly. Charged with maintaining international peace and security, the Security Council could address any situation it deemed to be a "threat to the peace, breach of the peace, or act of aggression," and had the power to take a range of actions from simply calling on the parties in dispute to seek a negotiated settlement to deploying "air, sea, or land forces . . . to maintain or restore international peace and security." While technically each member of the Security Council had one vote, the five so-called "permanent members" were more equal than others, keeping a tight grip on these expansive powers through the exercise of an unqualified veto unique to them. Perhaps the single most divisive issue of the conference, this veto power indicated that the Great Powers would allow the egalitarian spirit of the new United Nations Organization to extend only so far. When it came to the coercive power to enforce peace, the UN would preserve and legitimize the predominance of some states over others. Although the small powers did not simply acquiesce to Great Power supremacy in the Security Council—indeed the fight over voting procedures produced the most heated exchanges of the conference—the fact that the U.S., UK, and USSR all made the issue the sine qua non of their participation in the organization (meaning the sin qua non for the UN's very existence) meant that very little could be done to alter those plans.[54]

Forced to concede that the coercive maintenance of international security would continue to be the province of power politics, the small states had more success with expanding the General Assembly's right to debate. The adoption of this amendment—the only substantive change achieved over the combined opposition of the Big Three—was a symbolic victory for democratic principle at the UN that was to have real consequences for the UN human rights activities and more. Seeking to ensure that the Security Council had exclusive authority over anything related to security, the Soviet Union, with the tacit support of the United States and Great Britain, introduced language that would have confined General Assembly discussion to only those matters over which it had authority to take action. This proved a bridge too far for the vast majority of smaller nations, who regarded the General Assemble and the Economic and Social Council—which were to lack the Security Council membership and voting structure—as the fora where their influence on world affairs would be best assured. Behind the leadership of Australia's Herbert Evatt, most small nations voted to adopt new wording over unified opposition from the United States, Soviet Union, Great Britain, China, and France.[55] As it finally emerged, Article 10 of the charter grants the General Assembly the right to discuss anything "within the scope of the Charter."[56] This expansion of General Assembly power was designed with the hope that the body would function, in the words of Carlos Romulo, as the "conscience of the world," calling on not only individual nations to live up to their obligations under the Charter, but also the Security Council to carry out its mandate to keep the peace.[57]

Small nations were less successful in achieving expanded or more specific commitments to human rights. Rather, it was the United States delegation that proposed the insertion of paragraphs dealing with human rights into the preamble and Chapters II, IV, IX, and XII. But while it is true that the American proposals were the ones that eventually made their way into the charter, the small nations did more than simply provide a solid voting block in favor of these amendments when they arrived in committee. Many outside the inner circle of the Big Four came to San Francisco with specific human rights proposals of their own, and many more arrived with a general commitment to increasing the prominence of human rights within the new organization's mission.

Among those who arrived in San Francisco with specific human rights amendments to the Dumbarton Oaks Proposals were Colombia and South Africa,[58] both of whom submitted draft preambles declaring that the desire to promote rights was one of the key catalysts for establishing an international organization. Mexico, Brazil, and the Dominican Republic submitted a joint proposal—the first to be made public—that made the guarantee of human rights among the core purposes of the organization.[59] Beyond these proposals, which would be revisited in committee, two delegations also came forward with specific lists of rights. The delegation from Panama submitted a "Declaration of Essential Human Rights" containing eighteen articles protecting the freedoms of religion, speech, and assembly as well as the right to a fair trial and equal protection. Also included in the Panamanian draft were articles guaranteeing the right to work, adequate food and housing, and social security.[60] Representatives from Cuba drafted a Declaration of the International Rights and Duties of the Individual which, although less concise than the Panamanian draft, recognized a similar range of rights. The Cuban proposal also distinguished between two categories of rights, civil and social, although no distinction was made as to implementation (as would happen during the drafting of the human rights covenants).[61]

More than any other bloc of countries, those from Latin America arrived at San Francisco determined to elevate human rights. Having met at a conference of the Organization of American States in February, this bloc benefited from a level of regional organization that would be copied and surpassed by others (notably in Europe) in later years. There, the Dumbarton Oaks Proposals had been harshly criticized for seeking to institutionalize Great Power dominance and for failing to give due consideration to human rights promotion.[62] The government of Mexico, which had hosted the conference in Chapultepec Castle in Mexico City, proposed adding the promotion of "respect for human rights and fundamental freedoms" to the purposes of the new international organization, citing, among others, the CSOP report on human rights authored by Quincy Wright. The Cuban delegation even managed to submit a draft "Declaration of the International Duties and Rights of Individuals" at the Mexico City gathering.[63] The Final Act of the conference endorsed the Dumbarton Oaks Proposals, but called for revisions and amendments that would, among other things, ensure that promotion and protection of human rights would be a priority of the new world body.

Under the rules of the UNCIO, however, the voting bar was set quite high for amendments (adoption by a two-thirds majority in all but procedural matters), and none of the specific amendments offered by the Latin American delegations met with success in the drafting committees. Such was the case when several small nations attempted to insert "justice" alongside peace and security as the very first listed purposes of the organization (Chapter 1, Article 1, Paragraph 1). The majority of delegations felt, as Malik had announciated in his opening address, that the omission of the term "might mean that the Organization intended to impose a peace of expediency rather than a peace founded on justice." Those opposed to listing "justice," including the United States, held that such an addition might hamper the UN's ability to act, bogging the organization down in debate over what justice might mean in particular circumstances. In an allusion to the U.S. Senate, the American representative more ominously warned that such a change might render the charter unacceptable to "those parliaments which are prepared to accept an Organization whose primary purpose is clearly stated as the maintenance of peace and security." When the vote was taken, the addition of justice was supported 19 to 15, but failed to be reach the required two-thirds majority.[64]

During the next session, the Panamanian delegation attempted to strengthen Paragraph 3 of Article 1 to read, "promotion and protection of human rights and fundamental freedom" as opposed to "promotion and encouragement of respect for human rights and fundamental freedoms." The latter wording had been inserted earlier by the drafting subcommittee and was based on language contained in the Big Four joint amendments. In raising the amendment, the Panamanian delegate suggested that such a change would bring the stated intent of the organization more into line with the views expressed by U.S. Secretary of State Stettinius just four days earlier, when he said "the protection and promotion of individual human rights" was a "fundamental purpose of the world organization." The May 28 speech had been given by Stettinius in response to growing public criticism, much of it orchestrated by members of the consultant group mobilizing their constituencies back home, of the half-hearted efforts of the American delegation in support of their own human rights proposals. In committee, the Americans, backed by the British, were now taking the position that such a change would imply that the UN would "actively impose human rights and freedoms within individual countries," an implication that would unduly raise expectations of what the organization could realistically accomplish.[65] The American delegate went farther and suggested that the secretary was stating the *unilateral* policy of the United States to promote and protect human rights around the world, rather than proposing a major principle to be enshrined in the charter. While attempting to obfuscate the secretary's statement, the delegation hit on what would become perhaps the quintessential formulation of U.S. human rights policy over much of the next seventy years: America is happy to dispense wisdom from on high, but reluctant to engage in collaborative norm-setting on the ground. Whatever Stettinius had meant, the attempt to change the paragraph was unsuccessful and the earlier U.S.-sponsored wording prevailed.[66]

Despite the fact that the Great Powers had succeeded in containing efforts to prioritize justice and expand the organization's general commitment to human rights, the changes insisted upon by the American consultants combined with those supported by the small nations meant that the charter was becoming significantly more progressive than the Dumbarton Oaks Proposals. This fact made all the more important the elevation of the "domestic jurisdiction" clause to a cardinal principle of the organization. As noted in the previous chapter, the UK, China, Soviet Union, and U.S. formulated a general domestic jurisdiction clause in response to the human rights provisions insisted upon by the consultant group.[67] This connection was made explicit and public during a late drafting session, when the sponsoring governments tapped John Foster Dulles, co-author of the amendment, to present their case for the new clause to the conference as a whole. He suggested that respect for the priority of domestic jurisdiction needed to be made a basic principle of the United Nations Organization precisely because of its far-reaching role in social and economic matters. Such a role raised serious questions about the relationship between the UN and national governments. "Would the Organization deal with the governments of the member states," Dulles asked, "or would the Organization penetrate directly into the domestic life and social economy of member states?" The new paragraph proposed by the sponsoring governments would answer the question by requiring the UN "to deal with governments" in recognition of the "distinct value of the individual social life in each state." Dulles left the door open that the strict construction he was offering of the paragraph might be "subject to evolution" over time, citing the example of the United States and noting that over the years the Constitution had been interpreted in such a way as to give increasing authority to the federal government instead of states.[68]

On the whole, making the domestic jurisdiction clause one of the organization's general principles was widely supported, although the Bolivians attempted (without success) to change the language from prohibiting intervention in matters that were "essentially" domestic to only those that were "solely" domestic. Whether they represented great or small powers, the government officials negotiating the charter all were loath to give up sovereign authority within their own borders—an unsurprising fact that should have tempered overly idealistic accounts of small-power enthusiasm at San Francisco for establishing the kinds of international human rights protections that limited state sovereignty. The uncontroversial adoption of Article 2(7) also makes clear the divergence in the understanding of human rights between the CSOP and other civil society advocates on the one hand, and the small power governments on the other. While the wartime reports of the CSOP had explicitly sought to include human rights protections in the international organization as a limit on state sovereignty and as a direct relationship between individuals and global institutions, many small powers supported the human rights elements of the charter to promote a more just and ethical interstate system. These two conceptions were not necessarily mutually exclusive, but they were (and are) distinct enough to mean that the charter's human rights provisions cannot be regarded as either inherently advancing state sovereignty or abridging it. Rather, those provisions establish a tension between the two that remains unresolved in the UN human rights system to this day.

While nearly all delegations agreed that a general domestic jurisdiction clause was a good idea, the United States was exceptionally concerned to ensure that "there would be no interference . . . in the domestic affairs of any country." During the debate on the powers and structure of the Economic and Social Council, Virginia Gildersleeve sought an amendment that reinforced and restated Article 2(7) as it applied to the council's work. Despite the fact that the committee had already voted to adopt a draft, Gildersleeve asked that the change be made "in order to dispel fears which might arise when the Charter [comes] up for Congressional ratification." Most members of the drafting committee, even the Soviet delegate, thought this would be overkill. The Australians argued that such a change would "seriously weaken" the moral standing of the United Nations.[69] At the next meeting the U.S. agreed to withdraw the proposal, but only if the committee agreed to attach an official note to its report stating that the members of the drafting committee "are in full agreement that nothing contained in Chapter IX can be construed as giving authority to the Organization to intervene in the domestic affairs of member states."[70] Thus even as the U.S. was sponsoring language, including the specification of a Human Rights Commission, that enhanced the basic authority of the Economic and Social Council to deal with human rights issues, it was shoring up the bulwark of domestic jurisdiction.

The Charter, Colonies, and "Independence"

The tensions, ambiguities, and potential consequences surrounding human rights at the birth of the United Nations were nowhere more apparent than in discussions of the colonial world. Although on the original Dumbarton

Oaks agenda, the issue of the place of colonies and colonialism in the new world order had been deferred, much to the chagrin of many observers such as Clark Eichelberger and W. E. B. Du Bois. It was, however, discussed at the Big Three summit at Yalta, which meant, among other things, that the Chinese viewpoint was excluded. Roosevelt, Churchill, and Stalin agreed that the new United Nations Organization would take over the oversight of the League of Nations Mandate Territories and establish some mechanism for a similar administration of territories "detached" from the Axis powers. A more challenging and significant dilemma arose when the U.S. military began to insist on maintaining bases on, and therefore having unfettered control over, the Pacific Islands taken from the Japanese.[71] This issue remained contentious throughout the San Francisco conference and would ultimately be settled in favor of the United States, but the basic outlines of the UN Trusteeship system were essentially in place by early 1945. The main point of discussion at San Francisco, therefore, involved the question of the rest of the colonial world, or what were referred to euphemistically as "non-self-governing territories."[72]

The most outspoken delegate seeking an end to colonialism was Carlos Romulo, who had been made a brigadier general and aide-de-camp to Douglas MacArthur during the war, and was now the head of the Filipino delegation. As had Charles Malik and others, Romulo invoked human rights as a marker of and mechanism for a progressive peace, but he also pointed toward a future without colonialism and the specific changes that respect for human rights would require. In his opening address to the conference, Romulo called on representatives to remember the "one billion Oriental faces" who now looked to this conference and the organization that would result from it "for recognition of their human rights." Romulo then offered his view of what such recognition would entail:

> It is their hope and their prayer that the peace which this Conference is seeking to secure is one that will not neglect the uplift and development of all socially and economically depressed areas and peoples, but one that will help raise them to a plane of living where they can become not merely bystanders but effective collaborators in the promotion of human welfare and advancement. Theirs is the plea, my Fellow Delegates, that such a peace may not be appropriated for the purpose of freezing the political, economic, and social order of that part of the world.[73]

Most of his audience would have been well aware that the "political, economic, and social order" to which Romulo referred was not Japanese militarism but European colonialism. If others before and during the San Francisco
conference had made human rights a metonym for peace with progress, Romulo now added the expanded meaning of the Atlantic Charter to the chain
of association, making decolonization and development of Asia the specific
content of those rights.

In committee, Romulo worked to see "the principle of trusteeship" extended to all colonial territories. He argued that extending this principle did
not necessarily imply placing all colonies in the UN Trusteeship system, but at
a minimum it meant the progressive evolution of colonial territories toward
independence with some sort of international involvement or oversight.[74]
Wellington Koo joined Romulo and proposed, in addition to an expanded
international role in non-trust territories, increasing the authority of the
Trusteeship Council to include the publication of reports and the making of
recommendations. Such ideas were anathema to the French, who argued that
the principle of "nonintervention in the domestic affairs of member states"
included the administration of colonies. The Dutch also opposed the idea
of increased international involvement in colonial affairs, noting that "the
superimposition of such a system would be a backward step from the point
of view of the more advanced colonial territories," although by what measure
colonies such as the Dutch East Indies might be considered "advanced" was
not specified.[75]

The Chinese and Filipinos also pressed for the inclusion of the word "independence" as one of the basic objectives for both the Trusteeship system
and the administration of non-self-governing territories. As Koo told the
other delegates, the League covenant had included independence as a goal
for Mandate territories and any move away from this standard would provide
propaganda material for the Japanese, who were still fighting in Southeast
Asia. For Romulo, it was simply a question of living up to the promise of
the Atlantic Charter, a betrayal of which would crush the hopes and aspirations of millions of people around the world.[76] The British, however, were
unconvinced that independence was the universal goal of dependent peoples.
Lord Cranborne warned that the inclusion of independence might sow "con-
fusion" and "political uncertainty" in colonial territories and might have the
negative effect of scaring off "capital development" of colonial territories by
metropolitan governments. In any case, the British admonished, independence should not be confused with liberty as it was entirely possible that the

"natural evolution" of colonial territories might end in something other than full independence.[77]

In their effort to have the word "independence" included in the charter, Romulo and Koo received no help from a delegation they assumed would be a natural ally, India.[78] Technically, neither India nor the Philippines were sovereign states. The Philippines were scheduled for independence the following year. On the other hand, Churchill's government—in power only for a few more weeks—still refused to concede an inch to the Indian independence movement.[79] India was granted representation at the conference based on the fact that it was an original signatory to the Declaration by United Nations (an early and perhaps regretted concession by Churchill to Roosevelt). The Indian delegation, however, was hand picked by the Colonial Office and under strict orders not to broach the subject of colonialism.[80] Two years later, India would emerge as the leading anticolonial voice at the UN, but at San Francisco—much to Romulo's disappointment—the Indians demonstrated exactly the lack of autonomy inherent in the colonial relationship.

Significantly, however, among the first to invoke human rights at the conference was the chairman of the Indian delegation, Sir A. Ramasamy Mudaliar. A member of the Justice Party, which had opposed much of the independence movement out of concern it would lead to a Brahmin-dominated India, Mudaliar had been on the Viceroy's Council and was currently one of two Indian members of Churchill's War Cabinet. His opening speech stressed global interdependence rather than national independence, and contained the most eloquent statement of the universality of human rights made at San Francisco. Mudaliar cautioned against indulging in a version of political "realism" that would lead the conference to overemphasize the military enforcement of peace, and privilege the Security Council over the General Assembly. Instead, he called attention to what he saw as a deeper reality, one that "all religions teach[:] the dignity of the common man, the fundamental human rights of all beings all over the world." He continued:

> Those rights are incapable of segregation or of isolation. There is neither border nor breed nor color nor creed on which those rights can be separated as between beings and beings. And, speaking as an Asiatic, may I say that this is an aspect of the question which can never be forgotten, and if we are laying the foundations for peace we can only lay them truly and justly, to last for some time—for a couple of generations at least. Those fundamental human rights of all beings all

over the world should be recognized, and men and women treated as
equals in every sphere, so far as opportunities are concerned.[81]

Here, human rights were bound up in a transnational moral sense of equality
and mutual obligation, not in decolonization and self-determination. Mudaliar was one of the few to insist, during the debate on the domestic jurisdiction clause by the Economic and Social Council, that some sacrifices in
sovereignty were necessary if there was to be an effective and just peace.[82]
Ironically, the fact that Muladiar was politically unable to emphasize national
independence allowed him to articulate a vision of what an international
human rights system might mean for state sovereignty that was closer to the
version outlined by civil society organizations than to the one expressed by
most other governments at San Francisco.

The United States was represented on the committee dealing with trusteeship and colonies by former Minnesota governor turned naval commander
Harold Stassen, who, after he had secured a free hand for the military in the
Pacific, was largely without direction from above. On the question of a general statement of principles regarding non-self-governing territories, the U.S.
was uncharacteristically without a clear policy and had not submitted any
draft proposals. Into the breach rushed the consultant group, which mobilized to pressure the American delegation to become more engaged in the
debate between the colonial powers and the Asian representatives. On this
issue, the NAACP led the way; Walter White, W. E. B. Du Bois, and Mary
McLeod Bethune represented the NAACP at the conference. In fall 1944, Du
Bois had been among the first to excoriate the Dumbarton Oaks Proposals for
their neglect of the colonial issue in his book *Color and Democracy*, and the
preeminent African American intellectual had agreed to come to San Francisco mainly to lobby this issue.[83] Now, he along with White pressed Stassen
and the rest of the American delegation to ensure that the future peace would
not be imperiled by the ongoing injustice of colonialism. White even took
his lobbying efforts to Washington after he left the conference in late May,
discussing with President Truman the need to highlight concern for colonial
territories in his closing remarks to the conference.[84]

Truman's final speech to the San Francisco conference did, in fact, mention the need to address the problem of colonialism, but the real impact of
the NAACP efforts came through their access not to the president but to a
lowly technical advisor to the American delegation, Dr. Ralph J. Bunche.[85]
A longtime member of the NAACP and future recipient of the Nobel Peace

Prize for his work with the UN, Bunche was brought to San Francisco to advise the delegation on trusteeship matters. Having worked under Benjamin Gerig in the wartime Office of Strategic Services, Bunche served as the intelligence service's expert on colonial affairs and was thought to be a rising star in certain State Department circles. Despite a growing rivalry with Du Bois, his one-time idol, Bunche met regularly with the NAACP contingent, keeping them abreast of the intra-delegation developments on trusteeship.[86]

Bunche's efforts went well beyond giving White and Du Bois inside information on U.S. delegation deliberations. In addition to helping to coordinate the NAACP's public lobbying effort with the private advice he and Gerig were giving to Stassen, Bunche secretly passed a draft of the chapter on non-self-governing territories to the Australians, who used it as the basis for a compromise proposal between the colonial powers and the Asian delegations.[87] As it was eventually submitted to the committee, the draft avoided the taboo word "independence" but pledged administering authorities "to develop self-government, to take due account of the political aspirations of the peoples, and to assist them in the progressive development of their free political institutions." The draft's other important addition involved the issue of international oversight. In what Bunche regarded as a personal triumph, governments administering non-self-governing territories agreed to send the secretary-general "statistical and other information . . . relating to economic, social and educational conditions in [their colonies]."[88] Bunche wrote his wife Ruth at the conclusion of the conference that it was quite a thrill for her "blasé old hubby" to see his hand throughout the charter's colonial provisions. Later, the mechanism of reporting would become an important model for the implementation of international human rights norms, in both the intergovernmental and nongovernmental sectors.[89]

For Carlos Romulo, these paragraphs "carried the whole concept of independence without specifically mentioning the word independence." Romulo had been the most insistent in the committee on using the term and tried to get the United States to support it in a series of private conversations with Stassen. The two ultimately reached a deal whereby Romulo would back off on his demand that the chapter use the word "independence" in exchange for a public endorsement by Stassen of Romulo's interpretation of the chapter.[90] At one of the final drafting committee meetings, Romulo declared his support for the Bunche/Australian draft proclaiming that it carried "the spirit and meaning of independence."[91] Stassen, who had to work to convince the British and French to accept the phrases on developing "self-government" and "free political institutions," was equivocal enough in his own endorsement of the formula so that both sides felt vindicated.[92] The British delegation, tele-gramming London, expressed satisfaction that Stassen had "squared" the up-pity Romulo.[93] For his part, Romulo seemed satisfied that this compromise placed the U.S. on the side of the postcolonial states rather than the colonial powers.

Writing to Filipino president Sergio Osmeña after the signing of the char-ter in late June, Romulo recalled the main objective of the Philippine delega-tion: "to voice the aspirations of the small nations of the world namely: to establish the guarantee of the fundamental freedoms; to assure to all peoples the blessings of the Bill of Rights." It would have been more accurate to say that Romulo had worked to extend the blessings of the Declaration of In-dependence rather than the Bill of Rights, but his conflation of the two was not only commonplace but indicative of the emerging articulation of antico-lonialism and human rights at the end of the Second World War. He could, therefore, trumpet his achievements at San Francisco, citing as the main markers of his success in the field of human rights not the inclusion of those rights as a fundamental principle of the UN, nor the mandate for a human rights commission, but the chapters dealing with colonialism. "They are the soul of the Charter," he wrote, for they legitimated the yearning for freedom on the part of colonial peoples worldwide. Human rights and decolonization were inextricably linked in Romulo's mind, and to the degree that the UN Charter promoted both, small nations like the Philippines could have a major impact on global politics.[94]

Of course, an accurate assessment of the chapter on non-self-governing territories would have given more credit to Ralph Bunche and the NAACP consultants as major facilitators in the evolution of American policy, even though the Filipino pressure had been the most public. Taken together, the process by which the chapter was drafted and adopted illustrates several as-pects of human rights politics as they had developed during the war, and as they would continue to function in the postwar period. First, the essen-tial role of civil society organizations is readily apparent, especially when given access to channels of influence in the U.S. government, and it serves as a reminder that while the international system continued to be designed to benefit states—and in particular, powerful states—the rhetoric of human rights presented opportunities for non-state actors to engage with the sys-tem. Second, Romulo's advocacy on behalf of colonial peoples demonstrates the malleability of that rhetoric, as he worked explicitly to bring the Atlantic

Charter's right of self-determination into the UN Charter under the banner of human rights. Third, the integration of self-determination with human rights was central in the minds of Romulo, Koo, and others to ensuring that the United Nations Organization would serve, at least in some respects, not to preserve the status quo but to actively promote a more just world order—an order often articulated with reference to human rights. And finally, the ambiguous position of the U.S. government, which had been initially inclined to close ranks with the colonial powers, suggests how little American leadership there was on human rights at San Francisco, despite what one observer called "America's historic identification with independence as a 'law of nature.'"[95] And yet, precisely because of America's historic self-identification with human rights, the rise of the United States as a world power was a necessary though insufficient condition for human rights to become a politically potent discourse. How potent would only become apparent in the years following the San Francisco conference.

Chapter 3

Carlos Romulo, Freedom of Information, and the Philippine Pattern

Carlos Romulo left San Francisco buoyant about the future. The new United Nations Organization was far from perfect, but he believed the charter and the process by which it was negotiated signaled the advent of a new global order. As he had told his fellow UNCIO delegates at the closing plenary session, "the fact that fifty nations, representing perhaps fifty basic divergences of self-interest, could for once distill from those divergences the purest essence of fundamental accord—that . . . is the achievement."[1] In his report on the conference to Philippine President Sergio Osmeña, Romulo highlighted the fact that the Philippines managed to insert anticolonial sentiments into the charter as evidence of the possibility that through careful and considered diplomacy, coupled with moral rectitude, the Philippines could have an impact on the world stage far in excess of its economic or military station. The Philippines, advised Romulo, should make participation in and strengthening of the United Nations a cornerstone of its postindependence foreign policy.[2]

Whatever his hope in the potential for the UN to allow the Philippines to punch above its diplomatic weight, Romulo had another reason for optimism. As he privately confided to a friend less than two weeks after the unconditional Japanese surrender aboard the *U.S.S. Missouri*:

> The supreme position of America these days is an encouraging sign of the trend of a world that is weary and tired of turmoil and strife. While it is true that Russia is assuming every day a more important role, still it will be hard for her to overtake the United States. Great

Britain has been relegated to a secondary position whether she likes it or not. . . . The dawn of a new day is therefore here, and in the Philippines we must get ready for the advent of more prosperous times.[3]

Any prosperity that was to come would be hard won for the Philippines as it sought to recover from wartime devastation as great as any suffered in Europe or Asia, a fact that Romulo—famed as the "last man out of Bataan"—knew all too well. And yet, he could look forward to a brighter future because the ascendancy of the United States promised, it seemed to him, a departure from an old imperial order symbolized by Great Britain. The UN was but one manifestation of the new Pax Americana.

Another was the newfound relevance of human rights as a framework for advancing his agenda of decolonizing and developing Asia. Romulo was among those who took up the language and the law of human rights in the immediate postwar period, recognizing it as a way of extending and managing U.S. influence in the world. That recognition was rooted in his political and journalistic experience of American colonial rule in the Philippines, which had left him fluent in the language of American democracy, overawed by the potential of American power, and practiced in a politics of translation and rearticulation. After negotiating the charter provisions on non-self-governing territories, Romulo believed he could mobilize the language of human rights in a way that spoke to American sensibilities at the same time that it advanced the interests of colonial and postcolonial peoples. His sense of the potency of American power and of himself as a mediator of that power, led him to advocate that the United States not only support those interests but identify with and guide the development of those countries. While such a project was not necessarily typical of most of those engaged in the development of the postwar UN human rights program, Romulo's efforts demonstrate how the language and law of international human rights were, at least in part, a critical and contested space through which the meaning and direction of American influence in the world was negotiated from unequal positions of power.

As a member of the UN Human Rights Commission, Romulo was a prominent contributor to the drafting of the Universal Declaration of Human Rights and made a special mission of establishing an international freedom of information convention.[4] A gifted writer and orator, he articulated these and other efforts in terms of what he referred to as the "Philippine Pattern." This was a pattern based on American colonial policy in the Philippines, which

Romulo read, against the grain, not as an appeal for more imperialism but as a model for U.S. engagement with the world. Exemplified most explicitly in his pursuit of the freedom of information convention, Romulo's application of the Philippine Pattern was, in fact, a creative and selective translation of the American rights tradition to align it with the aspirations and interests of less developed countries. The convention ultimately failed to be adopted as the disruption of the global order caused by the Second World War eventually settled into the divisions of First, Second, and Third Worlds. Nevertheless, the Philippine effort to extend "the blessings of the Bill of Rights" demonstrates some of the possibilities and limitations of human rights politics in the late 1940s.

The Philippine Pattern

The establishment of the Republic of the Philippines as an independent state, an event that took place on the unsubtle date of July 4, 1946, demonstrated the continuing bond between the islands and the United States as much as their separation. Manila was still mostly rubble when Romulo joined President Manuel Rojas (who had recently defeated Sergio Osmeña in the country's first presidential election), General Douglas MacArthur, U.S. ambassador Paul V. McNutt, and 400,000 Filipinos in a steady drizzle to watch the American flag lowered for a final time.[5] Philippine independence was long anticipated and closely choreographed, and encompassed much that represented continuity with the colonial era. Formally, the United States retained many of its old privileges in the economic sphere with the passage of the Philippine Trade Act, also known as the Bell Act, which exacted a variety of concessions from the newly sovereign Filipino government. In exchange for swallowing the Bell Act, the Philippines was given substantial reconstruction aid, in the form of the simultaneously passed Philippine Rehabilitation Act, which was to provide much needed economic recovery assistance for the catastrophic war damage sustained on the islands. Informally, the Philippines maintained close political, economic, and cultural ties with the United States through their work together in a variety of international arenas, including the UN. This "special relationship" would come to be known derisively as neocolonialism, but from Romulo's perspective, the cultivation of close ties with the United States was essential to the pursuit of the Philippines' international (and domestic) interests, including decolonization.[6]

No one embodied this special relationship more than Carlos Romulo. Asian American historian Augusto Fauni Espiritu declares him "a true 'Filipino-American'" who straddled and negotiated the U.S.-Philippine relationship in his biography, writings, and diplomacy.[7] From the moment he became a public figure as a young protégé of Manuel Quezon, Romulo was associated with those educated by and oriented toward the American system. He earned a master's degree from Columbia University, wrote in English rather than Spanish and, in 1935 received an honorary doctorate from the University of Notre Dame in recognition of his editorials on behalf of the Tydings-McDuffie Act.[8] When war came to the Philippines, Romulo spent three months broadcasting as "The Voice of Freedom" from the underground caves of Corregidor Island before being evacuated, only to return at the side of Douglas MacArthur to the Leyte beach in October 1944. Romulo remained in the U.S. for most of the war and achieved a measure of fame, authoring three books—*I Saw the Fall of the Philippines* (1942), *Mother America* (1943), and *My Brother Americans* (1945)—and traveling constantly, logging some 90,000 miles and speaking in over 466 cities. These efforts, along with his Pulitzer Prize and his widely hailed performance at the San Francisco conference, combined to make Romulo perhaps the most prominent Asian voice in the U.S. and a rising political star back home.[9]

As a product of the Philippine-American relationship, Romulo presented his anticolonialism as rooted in his assimilation of American values. "I am a nationalist," he wrote in *I Saw the Fall of the Philippines*, "because I was educated in America and have absorbed the principles of democracy and liberty that are so thoroughly a part of America."[10] He presented a narrative that resonated with the widespread American perception of the benevolence and exceptionalism of the U.S. project in the Philippines, calling the islands America's "masterpiece" and a model for the entire region.[11] During the war, Romulo emphasized how well the United States had prepared the Philippines for independence, in part to head off any backpedaling from the promise to grant the islands sovereignty in 1946. But more than simply reinforcing his old political goal of a sovereign and independent Philippines, Romulo used the narrative of the national journey to establish a place for the Philippines in postwar international society.

His celebration of the American colonial project in the Philippines drew sharp contrasts between the practices of the United States and of the other colonial powers in Asia. In *Mother America*, Romulo argued that the rest of Asia was condemned to an eternal midnight of ignorance and exploitation by European rule and, should it continue after the conclusion of the war, the world faced the possibility of a new, greater catastrophe: the "cataclysm" of "a racial war."[12] Averting such a disaster was possible, he suggested in a July 1944 *Far East Survey* article, only through establishment of a new order in the Pacific, an order based on "the Philippine Pattern."

> The pattern that applied to the Philippines can apply to every country in the Far East. The success of that American plan has been the greatest in the history of colonization. By following that pattern, by investing spiritually as well as economically in countries under their rule, and by gaining the loyalty and gratitude of the natives, England and the Netherlands will be the gainers in the Far East.[13]

In arguing for an expanded American role in Asia based on its Philippine experience, Romulo was attempting to deploy the rhetorical strategy that had been effective in the struggle for Philippine independence—flattery of American self-perception as a just and decent people with a challenge to live up to that self-perception—in order to affect broader U.S. foreign policy.

Romulo's Philippine Pattern implied that his country was not only a good model to be replicated, but that the new republic could also be a conduit for the broader transformation of Asia. One of his first ideas for a postwar Philippine role—an idea which never became public—included the establishment of a regional federation in the southwestern Pacific made up of the Philippines, the East Indies (Indonesia), Singapore and the Malay States, Thailand, and Indo-China. As "the most politically advanced nation in this area," the Philippines, Romulo suggested, would "inevitably take the leadership in striving for this goal." Once established as the center of the federation, the Philippines could guide the other nations to full political maturity. The political organization and governing structure were left unspecified in the thirteen-page plan for the massive new federation. What was included was a plan for an extensive public relations campaign to win American support through articles, speeches, books, radio programs, and even movies. However unlikely this proposed federation looks in retrospect, the plan indicates that as early as 1942 Romulo was thinking about what the institutional form of the Philippine Pattern might look like, and saw U.S. support as necessary and perhaps sufficient to realizing his aims.[14]

His experience at the San Francisco conference demonstrated to Romulo the potential of the UN to serve as an institution, and human rights to serve as a discourse, through which the Philippines could pursue its anticolonial and leadership ambitions for Asia. He titled a brief January 1946 article, "Human Rights as a Condition of Peace in the Far East." His focus, however, was not on the human rights provisions inserted by the consultant groups, but on the charter's chapters on trusteeship and non-self-governing territories, which he argued placed the problem of colonialism on new footing by acknowledging, tacitly, the aspiration toward independence of all dependent peoples. Still, Romulo warned that a festering animosity among colonial peoples would threaten peace—or, rather, was already threatening peace in places like Korea, Indo-China, and Indonesia—if it was not dealt with properly. Toward this end, Romulo wrote, the world must guarantee "universal recognition" of "the fundamental human right of each man to speak for himself, of each nation to speak for itself." The right to speak, to be heard, and to be considered, was granted to the Philippines and a select few other Asian nations at the San Francisco conference. Only by extending this right and the other human rights to all colonial peoples would the lasting peace to which the UN was dedicated be realized.[15]

A few months later, at the first session of the UN General Assembly, Romulo introduced a resolution to give colonial peoples a voice on the international stage. To the consternation of both the French and British delegates, Romulo asked the Assembly to adopt a resolution calling for the convening of a global conference of representatives from the non-self-governing territories, the favored UN euphemism for colonies not in the trusteeship system. Offering the resolution, Romulo noted that while the charter required administering powers to provide periodic assessments of the "welfare" of their colonial wards, there was no mechanism for the inhabitants of colonies themselves to be heard. Implying, not unreasonably, that colonial powers might not always offer objective assessments of their own administration, Romulo thought it essential that colonial subjects be allowed to give voice to their own aspirations as well as report violations of their human rights.[16]

Indian delegate Krishna Menon and Milan Bartos of Yugoslavia immediately declared their support for the conference, but the most important target of Romulo's argument was the United States. Once again, he invoked the Philippine Pattern.

We are asking, for the Non-Self-Governing Peoples today, exactly the same opportunity for self-expression that we Filipinos enjoyed for forty years, in our relations with the United States of America. We are proceeding on the assumption that what was done in our country can and should be done elsewhere, for the sake of the peace, progress and security of the world, and with similar benefits.

John Foster Dulles, representing the United States, was not so sure. Whatever the merits of the American rule of the Philippines as a model for other colonies, Dulles, speaking immediately after Romulo, felt "compelled to oppose the pending resolution" because, he reasoned, it seemed to insert the UN into the domestic affairs of member states. Dulles, as described in the previous chapters, had drafted the "domestic jurisdiction" clause of the charter and was keen to see the principle defended at all levels of UN work. Ultimately, both Romulo and Dulles (along with cosponsor India and co-opponent Britain) were able to support a compromise resolution offered by China, which "invited" administering powers to convene the conference rather than directing the Economic and Social Council to do so, but the episode indicated how Romulo would attempt to combine the Philippine Pattern with human rights to affect U.S. policy at the UN. As it had during Romulo's drive to include the word "independence" in the Charter, the United States declined to embrace a non-self-governing peoples conference, not only because it seemed to encroach upon state sovereignty, but also because it drove too much of a wedge between the United States and its European allies.[17]

Another of Romulo's human rights initiatives was more successful, drawing wide support—including from the United States—and exemplifying how the human rights discourse in the postwar period was contested through an engagement over the meaning and direction of American influence in the world. The second UN conference that Romulo proposed at the 1946 General Assembly session was one "to discuss methods of ensuring the unimpeded transmission of news throughout the world." As with the first, he took care to articulate this initiative in the language of human rights. "Freedom of information is a fundamental human right," the draft resolution read. "It is the touchstone of all of the freedoms to which the United Nations is consecrated."[18] This time, Romulo had the full support of the U.S. delegation—the result of a less public and more conciliatory lobbying effort. A version of the draft resolution was submitted by another member of the Philippine delegation during the first part of the General Assembly's first session, held in London. This original resolution was withdrawn after U.S. delegate Senator Arthur Vandenberg, who wanted the London session to focus on organizational matters, assured Romulo's deputy Salvador Lopez that the United

States would in the future support the calling of such a conference. The tabled draft resolution was revised and resubmitted by Romulo six months later, during the second part of the Assembly's first session.[19]

In the weeks before presenting the resolution, Romulo consulted with the U.S. delegation. The most significant contribution by the Americans was the expansion of the conference to cover not only the press (still understood in terms of print journalism), but other information media as well, specifically film and radio. As much about free trade as human rights, this change was a concession to the commercial interests of the major film studios and broadcast networks.[20] Protecting freedom of information through an international treaty would make it much easier for the purveyors of American popular culture to consolidate and enhance their expanded wartime access to foreign audiences. When the American Society of Newspaper Editors (ASNE) declared in 1944 their support for the elimination of "conventions and customs" and the removal of "all restrictions imposed for commercial or political advantage" on the flow of news and information worldwide, they were seeking universal markets at least as much as universal rights.[21] Buttressed by these commercial interests, the proposal for a freedom of information conference was well received by the United States.

The freedom of information conference attracted support from the American delegation both because the ideas of free speech and a free press fit well within the mainstream of what Truman administration officials believed to be traditional American rights, and because, as a challenge to colonialism, it was an oblique one. Romulo's call for a conference of colonial peoples caused consternation as it cut too closely to a more unsettled area of U.S. policy. The third significant human rights initiative at the first General Assembly session was even more problematic for the United States; this one was introduced by India and was far more confrontational.

Indian independence (and partition) were still a year away, but the new Labour government in London had already conceded to the political reality of Congress Party leadership in India.[22] Among other things, this meant that India was now officially represented by V. L. Pandit, who was persona non grata at San Francisco. Unlike in the Philippines, the master narrative of Indian independence was one of defiant struggle and confrontation,[23] and now Pandit struck a more combative tone than Romulo. Her draft resolution directly accused a fellow member-state of a specific human rights violation: it sought the condemnation of the Union of South Africa for the discriminatory treatment of the Indian minority in that increasingly racially structured country.[24]

The resolution was something of a flashback, as Indian rights in South Africa had been the issue through which Mohandas Gandhi had entered politics in 1907 on his way to joining the Indian independence movement. That past returned as well in the figure of the South African representative at the UN. An aged but unbowed Jan Christiaan Smuts, Gandhi's foil as colonial secretary four decades previously, rose to defend his country and denounced the Indian proposal as an untenable violation of Article 2(7). Mark Mazower has described Smut's "imperial internationalism," which, as an architect of both the League of Nations and the UN, he had sought to give institutional form in two successive international organizations. A leading proponent of the British Commonwealth system, Smuts saw nationalism as entirely compatible with a large, supranational system of governance. He certainly also believed that, as it was signed in San Francisco, nothing in the charter precluded the continuation of either the British Empire or white minority rule in South Africa. Like his British counterparts, Smuts understood the elimination of "independence" from the chapter on non-self-governing territories as proof that the UN would allow colonialism to continue unabated. As for the human rights provisions, including those he himself had written into the preamble, Smuts essentially saw them as a restatement of the old imperial ethic of the white man's burden. He was, therefore, genuinely shocked to see this attack on what he regarded as business as usual in Africa.[25]

Most other delegations agreed with Romulo, who argued that by signing the charter nations had agreed to "the observance of the principle that there should be no distinction as to race, sex, language or religion." Romulo had long admired Smut's trajectory from military opponent of the British Empire to a loyal subject capable of advancing national interests within the colonial system—a trajectory not unlike that of Romulo's own father.[26] The Filipino also admired the South African's performance at the 1919 Paris Peace Conference, where, as the leader of a delegation from a small, not fully independent country, Smuts was able to make an outsized contribution.[27] Now, however, Romulo was dismayed to see that the seventy-six-year-old Smuts failed to grasp the extent to which the war had begun to turn the tide of international opinion against the most vulgar forms of racism.[28]

That most UN members were loath to appear in any way complicit in South Africa's increasingly harsh racial discrimination—even to the point of rejecting a strict interpretation of the domestic jurisdiction clause in Article 2(7)—was evident in the final vote, which saw the Indian resolution adopted by a two-thirds majority. In the hours before the vote, however, Romulo worried that even though his side appeared to be winning the debate was beginning to break down along the color line and warned that they "will have solved nothing if, in this controversy, we each stand firm and unmoving upon the vantage point of our racial sympathies." He implored those opposed to the resolution to take another look at the issue, not from a narrow legal or political view, but from a moral perspective. Demonstrating both the provenance of his education as well as the particular audience he was trying to persuade, he ended with a paraphrase of Frederick Douglass: "He who places a chain of prejudice on another people's neck runs the danger of placing the other end of that chain on his own."[29]

His words were in vain. The United States could not but line up with South Africa, the British Commonwealth, and the majority of western European states (with the notable exceptions of France and Norway). Not only had Smuts invoked the holy writ of domestic jurisdiction precisely as Dulles had done when Romulo proposed the colonial peoples conference, but it was all too obvious to many—and would soon become obvious to many more—that the system of segregation and discrimination set up in South Africa very closely resembled the Jim Crow laws that operated throughout much of the United States. Even Arthur Vandenberg, part of the U.S. delegation to the UN, had to admit he could see little difference between the plight of "Indians in South Africa and negroes in Alabama." Romulo would have done better not to remind the U.S. of its own history of racial oppression—a history hardly consigned to the past.[30]

If Paul Gordon Lauren is correct that the UN Charter "opened up a veritable floodgate to new possibilities of expanding international human rights as never before in the history of the world," then the first General Assembly session began to dig some of the channels into which the waters of human rights would be allowed to flow.[31] Carlos Romulo tried to steer them toward the decolonization and development of Asia, but found success more readily when he aligned himself with U.S. interests. The label for that alignment was the Philippine Pattern, and in his effort to give concrete form to the charter's vague human rights provisions, Romulo hit upon the development of an international convention on freedom of information as a way of pursuing his agenda in the idiom of American empire. As he told the General Assembly in his opening address, his newborn nation was "a child of the marriage of the East and the West, heir to the traditional ways and aspirations of one and the social and political institutions of the other." Of those "traditional ways" he said little, but the Eastern aspirations—aspirations Romulo claimed were

held by the inhabitants of Asia, the Near East, and Africa—were national independence, which the Philippines had achieved, and economic modernity,
which it was as yet achieving. Among those Western social and political institutions was a free press, which could serve as an agent of global progress and
liberty if properly established throughout the world.[32]

Freedom of Information: Rights and Responsibilities

Given the way he foregrounded human rights in many of his UN initiatives,
it was no surprise that Romulo sought a seat for the Philippines on the UN
Human Rights Commission when it was formed in early 1947. He served for
two years and made some critical contributions to the commission's work,
not least of which was much of the wording for Article 1 of the Universal
Declaration of Human Rights.[33] He saw the commission's work, particularly
in the drafting of the International Bill of Rights, in much the same way that
Quincy Wright and the other members of the CSOP had—as a potential
"corner-stone" of a world government.[34] He supported an Australian push to
establish an international court of human rights and, once that possibility was
shot down, worked to make the Human Rights Commission itself a forum in
which specific complaints of human rights abuses could be heard.[35] The next
chapter considers some of the issues and controversies of the Human Right
Commission in more detail, but it is worth noting here that the effort to allow
the Commission to hear individual complaints—which finally succeeded
under the leadership of Salvador P. Lopez with the adoption of Economic and
Social Council Resolution 1235 in 1967—was seen by Romulo as an aspect of
his larger endeavor to guarantee the right to speak and be heard, particularly
by colonial peoples.[36]

At the third meeting of the Human Rights Commission, Romulo asked
the group to create a sub-commission to advise the Commission on freedom
of information in general, and, more important, to prepare the agenda for the
international conference, which would be scheduled for the spring of 1948.[37]
The UN Sub-Commission on Freedom of Information (SCFOI) met over several weeks in May and June 1947. Unlike the Human Rights Commission, the
SCFOI was made up of "independent experts" rather than government representatives, although some members were more independent than others. Romulo nominated his friend and protégé Salvador P. Lopez. A former student
of Romulo's at the University of the Philippines (Romulo was Lopez's English

professor), Lopez had followed Romulo into newspaper work and then into the Army. During the war and in the immediate aftermath, Lopez served as one of Romulo's most trusted and thoughtful advisors, and his subsequent career seemed in many respects an echo of his mentor's.[38] He served in a number of capacities for the Philippine mission to the UN, at times chairing both the Human Rights Commission and the SCFOI, and eventually succeeded Romulo as permanent Philippine representative. He also served as ambassador to the United States, foreign secretary, and president of the University of the Philippines, as had Romulo.[39] An able and effective advocate for the cause of freedom of information, Lopez earned the respect of John Humphrey, the first head of the UN Secretariat's Human Rights Division, who remarked, "no one did more to promote freedom of information at the United Nations."[40]

The U.S. government was also enthusiastic about the creation of the subcommission and the upcoming conference. The high priority given to the project was evident in the nomination of Zechariah Chafee to serve on the SCFOI. Professor of law at Harvard University, Chafee had literally written the book on free speech, *Freedom of Speech* (1920), and was the primary intellectual force behind the legal revolution in free speech jurisprudence over the past quarter century. Legal historian G. Edward White credits Chafee with advancing the first modern legal argument for free speech in the United States, noting that, prior to 1920, the First Amendment was "marginal" to most interpretations of U.S. Constitutional law and that free speech was "undeserving of special judicial solicitude."[41] Chafee's arguments came in response to the arrests of thousands of Americans—most notably Eugene V. Debs—on sedition and espionage charges during the First World War. Although something of a nadir in the legal suppression of dissent, the wartime crackdown was hardly a departure from the way speech had been regulated in the past, and Chafee's claim that the First Amendment created broad protections for the press and individuals was a radical innovation.[42]

Chafee's prominence in the field had led him to be appointed in 1943 as vice chairman of the Commission on Freedom of the Press (CFP). Organized in early 1943 by University of Chicago President Robert Hutchins and funded by grants from Time, Inc. and The Encyclopedia Britannica, the CFP conducted a series of semipublic hearings, interviews, and surveys over the next three years in order "to discover where free expression is or is not limited, whether by government censorship, pressure for readers or advertisers, the unwisdom [sic] of its own proprietors or the timidity of its managers."[43] The group was made up primarily of intellectuals—including Reinhold Niebuhr,

Archibald MacLeish, and Arthur Schlesinger, Sr.— rather than journalists and its thought processes were led largely by Chafee and fellow Harvard professor, philosopher William Ernst Hocking. The result was a discouraging account of the current state of American journalism—declining competition and circulation, increasing sensationalism and "human interest ephemera," profit-driven owners, and an overly deferential attitude toward authority— and a more inspiring statement of principles and recommendations in the form of a report entitled, *A Free and Responsible Press*. Here and in several other more specialized studies published by the CFP (including a volume on international issues titled *Peoples Speaking to Peoples*), Hocking, Chafee, and the other commissioners outlined a concept of freedom of the press that emphasized the right of the press to be free from "compulsions from whatever source, governmental or social, external or internal," as well as the "overall social responsibility" of the press to provide the democratic citizenry with accurate, intelligent information about their world and a forum for the open exchange of ideas. While the CFP stopped short of recommending giving legal or governmental form to press responsibility (and Chafee was particularly adamant about the inviolability of the First Amendment in this regard), they thought that the "moral duties" of the press could be organized and enforced through more informal mechanisms.[44]

Chafee's presence on the SCFOI was thus a reminder both of the continued centrality of civil society organizations in the development of U.S. human rights policy, and of the fact that the American "tradition" of free speech was not all that traditional. In the subsequent debates over freedom of information at the UN, a polarization would emerge between the views of Western and Communist states and between First and Third Worlds, but going into the first discussions in the sub-commission Chafee knew as well as anyone that the status of free speech in the United States was an evolving and contentious process. Taking the lead in the SCFOI, Chafee presented an outline for the conference agenda, taken largely from proposals developed by the CFP, that focused heavily on measures designed to facilitate international newsgathering and transmission, including the elimination of censorship, special visa status for accredited news personnel, and the elimination of tariffs, taxes, and other restrictions on the production and import of news. More generally, Chafee proposed that the conference should also work to formulate measures designed to implement the universal rights of free speech and freedom of the press within countries, as well as explore methods for increasing the quality and quantity of domestic and international news available to publics worldwide. The U.S. proposals also included two "specific administrative mechanisms" Chafee felt deserved consideration by the conference: the creation of an international foreign correspondents organization with "strict, self-administered codes of ethics," and a "continuing machinery to promote the free flow of true information." The British and French members of the sub-commission also submitted proposed agendas—the British in the form of a long, somewhat rambling letter from the absent Robert J. Cruickshank—but there was sufficient overlap of the three that the decision was made to take the U.S. proposals as the basis for discussion.[45]

The consensus within the SCFOI had its limits. The Soviet nominee, Soviet consul to New York and former *Pravda* correspondent Jacob Lomakin, arrived with little in the way of prepared drafts, but managed to object to or propose ad hoc amendments for any number of agenda items, most of which were overruled and/or defeated. Lomakin's attempt, for instance, to remove state censorship from the agenda—suggesting it was not pertinent to freedom of information—left his fellow members particularly incredulous. The Soviet member found the sub-commission somewhat more receptive to his proposal for an agenda item regarding what he called "objectives" for the press. These included such things as promoting peace and friendly relations between nations as well as more militant objectives of "unmasking fascism" and combating "such press and information organs as engage in war-mongering." Still, many Western governments recoiled along with the Norwegian representative, who noted with alarm that the Soviet proposal would render the press a "weapon of the state," a reading Lomakin might well have been willing to concede.[46]

Salvador Lopez took the opportunity of Lomakin's proposal on press objectives to realign the discussion with the original Philippine resolution. As authored by Carlos Romulo back during the first General Assembly session, that resolution proposed a conference to find ways not only of promoting "the right to gather, transmit and publish news anywhere and everywhere without fetters," but also noted that such a right carried with it a responsibility "to employ its privileges without abuse." Continuing, the resolution as adopted asserted that freedom of information "requires as a basic discipline the moral obligation to seek the facts without prejudice and to spread knowledge without malicious intent."[47] The American proposals, despite their roots in the CFP work, emphasized the facilitation of the gathering, transmission, and dissemination of the news, and Lopez announced that he was "heartily in accord" with the basic idea behind the Soviet proposal because it brought the draft agenda closer to the original intent of the Philippine resolution. Discussion of the objectives of the press and other media was essential, he said, in order that the idea of freedom of information be properly understood. Here, as with all other aspects of UN human rights work, rights mixed with responsibility. "I understand freedom," he told the SCFOI, "to mean something more than the absence of restrictions. . . . I would say that freedom implies obligation and responsibilities at least in the same degree that it implies rights and prerogatives." As such, he supported the intent of the Soviet proposal, but decided to submit an amended version designed, he said, to bring it more fully into line with the resolution and to "tone down" what he called "the warlike phraseology" of the Lomakin draft.[48]

Lopez offered his revisions of Lomakin's "objectives" later that afternoon. Shorn of references to "daily struggle" and "unmasking," Lopez listed four objectives: "a) to tell the truth without prejudice and to spread knowledge without malicious intent; b) to facilitate the solution of the economic, social and humanitarian problems of the world as a whole through the free interchange of information bearing on such problems; c) to help promote respect for human rights and fundamental freedoms for all, without distinction as to race, sex, language, or religion; and d) to help maintain international peace and security through understanding and co-operation between peoples." After stating his strident opposition to the Soviet proposal, Norway's A. R. Christensen turned to warmly voice support for the Philippine draft as did Chafee, British member A. R. K. MacKenzie, and the observer from the American Federation of Labor, Toni Sender. Ferdinand Dehousse of Belgium grumbled about the "vagueness" of the Philippine version, but backed it in the end. When the vote was taken, the Philippine version passed on a voice vote of 7–1 with two abstentions.[49]

The Philippine strategy toward the SCFOI in many respects reflected the experiences of both Lopez and Romulo. Lopez was a gifted writer and critic, whose work in the 1930s helped lay the foundation of modern Filipino literary criticism, according to E. San Juan, Jr.[50] Before the war, Lopez's deep involvement with the nascent Filipino literary scene led him to develop a sense of both the importance of the right to free expression and its connection to a broader social responsibility. In February 1939, Lopez along with José Lansang, Federico Mangahas, and others formed the Philippine Writers League, which served at once as a literary society and an advocacy organization dedicated to the defense of "the democratic rights to education, to freedom of thought and expression." Inspired by and modeled on H. G. Wells's PEN Club in Great Britain, the Philippine Writers League published a manifesto that took note of the "menace to the free expression of the creative human spirit" posed by the rise of fascism, and insisted on the fundamental right of writers to both "artistic autonomy" and "political immunity."[51] But more than simply defending the civil liberties of writers to publish what they will, Lopez and the league also committed themselves to a political struggle "against injustice and oppression in every form." Only as part of a common progressive effort "to preserve the principle of freedom in other fields," could writers and artists hope to maintain and extend their own liberties.[52]

As a newspaper editor in the antipodes of American empire, the World War I-era controversies surrounding free speech were not just theoretical for Carlos Romulo. The U.S. Supreme Court decision in the Insular Cases had long established that the full protections of the U.S. Constitution did not extend to their colonial territories, and in some respects the censorship of the Philippine press in the decade before the First World War provided a template for the repression on the mainland after 1916.[53] Romulo's 1960 memoir, *I Walked with Heroes*, relates the story of his unlikely arrest and trial for sedition in 1916. Shortly before departing for the United States to study at Columbia, Romulo, then assistant editor of the *Citizen*, reprinted a satirical article clipped from *Life* magazine that, as he wrote in 1960, "made fun of the draft," albeit in "a humorous, good natured way." The American-owned rival to the *Citizen*, an organ of the Quezon political machine named the *Free Press*, seized upon the article as evidence of the treasonous sentiments of the editorial staff at the paper and pressed colonial authorities to bring charges. Although Romulo and the paper's editor-in-chief Conrado Benitez were eventually acquitted of the charges, the episode demonstrated the precariousness of free speech in the most liberal of empires, and the chilling effects even unsuccessful government repression of speech could have. The young Romulo came away, he would later say, even more convinced of the basic principle that "freedom of the press and freedom of speech are the very bulwarks of democracy."[54]

Limited and suppressed, the press in the American-administered Philippines was relatively more free than others in Asia and constituted an important forum for contesting the terms of U.S. rule. Romulo rose to prominence advocating for gradual independence in the pages of several newspapers and came to believe in the power of words to "move men and mountains."[55] But such a power was not his alone, and another experience depicted in his memoir describes how his opponents could be cast as irresponsible in their use of a free press. While he was a student at the University of the Philippines, an editorial appeared in the *Manila Times* that to Romulo embodied colonialist condescension and contempt for Filipino leadership. Written by the paper's American editor L. H. Thibault, who had ironically given Romulo his first job in journalism, the piece was an attack on University of the Philippines President Ignacio Villamor that Romulo regarded as racially motivated. More than just an isolated broadside against one prominent Filipino, however, the editorial was representative of a rising anti-Filipino racism that was increasingly apparent among the American population in the Philippines. Incensed, Romulo penned a scathing retort in the student newspaper and led a student protest march from the campus to the offices of the *Manila Times*. Although Thibault was not forthcoming with the demanded retraction, the editor did agree to publish Romulo's response in the *Times*, a modest victory that helped raise Romulo's profile. This episode also indicates the degree to which Romulo—certainly by 1960 when *I Walked with Heroes* was published—was sensitive to the idea that the press had responsibilities as well as rights in a democratic society.[56]

Informed by these experiences, the original GA proposal for an international freedom of information conference and Lopez's intervention in the SCFOI debate were intended to be an implementation of the Philippine Pattern, but one that was an active rather than passive form of assimilation, interpretation, and rearticulation. Writing on the emergence of Filipino nationalism in the translation of regional dialects into Castilian, historian Vincente L. Rafael contends that it is only through a common engagement with the "foreign" that the diverse Philippine nation could be imagined as a single entity.[57] Translation, particularly as it involved the resituation of what Romulo referred to as "American ideals of freedom and equality" to the colonial world, could be a challenge to the American hegemony as much as an extension of it.[58] In a similar vein, the insistence that freedom of information required both rights and responsibilities implied that the "gift" of free speech and a free press the Philippines had received from the United Stated had been altered just enough to reflect a new range of ideas and interests before being "re-gifted" to the world. If Stuart Hall is right that "politics actually works more like the logic of language: you can always put it together another way if you try hard enough," then the politics of human rights is constrained only by the discursive skills of its practitioners.[59]

The SCFOI discussion of the conference agenda demonstrated the potential of this discursive human rights politics. Lopez and Romulo both established themselves as stalwart allies of the United States, with deep appreciation for the tradition of free speech and a free press as learned under American tutelage. Romulo seized the initiative in calling for the conference, but co-ordinated carefully with U.S. representatives to ensure backing for the plan. As author of the General Assembly resolution, however, Romulo was able to include his own translation of freedom of information, which included a notion of press responsibilities that the U.S., had it been the author, might not have included. In the sub-commission, Lopez was content to let Chafee take the lead in offering an agenda for the coming conference. Still, drawing on the Philippine Pattern, he was able to make a critical intervention that turned the discussion toward a version of freedom of information that was rooted in the ambiguous colonial experience of a free press, rather than sim-ply the legal arguments of First Amendment jurisprudence. That Chafee and the other SCFOI members broadly agreed to press forward with a rights and responsibilities approach to freedom of information suggests how fluid the boundaries were between different approaches to human rights, at least in summer 1947.

The Cold War and the Geneva Freedom of Information Conference

The consensus Salvador Lopez created in the SCFOI quickly unraveled as the discussion of an international freedom of information convention moved first to the Geneva conference and then on to the General Assembly's Third Committee. The Geneva conference on freedom of information had the great misfortune of being scheduled in the spring of 1948—the white-hot moment of conception for the Cold War. The United States and its newly consolidating European allies shifted toward a position that more sharply differentiated be-tween a "Western" and a Communist view of freedom of information. When the draft conventions returned to the UN, another distinction emerged, this time between the West and the as-yet unnamed Third World; a number of Latin American, Asian, and Arab delegations banded together to push their own vision of freedom of information. Romulo and Lopez continued their ef-forts to articulate the interests of the U.S. and the developing world together, but as the brief moment of global plasticity hardened into the divisions of First, Second, and Third Worlds, the possibility that the Philippine Pattern would inform the postwar human rights system diminished accordingly.

The International Conference on Freedom of Information opened on

March 24, 1948, amidst a darkening world. Over the previous twelve months, the Grand Alliance that had saved the world from Nazi tyranny fractured and split into two opposing, hostile camps.[60] The previous March, U.S. president Harry Truman placed anticommunism at the center of U.S. foreign policy when he announced the Truman Doctrine in the form of aid for Greece and Turkey. In June, secretary of state George Marshall revealed an ambitious economic recovery plan for Europe targeted, many believed, at preventing further Communist encroachment through the ballot box. By early 1948, the Marshall Plan had succeeded in consolidating British, French, and Italian support for the U.S., which seemed to confirm the Soviet view, expressed by ambassador to the U.S. Nikolai Novikov when the plan was announced—that massive U.S. aid was the first step in creating "a West European bloc directed against us."[61] The Soviets too were busy consolidating their influence in the areas first liberated and then occupied by the Red Army—defined and formalized by the creation of the Cominform in September 1947. Days before the conference, a Soviet-backed coup overthrew the moderate Benês government in Czechoslovakia, clarifying and hardening the front lines of the conflict. The state of U.S.-Soviet relations was sufficiently dire for UN Assistant Secretary-General Benjamin A. Cohen to remark in his opening address to the conference, "mankind [is] on the brink of a third world war." Cohen's remark seemed all the more prescient three months later when the Red Army blockaded all road and rail routes to the western zones of Berlin, provoking the greatest European crisis since the end of the Second World War.[62]

These developments caused U.S. officials to retreat from the more progressive plans of the CFP and to concentrate only on eliminating barriers to the free flow of information across borders.[63] The U.S. delegation, led by former ad man and future Connecticut Senator William Benton, regarded the conference as an "unhappy necessity" and braced for an all-out assault by the Soviets on the "war mongering" American press. Given the fact that much of the world's communications infrastructure lay shattered by the war or still undeveloped, Benton feared that the "middle group of states" would prove susceptible to Soviet propaganda about the dangers of U.S. cultural imperialism. "The fear of the flood of American material—comic strips, films, news services, magazines and even popular songs which might swallow up their culture—is widespread," Benton wrote to Secretary of State Marshall; "Soviet propaganda has learned to make the most of this fear." As such, the U.S. representatives arrived in Geneva expecting the Soviets to call vociferously for restrictions on press freedoms in the name of exposing fascism and war mongering, and protecting and enhancing "democratic control" of media resources.[64]

What began to emerge at Geneva was a "Western" theory of freedom of information that emphasized its value as an individual right, rather than as an important part of a democratic society. Speaking to the conference as a whole, Benton denounced what he called "the three-fold sequence of dictatorship, control of information and aggression," and declared that the United States would agree to an international convention only if it protected "the rights of individuals to receive and transmit news without constraint."[65] The British representative, Minister of State Hector McNeil, was more prepared to cast his position in terms of a common Western identity, noting that the UK, like "those communities based on the Anglo-Saxon model," was opposed to any form of "dictated thinking." Only a week before, the British had signed the Treaty of Brussels along with Belgium, France, Luxembourg, and the Netherlands, seeding both the North Atlantic Treaty Organization and the Western European Union and, according to A. W. Brian Simpson, spurring British Foreign Office lawyer Eric Beckett to begin work drafting what would become the European Convention on Human Rights.[66] The Brussels pact also began to give institutional shape to a reimagined "West" opposed to the Communist east, and McNeil suggested there was a common view on freedom of information. "The peoples of Western Europe," he said, "[consider] no idea incapable of improvement, but that its individual author [is] potentially noble and more important than the idea."[67]

Viewing the freedom of information conference through the prism of the Cold War gave the Americans a significantly distorted understanding of the nature of the support for discussion of press obligations. While acknowledging the economic material conditions that lay at the root of resistance to a monological insistence on a laissez faire view of freedom of information, Benton and other officials saw the discussion of press obligations only as "fertile ground" to be exploited by Soviet machinations rather than as a legitimate alternative perspective. This was despite the fact that Romulo's original proposal and Lopez's sub-commission interventions had indicated that even demonstrably pro-American voices—Romulo was already being denounced by Moscow as a Washington shill—were insisting on equal priority of rights and responsibilities.

In Geneva, Romulo served as president of the conference and attempted to disentangle the conference's work from the Cold War. Even though the Soviet Union tried to derail his selection as president, Romulo used his opening address to express the hope that the proceedings could avoid becoming overly politicized and make a real contribution to the promotion of peace. That contribution would hinge in part, Romulo told the assembled dignitaries, on their willingness to consider not just press freedom, but press objectives as well. "Rapidity of transmission of information [has] tended to aggravate the dangers of another war," he cautioned. It was the duty of the conference, therefore, "to provide adequate defenses against the ignorance and misunderstanding which [poison] relationships between nations. This [is] the place to establish a precedent, in the heart of a continent threatened by another conflict."[68]

In the committee negotiations, the Philippines continued to play the role of mediator. During the discussion of a U.S. draft resolution of general principles, Cipriano Cid, a Philippine labor organizer, declared his strong support for the draft, but then asked the committee to revise a passage noting the problems caused by "monopolies, but particularly those of a governmental nature" to read, "monopolistic practices of a public or private character." He also suggested the resolution be changed from calling on the press to "accept" their moral obligation to an admonishment that they "accept and comply" with those obligations. A British move to strike all references to monopolies was upheld, rendering the first change moot, but Cid's second suggestion was adopted, implying that there was still some interest beyond the Communist bloc countries in seeing the responsibilities of the press defined—and possibly enforced.[69]

This small change aside, the Philippine effort to once again achieve some consensus fell on deaf ears as the Americans had come not to negotiate but to win. Benton early on dismissed any talk of "responsibility" as the label dictators always use to describe their restriction of freedom of information.[70] Some of the Communist bloc delegations were even willing to concede most of the U.S. positions in exchange for language condemning war mongering. John Humphrey attempted to facilitate a backroom effort by Yugoslavia's Vladislav Ribnikar to seek a private meeting with the Americans. Benton refused to even consider it and concentrated instead on pressuring the "middle countries" not to support any of the Soviet initiatives. The result was a final communiqué that contained three separate draft conventions and no mention of war mongering. The U.S. had proposed and backed a convention to facilitate international gathering and transmission of news, the British had sponsored a convention designed to promote freedom of information domestically, and the French had promoted one establishing an international "right of reply," which would have provided a mechanism for governments to offer "corrections" to international reporting they deemed false or misleading. Given what Humphrey called the "political imbalance" of the originators of these drafts and the successful sidelining of the Soviet proposals, Benton was satisfied in describing the U.S. effort in Geneva as a "victory of limited objectives."[71]

But if the United States had achieved a victory over their incipient Cold War adversaries, they had not yet succeeded in excluding explicitly defined responsibilities or limitations of press freedom from international law. The French draft "right of reply," was one such instance, despite Benton's claims to have successfully modified an earlier, more "troublesome" version. More significantly, the draft conventions produced by the conference were not opened for signature there, instead being forwarded on to the UN for further consideration and approval. This meant that Geneva was the beginning and not the end of the drafting process, a point emphasized by Romulo after the close of the conference on April 21. Implausibly, Romulo suggested a consensus on freedom of information had "begun to crystallize" and would be built upon at the UN. Speaking to news reporters, his assessment of what was agreed to in Geneva would have come as a surprise to the U.S. delegation: "Everyone [has] agreed no right [is] absolute, since the exercise of any right [is] necessarily limited by respect for the rights of others." Freedom of information required:

> the proper balance between freedom and responsibility, between the freedom to gather, transmit and disseminate news and the right to receive truthful information, between the general obligation to tell the truth and the special duty to observe public decency and to help maintain national security and peace among nations, and between the traditional concept of national sovereignty and the requirements of the new international order.

This was a rather bold act of translation. When the UN took up the draft conventions in the next several years, it would become clear that everyone had *not* agreed to this philosophy, regardless of Romulo's insistence that it was fully in keeping with a Western rights tradition.[72]

The Third World and a "Third Concept"
of Freedom of Information

Later debates on the freedom of information convention at the UN continued in acrimony. The split was most significant not between Cold War enemies, but between Western states and an increasingly unified coalition of Asian, Arab, and Latin American states. Kenneth Cmiel has written convincingly on how these debates were a critical moment in the development of Third World solidarity at the UN.[73] Several years before the French economist Alfred Sauvy coined the term "Tiers Monde" in an article describing the inadequacy of thinking only in terms of the Cold War binary, figures like Raúl Noriega of Mexico and Saudi Arabia's Jamil Baroody joined forces to press for changes to the three draft conventions passed on from the Geneva conference.[74] In the General Assembly Third Committee, Noriega proposed a whole barrage of amendments seeking to limit the license of the press to insult a nation's "honor," publish obscene or morally objectionable material, or incite public disorder or criminal behavior. American representatives argued that such amendments were authoritarian, but many other delegations felt they addressed legitimate concerns of their "younger peoples" or "less-developed nations."[75] Baroody, who would come to be almost universally disliked at the UN, was the closest to rejecting the entire premise of the international human rights project, and was among the small handful of delegates to speak out against adopting the Universal Declaration of Human Rights a few months later. He linked democratic free-press practices with a covert form of imperialism, which used "propaganda, political pressure, the installation of puppet governments, [and] economic and financial monopolies" as a means of "penetrating and controlling foreign countries."[76]

For their part, the Cold War belligerents did their best to turn the freedom of information debate into a struggle between war-mongering capitalists and totalitarian communists. U.S. delegate Erwin D. Canham, editor of the *Christian Science Monitor*, spoke of the clash of "two divergent conceptions of the role of the Press in the modern world" and warned of the slippery slope "leading to despotism and slavery" should state control of the press be enshrined in the freedom of information conventions.[77] Moscow's hard-edged UN ambassador Andrei Gromyko dismissed the entire UN agenda on freedom of information as "designed to enhance the role played by the U.S. newspaper syndicates in the dissemination of war propaganda."[78] The efforts of the U.S. and Soviet Union to place their struggle at the center of the debates could not overshadow the fact that, as Renuka Ray of India put it, "a third concept" of freedom of information had emerged.[79]

However real the emergence of "Third World solidarity" was, focusing on Noriega and Baroody runs the risk of overstating and naturalizing the cultural and political divisions manifested in the freedom of information debate. Although he ultimately failed to convince anyone, Carlos Romulo expressed support for an expanded freedom of information convention inclusive of some version of Noriega's amendments by casting the notion of press responsibilities as central to the Western tradition of a free press and a key component in the struggle against communist expansionism. During his speech before the General Assembly in support of the draft conventions that emerged from the Third Committee, Romulo returned to the well of Roosevelt's Four Freedoms, telling the delegates that freedom of information was essential not only for peace, but "to liberate men from want and hunger, [and] to give them the means to fight against any threat directed against freedom of religion or freedom of expression."[80] As articulated by Romulo, emphasizing responsibility was not part of a new "third way" alien to the Western tradition of freedom. Rather, it represented the proper translation of freedom of the press from the developed Western to the less-developed Asian context.

Despite Romulo's best efforts, the disagreement on freedom of information continued. By the end of the GA third session, the UN had tentatively adopted language for the newly amalgamated Convention on the International Transmission of News and the Right of Correction, based largely on a compromise brokered by the French. Romulo argued it represented "the full responsibility and all the rights and obligations which normally belonged to the Press."[81] Despite the fact that Mexico had agreed to the new compromised language, Noriega noted he was still interested in ensuring that due regard was given to his full range of concerns, and suggested that the transmission convention be voted on only after the UN had also completed a review of the draft Freedom of Information Convention, which was still as the Geneva conference had left it. In hopes of maintaining whatever momentum was left for discussion of the issue, the GA decided not to open the former for signature until the latter was completed at the next session.[82]

When the subject was taken up at the fourth GA session, a schism within the Communist bloc helped to bring the Cold War adversaries together, if only for a moment, in opposition to the emerging Third World. A reliable ally to the Soviet Union through the first three sessions of the UN, Yugoslavia was expelled from the Cominform in late 1948 and Josip Broz Tito moved toward establishing an "independent" socialist state in the Balkans. During freedom of information discussions, the Yugoslav representative Vladimir Dedijer noted the way in which the Soviet press had engaged in "open and violent attacks" on the Tito government, and he argued in favor of a French proposal to appoint a small subcommittee to finish the draft Freedom of Information Convention.[83] In this rare instance, however, the U.S. sided with the Soviet Union in voting to shelve the convention on the pretext that they should wait for the UN Human Rights Commission to complete its draft of the general human rights covenant before going on to more "specialized" human rights treaties.[84] In fact, the U.S. had never been in favor of the Freedom of Information Convention, preferring to focus on the convention on international gathering and transmission, and in the Fourth General Assembly, the Americans succeeded in convincing the British to abandon what was originally called "the British draft," even as support for amending and adopting the convention picked up among the "third concept" countries.[85] This group was able to block a U.S.-led effort to have the Convention on the International Transmission of News and the Right of Correction considered separately from the Freedom of Information Convention, meaning that the stalemate of the Third General Assembly continued through the Fourth.[86]

The slow-motion collapse of the freedom of information initiative at the UN was particularly disappointing to Carlos Romulo, who had been elected president of the General Assembly for its fourth session and hoped to preside over the culmination of the effort he had begun at the first. The Philippines had supported the deferment of both the conventions as a compromise, in hopes that doing so would prevent the Freedom of Information Convention from falling into, as the French delegate put it, the "quicksands" of the UN bureaucracy, but it was also clear that Romulo continued to regard the problem of freedom of information as one of rights and responsibilities. Speaking at a roundtable discussion held at Carnegie Hall on the first anniversary of the adoption of the Universal Declaration of Human Rights, Romulo argued that the most significant barriers to the free flow of information were not political—that is, those addressed by transmission convention—but economic and social. It was, he said, the shortages of newsprint and printing presses along with the prohibitive costs of international cable and radio equipment that effectively kept the peoples in underdeveloped regions in the dark. He also chastised the press "in many parts of the world" for publishing nothing but "stories of revolutions and earthquakes in certain other areas."

As a human rights issue, freedom of information was as much about develop-ment as about legal reform.[87]

All this meant that, when it came time to vote, more often than not the Philippines lined up with the "third concept" group of nations coalescing around a rights-and-responsibilities approach to freedom of information. But what is significant here is that Romulo saw no reason why the United States should not line up there as well. It was undoubtedly a Western country, but, by his reasoning, so was the Philippines. The United States was also, despite its foray into European-style imperialism, fundamentally an anticolonial na-tion, having set the precedent for declaring independence from empire and taking a rightful and equal place among the powers of the earth. "America," Romulo wrote in a 1949 *New York Times* article, "should seek to befriend, influence and guide the forces of freedom and social progress in Asia along democratic channels instead of trying to contain them within the inflexible mold of a negative anti-Communist policy."[88] As strident an anti-communist crusader as could be found in Asia, Romulo nonetheless acknowledged the appeal of communism to some in Asia at the same time that he sought to dis-tinguish between Moscow-inspired anti-Western agitation and the legitimate anti-European sentiments of most national movements. A month later, U.S. Secretary of State Dean Acheson poured cold water on Romulo's hope for a New Deal—or at least a Marshall Plan—for the world when he declared that the U.S. could offer, at best, "marginal assistance" to struggling nations. As if in direct reply to Romulo's plea, Acheson promised to help those who would help themselves, but "we cannot direct or control; we cannot make a world, as God did, out of chaos. There are some, apparently who think we should do this—and in less than six days."[89] Romulo was unlikely to confuse the U.S. with God, but he was convinced it could do much more to foster the legiti-mate aspirations and interests of developing nations.

The two conventions did, in fact, disappear into the quicksands of the UN. Those same quicksands also soon absorbed the SCFOI and the rest of the UN effort in this area, but not before Salvador Lopez caused almost everyone in the First, Second, and Third Worlds to unite in defense of keeping their do-mestic practices off the agenda. In 1950 the SCFOI had come under criticism for discussing "political" rather than "practical" questions—from the Soviet Union for condemning its practice of jamming Voice of America broadcasts and from the United States for drafting a "code of ethics" for journalists.[90] Be-fore it was disbanded by ECOSOC in 1952, ostensibly for budgetary reasons, the SCFOI recommended that the UN establish a Freedom of Information

Commission.[91] This new unit was rejected, but as a consolation the UN did appoint Salvador Lopez as special rapporteur on freedom of information—a position Lopez had lobbied for and won, mainly on support from developing nations from the General Assembly. When, however, he issued his report the following year, it was broadly critical of a number of specific governments, enough to ensure that another rapporteur was not appointed.[92] Freedom of information was essentially dead as a distinct human rights issue at the UN.

Conclusion

In a 1992 interview with literary scholar Roger J. Bresnahan, Salvador Lopez described the Philippine involvement in the development of the UN human rights program in these terms: "We contributed a lot, because we worked with the [U.S.] delegation very closely." Romulo and Eleanor Roosevelt were acquaintances from his days as Philippine commissioner during the war, and this relationship formed the basis of an "agreement" between the two. "The idea," Lopez told Bresnahan, "was to ensure that the principles [of the UN human rights program] were the fundamental human rights which were common to us, since we share your Bill of Rights." This collaboration was particularly effective, because it allowed for the diffusion of American influence through the medium of the Philippine representatives. "It was very fortunate that we were on that commission," Lopez surmised, "because through us it was easier for the U.S. to ensure that the principles embodied in the Bill of Rights were included."[93]

As described by Lopez, the Philippines and the U.S. shared a nearly identical perspective on human rights, and their combined efforts at the UN served to extend this perspective into the international sphere. Freedom of information was an ideal starting point, not only because it was a critical component of the human rights initiative—the "foundation" of all other rights, as Romulo put it—but because it was an institution the two countries shared and one that was amenable to international intervention. Indeed, there was little doubt among the Filipinos at the UN that the Bill of Rights was as much theirs as the Americans,' and both Lopez and Romulo were assiduous in their attempts to ensure a consonance between that tradition and the emerging UN rights regime. The Philippines was, in this respect, not only a pattern but also a conduit.

And yet, Lopez's reflections leave unstated the degree to which principles and presumptions of the American rights tradition were altered as they were refracted through the prism of the Filipino colonial experience and translated into a form that was appropriate to the global context. Once again, the practice of translation worked not merely to communicate, but to amend and augment the ideal of human rights. Nowhere was this more apparent than on the question of responsibilities. Built in by Romulo to his initial freedom of information resolution, the notion that the press had responsibilities as well as rights was resisted by U.S. representatives, reinserted by Lopez into the conference agenda, only to become an unbridgeable fault line in the effort to secure an international convention. In this regard, the skills of discursive politics that Romulo and Lopez had developed during the colonial period demonstrated their continued relevance, but not necessarily their effectiveness, in the postwar, postcolonial context.

Beginning before the San Francisco conference, Romulo had worked to convince the United States not only to accept the notion of a robust international human rights program inclusive of a broad range of specific rights, but also to lead the charge for such a system based on the Philippine Pattern. As articulated by Romulo, that pattern was a paradoxical form of neocolonial anticolonialism that involved the U.S. "guiding" the development of much of Asia, and perhaps Latin America and Africa as well. If such a vision of the American role in the world was something more than a continuation of the "white man's burden," it was only because, in pleading for the U.S. to "befriend, influence and guide" the lesser countries of the world, Romulo was befriending, influencing, and guiding the U.S. That U.S. officials were ultimately unwilling to be so guided reveals not so much a reluctance to shoulder the burden of global hegemony, but rather their ambivalence about what the discourse and structures of human rights might mean for U.S. society at home and the pursuit of its interests abroad.

Some of the sources of that ambivalence will be explored in Chapter 5, but it should be noted here that the "uncertain" American approach to human rights contributed to Romulo's steady shift away from emphasizing the universal applicability of the Philippine Pattern of social and political transformation—even for the Philippines themselves. By the mid-1950s, Romulo was insisting that anticolonialism was an extension not of the U.S. ideal of universal human rights, but of anti-communism. While advocating for a Southeast Asian collective defense treaty similar to NATO, Romulo found himself defending the authoritarian regimes in Taiwan and South Korea. He wrote in his 1955 book, *Crusade in Asia*, that while "democracy in the Western sense, based on the fundamental principle of the rights and freedoms of the individual, has gained a foothold in only a few countries in Asia," notably the Philippines, "we must bear in mind, that the word 'democracy' does not necessarily strike a responsive chord in the heart of every Asian."[94] By 1962, amidst a stagnating economy and a bitter fight over U.S. military bases, Romulo as president of the University of the Philippines called on his students to forget "the so-called hybrid quality of our culture" and focus instead on "tradition" and "our roots as a nation and as a people."[95] By 1967, he had concluded that Asian identity included the fact that "we are really an authoritative society: we want freedom but we look up to leadership for guidance even in personal matters."[96] He was, by then, a member of the cabinet of the new young president, Ferdinand Marcos, and continued as the government's foreign minister before, during, and after the brutal marshal-law dictatorship from 1972 to 1981. No doubt, it was an ignoble end to an otherwise illustrious career, and Romulo's service under the notorious kleptocrat irreparably compromises his reputation as a proponent of international human rights.

Chapter 4

Charles Malik, the International Bill of Rights, and Ultimate Things

S hortly after the conclusion of the first session of the United Nations General Assembly, members of the U.S. delegation submitted a memorandum to the State Department detailing their assessment of the "politics and personnel" of the UN. Lebanese representative Dr. Charles H. Malik, they reported, had become considerably more skilled as a diplomat since the San Francisco conference, and while he could not always be counted on to line up with the United States when the votes were counted, he came closest of all the Arab delegations to "speaking our language." Of Carlos Romulo, the American advisors admitted that despite his obvious conceit and intense ambition, the Filipino general was "one of the outstanding personalities of the whole Assembly." Romulo had positioned himself as the champion of "those colonial peoples of the world who want freedom and independence," but, the memo happily reported, he was also committed to "working with the white man, providing the white man is at all reasonable." In a conclusion that might well have applied to the head of the Lebanese mission as much as the one from the Philippines, the U.S. delegation assured their superiors at the State Department that Romulo and his team would be "valuable friends of the United States providing we continue with a forward looking, progressive policy in our relations with the less advanced nations of the world."[1]

Neither Malik nor Romulo would have found much to disagree with in the secret profiles of them offered by the American delegation. Indeed, both would have been gratified to be counted as friends of the United States— worthy and important friends at that. The previous chapter made clear that Carlos Romulo would have been particularly satisfied to know that the

American delegation felt a subtle and friendly pressure to maintain their lead in colonial policy as the most liberal colonial power. Like Romulo, Charles Malik placed his ability to influence American policy at the center of his diplomatic strategy, mobilizing his affinity for and experience with the United States in the service of his particular global agenda. Also like Romulo, Malik's close association with the U.S. led many to assume his subordination to the dictates of Washington. In later years, his critical facilitation of the 1957 U.S. invasion of Lebanon only solidified his reputation as a proxy for American power in the Middle East.[2] And yet, he, like Romulo, cultivated his friendship with the United States not simply to do the bidding of successive American administrations, but to have the opportunity to shape the terms of American engagement with the world.

Nowhere was this strategy more evident than in his work on behalf of international human rights, a cause with which Malik was closely identified in the first decade after the Second World War. In this too, he was like his Filipino counterpart, but Malik's engagement with human rights was more profound than Romulo's. Certainly, Malik played a larger role in the Human Rights Commission. At the first session, on Romulo's nomination, he was elected rapporteur of the commission and served alongside Chairman Eleanor Roosevelt and Vice-Chairman Peng Chun Chang during the drafting of the Universal Declaration of Human Rights. As rapporteur, Malik was in a unique position to prepare and present the reports of the commission's work to the Economic and Social Council and General Assembly, as well as author a number of articles on human rights in various UN publications. Malik succeeded Roosevelt as chairman in 1952, and while only serving for two sessions he was critical to keeping the work on the human rights covenants from stalling out, as it had for the freedom of information convention. From these positions, Malik made seminal contributions to both the content and structure of the International Bill of Rights, advocating for a legally binding international human rights law, stressing the priority and autonomy of the individual and what he called "intermediate institutions," protecting intellectual and spiritual freedoms (including the right to change deeply held beliefs), and establishing a coherent philosophical foundation for the UN human rights program. With the possible exception of John Humphrey, no individual contributed more.

Malik's engagement with human rights was uncommonly profound for another reason. Certainly he, like Romulo, viewed the international human rights system as both a symbol and a channel of U.S. global ascendancy. But for the Lebanese philosopher, the stakes were considerably higher. His ambitions went beyond decolonization and development to an almost millennial desire to remake the modern world. Properly defined and institutionalized, human rights, Malik thought, could express the "authentic spiritual tradition" of the West and foster the social and political conditions that would allow for the full development of the human person worldwide. Both this tradition and his sense of personhood emerged as his philosophical training and deep Christian beliefs combined with experiences in the United States, Europe, and the Near East to produce an impression of global crisis symbolized by but not limited to Nazism and communism. Called from academia to diplomatic service on the eve of the San Francisco conference, Malik spent the better part of a decade struggling to awaken the "giant" of the United States to the responsibility of leading a human rights crusade. In his failure to do so, he yet succeeded in helping to establish an international bill of rights.

The UN Commission on Human Rights and an International Bill of Rights

If it had been up to him, Charles Malik would not have been a founding member of the UNCHR. His view, like that of the CSOP which had originated the idea of a UNCHR, was that the body should be constituted as a widely representative group of independent experts. Duly appointed by the government of Lebanon as their official representative to the UN, Malik argued in ECOSOC that he and his fellow government representatives should not serve on the UNCHR. Given that international human rights standards were understood by many to constrain and perhaps criticize state practice, an independent UNCHR would have been, as British delegate and future Nobel Peace Prize winner Philip Noel-Baker put it, more "free to raise questions which might embarrass governments."[3] Malik, as will be described at length, regarded the promotion of human rights as a challenge to state sovereignty and an important resource for individuals and civil society organizations to retain their autonomy from governments. He thought it obvious that the primary UN human rights body should enjoy a similar autonomy.[4]

   The majority of ECOSOC members, however, agreed with Soviet representative Alexander Borisov that, given how broad its mandate was, the UNCHR needed to be made up of officially empowered and directed state representatives.[5] In establishing governmental membership for the UNCHR,

ECOSOC helped to ensure that in the first several years, the commission's work would focus primarily on drafting international norms, such as the Universal Declaration and covenants, not on investigation of violations or enforcement of standards. The move also encouraged the work of the commission toward a bias in favor of states, meaning that the norms set and implementation mechanisms established generally deferred to state sovereignty and the power of governments to control what and how human rights were implemented within their borders. And yet, despite these structural and practical limitations, the discourse of human rights, particularly as articulated by Charles Malik, proved irreducible to the interests of state power. This resistance enabled the International Bill of Rights to serve as more than just a ratification of the inviolability of domestic jurisdiction. By attempting to give institutional and legal form to the charter's vague human rights provisions, Malik, in conjunction with several other members of the UNCHR (including Carlos Romulo), helped create a novel space in the international order for a "human rights subject."[6]

With the possibility of a nongovernmental commission foreclosed for the time being, Malik's was perhaps the most independent voice on the UNCHR, as he received little in the way of instruction from his foreign ministry with regard to human rights policies, and consulted closely with John Humphrey and the secretariat staff, particularly once he took the chair of the commission. Negatively, such independence was enabled by the particular weakness of the Lebanese state, as well as by the fact that his country lacked the kinds of global strategic interests that kept the representatives from "great power" nations—Eleanor Roosevelt included—closely tethered to their governments. Positively, Malik's human rights work at the UN constituted both a personal and a national calling. "The Lebanon," Malik wrote in 1949, "has a positive vocation in the international field. It is not political. It is spiritual and intellectual."[7] At San Francisco he had asserted much the same point by claiming that Lebanon, by virtue of its "traditions, educational institutions, potentialities, and geographic position," was uniquely suited to lead in the UN human rights efforts, and during the first General Assembly session he actively sought a seat on ECOSOC, outflanking a U.S. State Department move to elect Turkey.[8]

Malik's sense of this "positive vocation" was rooted in a version of Lebanese nationalism articulated by Michel Chiha. A generation older than Malik, Chiha was a prominent banker and intellectual, serving as an informal advisor to his brother-in-law, President Bishara al-Khoury. Chiha was known as the principal drafter of the 1926 Lebanese Constitution, and had spent much of the French mandate period advocating for a unique Lebanese identity based on a shared Phoenician history, open mercantile economy, and a culture of tolerance and religious diversity. For Chiha and his many supporters, particularly among the Francophone Christian elite, this identity distinguished Lebanon from the wider Arab world and served as a basis for a modern nationhood.[9] Malik adopted a similar view of the Mediterranean orientation of Lebanon and of its status as a zone of interaction and exchange on the border between East and West. Yet Malik's experience as a philosopher educated in American missionary institutions, gave him a different opinion of how that orientation and status should be expressed. While the banker Chiha emphasized the inherently commercial nature of Phoenician society and translated that into a view of Lebanon as a land of economic opportunity,[10] Malik rejected such materialism and proclaimed Lebanon's mission in terms of human rights. Lebanon was "a corner of complete freedom of thought and conscience in the Near East," he wrote, and as such could serve as an engine of spiritual and intellectual—rather than financial and economic—development.[11]

If the nation of Lebanon was gifted with the special mission of "mediation and understanding" between East and West, it was because the archetypical "man from Lebanon" was someone who had extensive roots in both the Eastern and Western worlds, spoke numerous languages fluently, and whose diaspora of family and friends stretched across continents and oceans. "He is thus," Malik reflected, "related to the outside world not externally and by accident, but internally and in essence."[12] Malik was just such a man. Like Carlos Romulo, he had been educated in American-run institutions, first in the Protestant missionary schools of the Near East and then as a graduate student in philosophy at Harvard University. Beginning as a boarding student in 1924, Malik's education was spiritually and intellectually transformative, producing in him a sense of individual responsibility for the collective development of the Arab world. Both at Tripoli Boys School and the American University of Beirut (AUB), Malik found teachers dedicated to a pedagogic model that asked students to "be original," and an administrative commitment to, as AUB President Bayard Dodge put it, Protestantism as "freedom of conscience." Malik emerged from these ostensibly missionary institutions devoutly Greek Orthodox—the religion of his ancestors stretching back, as he sometimes liked to say, to the days of Christ himself—and a firm believer in the individual's capacity to shape his own life. At Harvard, Malik managed to synthesize the intellectual traditions stretching, as he put it, from Socrates to Alfred North Whitehead (Whitehead was his dissertation advisor) into a coherent story of "the West." And, thanks to a traveling fellowship that sent him to Germany to study with Martin Heidegger in 1936, Malik's graduate education included a "suffocating" experience of the radical rejection of an open political and intellectual culture. The ascendance of a ubiquitous racism and the pervasiveness of an all-powerful German state were shocking to the Semitic-looking Lebanese student, and he left Germany even more certain of the necessity not only of legal protections for individual rights, but of free and independent "intermediate" institutions—church, university, and other voluntary organizations—distinct from the state.[13]

After graduating in 1937, Malik returned to Lebanon where he joined the AUB faculty and began imagining a new transformative role for himself and the university at the center of an Arab renaissance. Over the spring of 1942, Malik produced an extended essay on his plan to develop the School of Arts and Sciences to ensure that the liberal arts were as important as medicine and engineering in the AUB curriculum. He proposed the AUB as a "meeting-place between East and West" that would function, on the one hand, to teach the fundamentals of the "Greco-Roman-European humane tradition of thought and being," and on the other, to promote the ideal of Arab citizenship through the cultivation of Arabic culture, language, and heritage. The lynchpin of his plan was a commitment on the part of the AUB to consciously defend itself as an "oasis" of freedom of thought in the Near East—that freedom being the same issue he diagnosed at the heart of the Second World War. The war was, according to Malik, a war for the soul of the West. Germany, on the one side, represented a "radical revolution" against the "highest recognized values of the last three thousand years," while the United States and Great Britain (Malik, perhaps intentionally, forgot the Soviet Union), on the other side, represented the defenders of "the Western positive tradition from Plato to the present day." This construction of the conflict ensured that force of arms would not settle the core question. The Nazi war machine might be defeated, but the intellectual and spiritual danger it represented—the total abrogation of the "highest values"—would continue.[14]

Malik felt his American education had given him special insight into the current global crisis and, by the onset of the Second World War, he had begun to articulate a vision of a new world order. Malik imagined a different role for the United States in the Near East, one that hinged on his articulation of a new Western tradition that went beyond the technical mastery of economic and political formulae. The military and economic power evident in European colonialism had clouded this "truth" for many, but Malik believed it was a commitment to individual freedom and spiritual, rather than material, progress that was the font of Western greatness. This new West could be mediated to the East through institutions like the AUB and by individuals like Malik himself, who had a creative and dynamic understanding of what lay at the core of Western values.[15] Alternatively, the expansion of these ideals might also find support in any new postwar international organization, broadening the dissemination beyond the Near East to the entire world. When Malik was tapped by president Bishara Al-Khoury to represent Lebanon at the UN and in the U.S., it was the latter program that became the focus of Malik's efforts.

Unsurprisingly, Malik's commitment to freedom of thought and conscience manifested itself in a particular insistence that protections for these freedoms be included in the International Bill of Rights. More surprisingly, it was precisely these freedoms that provoked some of the first murmurs of a cultural opposition to the human rights project. Freedom of thought and conscience were, of course, included in the first draft of the international bill of rights (prior to its division into a declaration and a convention) produced by John Humphrey, but Malik ensured that the language of what became Article 18 of both the declaration and the International Covenant on Civil and Political Rights (ICCPR) specified the right to "change religion or belief" and, in the ICCPR, prohibited "coercion" in matters of faith.[16] Relatively uncontroversial in the UNCHR, Article 18 was one of two articles (the other being Article 16 dealing with marriage rights) that caused Saudi Arabia to abstain from voting for the Universal Declaration of Human Rights.[17] Saudi delegate Jamil Baroody, who was also a Lebanese Christian, argued that "the draft declaration [has] for the most part taken into consideration only the standards recognized by Western civilization and [has] ignored more ancient civilizations which [are] past the experimental stage." Going further, he suggested that specifying the freedom to change religions was unnecessary and perhaps even indicative of the kind of overzealous proselytization that had led to the Crusades.[18] The Pakistani delegate, Sir Muhammad Zafrulla Khan, offered an impassioned defense of Malik's principle of change, arguing that the Koran enjoined against compulsion to faith and that Islam itself was a "missionary" religion in search of converts, but the genie of cultural relativism was out of the bottle.[19]

That a robust human rights program would pose a threat to "ancient civilizations" was for Charles Malik part of the point. If it was to be worth the effort, the UN human rights regime would have to have a transformative effect on societies and cultures. During the first General Assembly in late 1946, Malik threw his support behind a Danish resolution calling on member states to ensure equal political rights for women. Speaking before the Assembly's Third Committee, Malik conceded his country "has not yet granted women political rights equal to those enjoyed by men" but, he argued, this should only lend all the more weight to his support for the resolution:

> The position is often stated that this question had better be left to natural evolution, that the normal development of a people will in time take care of it. But natural evolution left to itself is dumb and blind. . . . Social progress never comes by nature. It is the result of human design. Things left to take care of themselves will deteriorate. . . . And when people then begin talking about "practical wisdom" and "going slow" and "the inevitability of evolution," they are really conscious or unconscious apologetics for the mistake of their grandfathers.[20]

Adopted without a vote, it is unclear how many of the fifteen other member states that granted women fewer political rights supported the resolution. What is clear, however, is that Malik considered the progressive and reformist imperative of international human rights norms as valid and important in his own country as abroad—undoubtedly a minority position for most of the governments then as now.[21]

When the UNCHR met for the first time in January 1947, Malik pushed for a UN human rights program that would be an agent for this kind of "social progress." He was joined by Eleanor Roosevelt, Carlos Romulo, and fifteen other representatives to begin work on giving form to the charter's human rights pledges. This included a discussion about the commission's role in addressing allegations of specific human rights violations. In the eighteen months since its founding, the UN had received hundreds of individual communications, including protests against the Franco regime in Spain and the Trujillo regime in the Dominican Republic, accounts of lack of rights in colonial Indonesia, and a letter from an individual in Austria pleading for better treatment for "German nationals who have been settled in countries like Hungary, Czechoslovakia, Yugoslavia and Rumania."[22] As discussed in the next chapter, among the most prominent communications received was a petition by the National Negro Congress, given to the secretariat in June 1946, describing the widespread and systematic violation of African American human rights in the United States. Clearly, the UN Charter, like the Atlantic

Charter before it, was being taken seriously by some, regardless of the intentions of those who signed it.

During the first UNCHR session, the United States sought to preclude consideration of such communications as beyond the scope of the commission's mandate.[23] The move put Roosevelt at odds with both Carlos Romulo and Charles Malik, each of whom supported a proposal to set up a permanent sub-commission to review and respond to the incoming letters, telegrams, and petitions. Even if most of the communications reviewed by this sub-commission "will be thrown in the wastebasket," Malik argued, at least the UNCHR would have demonstrated to the world an interest in concrete violations of human rights.[24] Romulo also supported the idea of a sub-commission, noting that while the commission might not be able to function as a "supreme court of appeal" for those suffering human rights abuse, it could at least act as a sort of "world conscience."[25] The thought that the UNCHR might exercise some "power of inquiry or judgment" over states was rejected by Roosevelt, although she recognized that it would be a betrayal of public trust not to "take notice" of the communications in some fashion. Roland Lebeau of Belgium then suggested a compromise that gave commission members who were squeamish about addressing actual violations an alternative to simply ignoring the letters. He thought that the UNCHR could receive and review the communications, but only in connection with what he called the "principal task" of the group, the drafting of an international bill of rights.[26] As adopted, the plan was to have the chairman and one or two members meet to review and bring to the attention of the UNCHR "such communications as might assist it in its work." More significantly, the UNCHR also included in the plan a rather remarkable statement of its own limitations. Insisted on by the British and Soviets and supported by the United States, the report, which was passed on to the Economic and Social Council and became the definitive policy on communications, declared that "the Commission recognizes that it has no power to take any action in regard to any complaints concerning human rights."[27]

The move certainly aligned UNCHR work with the terms of reference established for it by the ECOSOC, and confirmed the fears of those who had advocated for a human rights commission constituted of independent experts. It did not help clarify, however, what exactly an "international bill of rights" entailed. John Humphrey of the secretariat suggested that the UNCHR could meet its obligation in one of three ways: "a declaration or other act of the General Assembly, a multilateral convention, or an amendment to the charter."[28] Negotiations on this point continued through the first two sessions of the UNCHR, with Malik among the most consistent supporters of a binding multilateral convention. In 1946, he told the ECOSOC that pious statements about respecting human rights were not enough and that all members of the UN should be bound by "the force of an international treaty" to promote and protect rights within their borders.[29] In the commission, Malik suggested that they pursue both "formulation of principle and the formulation of positive law." He made it clear which he thought most important: "I say this because we have enough principles suggested in the past. The UN Charter is full of them. The Atlantic Charter is an excellent declaration of principle. We want some positive results from all these pious declarations that have been made in the past."[30]

The Soviet Union, perhaps the most jealous guardian of the principle of national sovereignty, had consistently maintained through all of its representatives that they were uninterested in pursuing a legally binding convention. When the British introduced a draft international convention, Vladimir Koretsky warned against crossing "the border which divides international law from internal law," and suggested the commission concentrate on preparing what he called "a pre-pre-draft" of a nonbinding declaration.[31] To a lesser extent, these views were supported by the other Communist delegations on the UNCHR: the Ukraine, Belorussia, and Yugoslavia. Vladislav Ribnikar of Yugoslavia called national sovereignty "the oldest democratic principle in the field of State relations," opposed only by those who sought "international domination and generally represented reaction." At the end of the second session, all four countries would be the only commission members to both abstain from voting on the draft Universal Declaration and vote against adopting the draft international convention.[32]

Similarly, but much less stridently, the United States evinced a strong disinclination to pursue a binding international human rights treaty. As early as December 1946, the State Department decided to emphasize a declaration to the exclusion, or at least the deferral, of a convention. The problem with an immediate attempt to draft a convention, according to one strategy paper, was that the UN would "undoubtedly" have to "water-down" the rights and enforcement mechanisms in order that member states sign them (although it said nothing about which member states might be so squeamish).[33] However, once discussions demonstrated that many countries were willing to go further in their commitments than the United States, the argument changed, with the U.S. now claiming that any convention adopted would meet with such "flagrant, prolonged and repeated violations" that the effectiveness of the UN would suffer irreparable harm.[34] In the UNCHR, Roosevelt argued that while they could try to achieve both a declaration and a convention, the drafting of the latter was bound to be far more arduous and time consuming, involving "lawyers and experts" to hash out its minefield of technicalities. The American position was that a declaration, in the form of a General Assembly resolution, was the logical first step toward a more robust and enforceable set of human rights standards.[35]

Most other delegations, however, rejected prioritizing the declaration over a convention, and joined forces to thwart a combined U.S.-Soviet effort during the second UNCHR session to defer consideration of the convention. Malik was joined by Romulo (who called drafting a declaration "incidental to the main task of drafting the Bill of Rights and some form of international agreement to secure implementation thereof"), W. R. Hodgson of Australia, Hansa Mehta of India, Ferdinand Dehousse of Belgium, and Charles Dukes of the UK in committing to the simultaneous development of both.[36] In fact, the declaration would be adopted by the General Assembly almost twenty years before the covenants were opened for signature, but the early intention of the UNCHR majority was to quickly give legal form to the human rights provisions.

At the conclusion of the second session, clarity was finally achieved on what an "international bill of rights" meant. After Hodgson proposed that the term "bill of rights" should apply to the convention, C. H. Wu, alternate for UNCHR vice chair P. C. Chang, suggested that "bill of rights" refer to the trio of the declaration, convention, and machinery for implementation. This was taken as a stroke of genius, quickly becoming—and remaining—the standard definition of the International Bill of Rights.[37] Charles Malik made one final modification before this was officially adopted, substituting "covenant" for "convention." The term had earlier been suggested by Dehousse as the better English translation of the French "pacte," which conveyed for the Belgian representative the fact that the document was designed to "set a seal on friendly relations between States." Dehousse had not insisted on it after Wu introduced his triptych proposal, but Malik returned to it at the end of the debate. He had long held that the international bill of rights should be placed "above the sanctity of [ordinary] treaties," and the biblical connotations of the English term "covenant" (not as strong in the French "pacte") conveyed more of that sanctity, even if "convention" was a more accurate description of the multilateral treaty under consideration.[38]

Equally significant, in Dehousse's usage, "covenant" was intended to stress the international character of the convention, placing it squarely in the traditional realm of an agreement between sovereign states. In Malik's translation, however, he understood the sanctified term "covenant" to mean something different and more novel: "a document so clearly defined and so binding in character," he told the UNCHR, "as to occupy a level of its own; a document by virtue of which men could rest confident that they would secure redress under international law for any violation of rights."[39] The covenant was to accomplish more than sealing "friendly relations between States." For at least some members of the UNCHR, "covenant" meant giving individuals the right to have rights under international law. Famously, Hannah Arendt, writing at the same moment the International Bill of Rights was being deliberated in the UNCHR, heaped melancholic scorn on the "perplexities of the rights of man," noting that the only human right that mattered was the only one that was never guaranteed: the "right to have rights," which for her meant the "right to belong to some kind of organized community." But if, as she suggests, the real "calamity of the rightless" is "not that they are not equal before the law, but that no law exists for them," then the covenant, understood as something more than a compact between sovereign nation-states, was and is a law "for them"—even if only to be violated.[40]

"Ultimate Things" in the Universal Declaration of Human Rights

During these early debates over the mandate of the UNCHR and the form of the International Bill of Rights, Malik made a critical but ill-fated intervention that in many respects epitomized his work on behalf of human rights. Late on a Friday afternoon of the first UNCHR session, the Yugoslavian representative Vladislav Ribnikar, after flatly rejecting the possibility of an international convention, admonished the commission to take care not to reify the "social and political ideals of the middle classes" in the international bill of rights. These were principles "of another age" in the view of the Yugoslav government, which held that true personal freedom could come about only through a complete identification between the interests of society and the interests of the individual. All else, Ribnikar claimed, was merely "transitional."[41] Such views were consistent with a Marxist critique of rights, stretching back to Marx's own "On the Jewish Question," which insisted that "the so-called rights of man" were only the rights of "egotistic man . . . withdrawn behind his private interests and whims and separated from the community."[42]

After Ribnikar finished, Charles Malik was surprised and disconcerted to see that no other delegate rose to defend the principle that the kinds of protections for individuals embodied by a bill of human rights represented more than an outmoded philosophy. At the following meeting, Malik attempted to provoke a more spirited defense of what he regarded as an essential tenet of Western political philosophy, noting that the vision of human freedom presented by Ribnikar was opposed by that embodied in "the British Liberal tradition." The UNCHR had an absolute obligation to ensure that the international bill of rights drew upon this tradition and protected individuals from what Malik referred to as "the tyranny of the masses and the State." The British delegate Dukes—trade unionist, "crony" of Ernest Bevin, and soon to be the first Baron Dukeston—failed to take the bait, however, and declined to offer a defense of the tradition purported to be his own.[43]

It fell to Malik, some three days later, to revive the issue by formally proposing that the UNCHR adopt four principles, which in his mind were "in danger of being repudiated." As reported in the summary record, they were

1. The human person is more important than the racial, national, or other group to which he may belong;
2. The human person's most sacred and inviolable possessions are his mind and his conscience, enabling him to perceive truth, to choose freely, and to exist;
3. Any social pressure on the part of the State, religion or race, involving the automatic consent of the human person is reprehensible;
4. The social group to which the individual belongs, may, like the human person himself, be wrong or right: the person alone is the judge.[44]

"Madam Chairman," Malik intoned with all the gravity of a professor of philosophy, "these are ultimate things."[45]

The Soviet representative, Valentin Tepliakov, immediately and unsurprisingly voiced opposition to the proposal, claiming to be completely confounded by the notion of "social suppression or oppression, whatever he called it, on the individual." "Our principle," Tepliakov offered in alternative, "is that we cannot divide the individual from the society, from the group, or from the community." Such was to be expected from the representatives of the people's republics, but what Malik perhaps did not see coming was the reaction from the representatives of the West. Charles Dukes followed Tepliakov in rejecting Malik's principles, although he tried to stake a claim to the "middle position" between the Lebanese and Soviet views. In his remarks, however, he confined himself to rebutting Malik's arguments. Dukes did not think it possible that there could be "unrestricted individual liberty" in any modern society and he stressed "the co-existence and closely knit interdependence of the State and of the individual." So much for the British liberal tradition. The French too refused to endorse Malik's principles, with Rene Cassin holding that "the human being [is] above all, a social being," and suggesting that alongside a list of rights of the individual, the commission should draft "a list of the rights of the community." Colonel Hodgson of Australia suggested that there was, in fact, only a slight difference of opinion among the delegates and that there was a general consensus that "the individual's rights ought to be subordinated to those of the national community and of the international community."[46]

For her part, Eleanor Roosevelt acknowledged that "the rights of the individual are extremely important" and that they were "something you have to think about rather carefully when writing a bill of human rights." She did not, however, actually endorse the principles set out by Malik, instead taking the opportunity to highlight the fact that the United States had instituted "social-security measures" to protect the fundamental freedom from want. Carlos Romulo was somewhat wary of wandering into what Hansa Mehta had called "the maze of ideology," but perhaps came the closest to supporting Malik. "I only wish to go on record," he told the commission, "that we hold to the familiar Jeffersonian maxim that governments derive their just powers from the governed, that the natural rights of men are anterior to the authority of the state, that the people are sovereign, and the state merely the instrument of their sovereign will."[47] Romulo's translation of the American tradition notwithstanding, Malik was aghast at the abdication by the leading Western powers of what he regarded as their very political soul. Attempting to salvage something of his proposal, Malik distilled from his principles the basic contention that the UNCHR should at least recognize that "the human person had not been created for the sake of the State, but that the State existed rather for the sake of the human person." Even this proved too much to ask, and the commissioners moved on to other business with Malik's proposal left to die of near universal indifference.[48]

This episode illustrates how marginal classic liberalism was among most members of the UNCHR during the drafting of the International Bill of Rights, even if Malik cannot be characterized as Lockean in any strong sense.[49] On the question of the value of human rights for protecting the inviolability of the human person, Malik's prewar experience, particularly in Nazi Germany, was at least as important as his abstract philosophical commitments. He had spent nine months, between August 1935 and May 1936, studying under Martin Heidegger at the University of Freiburg. Whether or not he was, as some supposed, the world's greatest living philosopher, Heidegger was undoubtedly a card-carrying member of the Nazi Party and by the time Malik arrived he had successfully implemented the National Socialist higher education policies—including the sacking of several Jewish faculty— as rector of Freiburg. At the time, Malik was of two minds about Heidegger: on the one hand attracted to his undeniable genius and sympathetic to his treatment of Kant; on the other, repulsed by his rejection of any notion of "a transcendent God outside man" and the sense that beneath his "clever" philosophy there lurked "a defiant undercurrent of ugly Germanism."[50] Far more troubling and less ambiguous, however, was the political and social atmosphere that enveloped the whole of Germany like a fog. Just months after Malik's arrival, the German people voiced overwhelming support for the Nazi party, and in particular the personal leadership of Adolf Hitler in the March 1936 parliamentary vote. His grip on the German people was, in Malik's assessment, absolute and he recognized in Hitler's ascendancy the triumph of "systematic, controlled propaganda." Watching how it had transformed the German public into rabid, thundering nationalists (even his elderly, infirm landlady was a devoted admirer of Hitler and his policies), Malik understood that modern propaganda constituted "the most revolutionary single force in the world today." It was, as Germany was demonstrating, completely capable of remaking "human nature into any mode of being you pleased."[51]

Malik's sojourn in Germany was a spiritual, intellectual, and personal crisis. The absolute racial logic, for which Malik seemed little prepared, was the most unsettling aspect of Nazi rule. Not only did it manifest itself in the "terrible hatred" for Jews that seemed to characterize nearly every pronouncement of the party and its sundry spokesman, but the race-think of Germany made Malik racially self-conscious for perhaps the first time.[52] "Because I come from Syria, and Syria cannot show forth military splendor," Malik wrote to a friend, "I am nothing." To another, he wrote of the utter loss of individualism in the face of the worship of the Race: "In 1935 A.D. you must belong to a Group, with a brilliant history, if you want to *be at all*. Being is Group-being and only Group-being. The individual is dead, wholly dead."[53]

Dehumanized by the all-pervasive Aryan racialism of the all-powerful German state, Malik was surprised and dismayed to see how fragile reason could
be when faced with the combined influence of mass media, rigid political
censorship, and an anti-intellectual public culture. Malik's time in Germany
gave him an expanded and far more dire sense of what was at stake in the
protection of human rights.[54]

During the final drafting sessions for the Universal Declaration, Malik
responded to a provocation from Soviet delegate Alexei P. Pavlov—who declared the draft insufficiently antifascist and in need of a list of duties citizens
owed to the state—by again noting that the attempt to closely identify the
individual, the state, and society threatened to undermine what he regarded
as the very foundation of the human rights ethic. He argued that the renewed
postwar interest in human rights represented a broad-based reaction against
the rise of political "monstrosities" in the modern era that had "trampled the
dignity of human beings." A defining feature of these monstrosities was a "determination by the state of all relations and ideas, thus supplanting all other
sources of conviction." This statism left the individual entirely "overwhelmed
by the group" and exposed and vulnerable before an all-powerful state. If the
effort to establish international human rights law was about anything, it was
about mitigating this exposure by curbing the state's authority to dominate
the individual.[55]

And yet, the British delegation was off the mark when they described
Malik as "a fervent individualist" in a cable home to the Foreign Office. The
problem of statism, as Malik saw it, was not simply a question of the individual versus the state, but of civil society versus the state as well. Malik's
German sojourn had sharpened his distrust of state power and confirmed his
doubts about the individual's capacity to withstand the disintegrative forces
of modernity, but it was his experience of religious community and school life
that pointed him toward a theory of human rights emphasizing not simply
individualism, but a communitarian ideal rooted in what he called "intermediate institutions." As a youth attending first the Tripoli Boys School and
then the American University of Beirut, Malik not only developed close and
durable relationships with teachers, staff, and fellow students, but also came
to regard the institution of the school as the central locus for incubating freedom as an individual, social, and political goal. It was not simply a matter of
inculcating certain values—American or Presbyterian proselytization—but
of a social and geographic location where free inquiry could be combined
with new forms of social solidarity to produce an imagined community of

empowered yet responsible subjects. Undoubtedly, Malik's educational trajectory had separated him from a more traditional social integration into his natal village community, but it hardly left him alone in the world. Rather, he came to see the university, broadly conceived, as the source of community that was equally gratifying and more universal. "These intermediate institutions between the state and the individual," Malik said two months before the start of the UNCHR's third session, "are the real sources of our freedom and our rights. . . . Unless the proposed Bill of Rights can create conditions that will allow man to develop ultimate loyalties with respect to these intermediate sources of freedom, over and above his loyalty to the state, we will have legislated not for man's freedom but for his virtual enslavement."[56]

Malik's concern with protecting and promoting these "intermediate sources of freedom" led him to be one of the only defenders of including a minority rights provision in the Universal Declaration. In his original draft, Humphrey had included an article guaranteeing the rights of minority groups to "establish and maintain schools and cultural or religious institutions, and to use their own language in the press, in public assembly and before the courts and other authorities of the state." Oversight of minority rights, particularly in Eastern Europe, had been among the most innovative work of the League of Nations, and remained of sufficient international importance under the UN to warrant the establishment of a Sub-commission on the Prevention of Discrimination and the Protection of Minorities. Johannes Morsink has argued that the mood turned against the article when debate over the Genocide Convention's controversial prohibition of cultural genocide intersected with the declaration debates.[57] What is also true is that the United States stepped up its lobbying efforts to eliminate the article, turning several members who had previously supported the minority rights protection. During the third UNCHR session, Roosevelt proposed to delete the article, stating that minority rights "had no place in a declaration of human rights," which presumably was meant to deal only with the rights of individuals as such. She was joined by a majority of the other members for whom the solution to minority problems was primarily "one of tolerance and the strict application of human rights to members of minority as well as majority groups," as Roland Lebeau of Belgium put it. He went on to remind the commission that Hitler had used the pretense of concern for the rights of German minorities in neighboring countries "to further his political and material ends."[58]

As Roosevelt and the others moved to delete it, Malik defended the article by noting that while the model of assimilation and national homogeneity may predominate in the Americas and Western Europe, multinational, multicultural states in Eastern Europe and Asia were content with their heterogeneity, and groups in those places sought not only protection from persecution but guarantees of their "right to free self-development," as he put it. Along with Lebanon, Malik cited the USSR and India as just such pluralistic states, but only Pavlov and delegates from the other socialist republics spoke in support of retaining the minority rights article. Hansa Mehta, who had in previous years supported the article, now found it "unnecessary" given the declaration's many repetitions of the principle of nondiscrimination.[59]

Malik was more successful in defending what became—after the minority rights article was removed—the declaration's only group right. Article 16 of the UDHR gave the family special status as the "natural and fundamental unit of society," deserving of protection "by the State and society." Originally introduced by Carlos Romulo at the second UNCHR session in Geneva, the article was of particular importance to Malik, who called the family "the cradle of all human rights and liberties."[60] In the drafting committee, both the U.S. and the UK suggested removing it, Roosevelt because it was superfluous and Geoffrey Wilson because he preferred that the article focus on prohibiting forced or underage marriages. Malik, however, was joined by Pavlov and Cassin, who thought it was foolish to "disregard human groups and consider each person only as an individual." The article survived, as did the principle that human rights implied more than the defense of the autonomous, atomized individual.[61]

While he supported the group rights of families and minorities in order to protect affiliations with social groups other than the state, Malik also initially opposed including economic and social rights in the covenant for the same reason. In June 1948, John D. L. Hood of Australia moved to include economic and social rights in the covenant, and while he was supported by Hernan Santa Cruz of Chile, the majority felt that negotiating such rights would prove more difficult and time consuming than negotiating civil and political rights; even Pavlov gave only cautious support to the concept of "broadening the democratic aspect of the Covenant," and thought the provisions might be included "in subsequent conventions." The U.S., UK, and China framed their opposition to including social and economic rights around the idea that such rights either were nonessential or needed different enforcement mechanisms, but Malik couched his opposition in terms of antistatism. Voicing his support of the Australian proposal "in respect of the Declaration," Malik reminded the delegates that the covenant placed direct responsibility on governments to realize the rights enumerated therein. Such responsibility, Malik said, implied power "over the economic, social, and cultural agencies, such as universities, the arts, religion, the church," and even "the home, folklore, and folk songs." This would amount to "the destruction of free institutions in a free world." Autonomy for these "free social institutions" needed to be defended. "Governments," Malik concluded, "should see only that the material conditions of freedom [are] maintained."[62]

The dilemma presented to Malik by economic and social rights—that is, how to incorporate them in a way that made clear their importance without at the same time authorizing the state to assert control over every aspect of the economy and society—led directly to the creation of perhaps the most novel right in the Universal Declaration.[63] Article 28 of the UDHR states that "Everyone is entitled to a social and international order in which the rights and freedoms set out in this Declaration can be fully realized." Amidst a long debate over whether the article guaranteeing the right to work should include a paragraph declaring the state's obligation to create the conditions necessary for full employment, Malik noted more broadly that it might be useful to include a new article "calling attention to the need for establishing the kind of social and economic conditions . . . in which the individual could develop and in which his rights could be guaranteed."[64] The idea was, rather than list the specific duties of the state to realize each of the social and economic rights listed in the declaration—a possibility supported by France and the socialist bloc but opposed by the UK, India, U.S., and Philippines—that a general covering article could be inserted before or after this section. Almost all the participants spoke in favor of the concept of a new article—a rare agreement to expand the declaration during a session devoted to streamlining and editing—and a subcommittee of Lebanon, France, the U.S., UK, and Soviet Union was appointed to draft it.[65]

When the subcommittee presented its work to the full commission, however, there were two new articles on the table. One, authored by Cassin, fulfilled the original mandate of the subcommittee by declaring that everyone "as members of society" had certain economic, social, and cultural rights whose realization "should be made possible in every state separately or by international cooperation." Cassin explained that he sought to give form to the "practical difference" between social and economic rights and the individual rights listed in the previous sections of the declaration, namely, that they "required material assistance to be furnished by the State." Most delegations agreed, and after some significant revision of the language, what became

Article 22 of the UDHR was adopted without opposition.[66] More interesting was the second draft article, which also enjoyed relatively broad support. As drafted by the subcommittee, the proposed article reflected more of Malik's original language from the debate, but was now framed as a covering article for *all* the declaration's rights. "Everyone," it said, "[has] the right to a good social and international order in which the rights and freedoms set out in this Declaration can be fully realized." Although he had originally sought a new article to frame the social and economic rights of the declaration, after the subcommittee's meetings, Malik now argued that a singling out of those rights from the rest of the declaration amounted to "preferential treatment." It also allowed Malik to avoid singling out the state as the primary guarantor of human rights, opening up the possibility that a broader range of social actors could be held accountable for protecting and promoting the rights of the declaration. In addition, the article introduced the concept of a right to an "international order." In Cassin's article, "international cooperation" was invoked to authorize the UN and other intergovernmental organizations, such as the International Labor Organization, to participate in social and economic development initiatives. The "international order" of Article 28, however, was not simply a mechanism to achieve the rights in the declaration—although, on this point, it is an important gesture toward the question of implementation—but a right in and of itself. The implications of this right, which seemed lost on many members who regarded it as a fairly innocuous statement of principle or even as a tautology, were evident to Malik: each individual had a fundamental human right to live not just in a nation-state organized and committed to her "individual development," but also in a world that facilitated and enhanced realization of universal human rights. Like the right to have rights, the right to an international order dedicated to human rights is less a tautology than a foundational condition of the international human rights project itself.[67]

"The Crisis of the Declaration is the Projected Covenant"

Malik's contributions to the form and substance of the UDHR would have meant little if the various bureaucratic and political obstacles had been allowed to endlessly delay bringing it to the floor of the General Assembly. By a fortuitous alignment of bureaucratic stars, in 1948, Malik had been placed in both the presidency of the Economic and Social Council and the chairmanship of the General Assembly's Third Committee, both of which needed to give their approval before the declaration could be voted on by the full GA. The ECOSOC, perhaps more than any other UN body during this period, became a theater of the Cold War with Alexi Pavlov taking every opportunity to attack the United States and its allies, while U.S. representative Willard Thorp, then assistant secretary of state for economic affairs and a co-author of the Marshall Plan, returned fire to declare the Soviet Union "completely unfree."[68] During these meetings, John Humphrey was unimpressed with Malik: "He invites debate, does little to direct the discussion, and tries to be everybody's friend," he wrote in his diary. "As a consequence the delegates ride off furiously in every direction." Much to Humphrey's surprise, however, the end result was that the ECOSOC passed the declaration, unchanged and for the most part undiscussed, on to the General Assembly. Whether by intention or by accident, Malik had brought the declaration through the briar patch of the Economic and Social Council unscathed and intact.[69] In the Third Committee, Malik switched tactics. He was also joined by a more sympathetic group of delegates, including fellow UNCHR members Roosevelt, Chang, Cassin, and Hernan Santa Cruz. Unlike in the ECOSOC, Malik rarely interjected in substantive debates, content to let his deputy Karim Azkoul state the Lebanese position and his compatriots from the UNCHR defend the commission's work. Instead, Malik was much more heavy-handed as the chairman, scheduling night meetings, keeping discussions on topic and, when it began to appear as if the work might bog down as it had with the ECOSOC, acquiring a stopwatch and "mercilessly" enforcing a three-minute time limit on speeches. The tactics paid off and the Third Committee voted without opposition on December 7 to send the final draft of what was now titled "Universal Declaration of Human Rights" to the General Assembly.[70]

Two days later, Charles Malik introduced the text of the Universal Declaration of Human Rights to the General Assembly on the evening of December 9, 1948, just minutes after the assembly had adopted—without debate or dissent—the Convention on the Prevention and Punishment of the Crime of Genocide. He read a speech prepared for the most part by Humphrey and the Secretariat Division of Human Rights and summarized the drafting process that had begun over two years earlier. While more politically neutral than most of Malik's own statements on human rights, the address did include the assertion that the declaration was intended as "a potent critic of existing practice" and should help "transform reality"—sentiments very much in keeping with Malik's views.[71] He was followed by a parade of speakers that continued until the next day, and when the final vote was taken the results were 48–0 in favor of adopting the declaration, with 8 abstentions. As noted above, one abstention came from Saudi Arabia based on objections to articles it found in conflict with Wahabi interpretations of Islam. Another came from the Union of South Africa, which had already found itself the subject of human rights criticism in the UN. Under the leadership of Jan Smuts, South Africa had originally been a supporter of the international bill of rights project, but in May 1948 his relatively more liberal United Party was defeated by the unapol-ogetically racialist National Party, which expanded and institutionalized the policy of apartheid as, in the words of Nationalist M.D.C. de Wet Nel, "a di-vine task." Unsurprisingly, the new regime found the UDHR, with its promi-nent rejection of racial discrimination, anathema. The final six abstentions were from the Communist delegations of the Soviet Union, the Ukraine, Be-lorussia, Poland, Yugoslavia, and Czechoslovakia, which objected because the declaration, as Soviet deputy foreign minister and former Moscow show-trial prosecutor Andrey Vyshinsky put it, "completely ignored the sovereign rights of democratic Governments." In the Soviet Union, he said, "The State and the individual [are] in harmony with each other; their interests [coincide]." Any declaration of human rights that failed to recognize this could not be ac-cepted by an "advanced socialist State."[72] No doubt, Charles Malik agreed that the UDHR was incompatible with the Soviet system.

The declaration was only one component of the International Bill of Rights, and following its adoption, Malik set to work ensuring that the com-mitment to the deferred human rights covenant was not forgotten in all the self-congratulations of December 10. At an informal dinner hosted by the Commission of the Churches on International Affairs in April 1949, Malik spoke of the UDHR as an admirable "statement of principle" whose worth was attested to by the fact that it was vehemently denounced from the left by the Communist Party and from the right by the American Bar Association. "But," he continued, "the crisis of the Declaration is the projected Covenant." Pious statements needed to be backed up with real commitment to change. "Are we prepared to join with others not only in the elaboration of principle but also the establishment of law?," Malik asked. "This is the real test of our moral courage and fundamental convictions."[73]

When the fifth session of the UNCHR began in May, Malik's concerns regarding a postdeclaration loss of momentum proved prescient. Charged with completing the draft of the human rights covenant, the UNCHR moved at a snail's pace, completing little more than a review of the work already accomplished over previous years. Eleanor Roosevelt, who had been essential in keeping the commission on track during the drafting of the declaration, missed several meetings, leaving vice chair P. C. Chang to run the proceedings. Although a brilliant mind and an essential contributor to nearly all the discussions of the commission, Chang lacked the bureaucratic acumen of either Roosevelt or Malik and allowed the UNCHR to wallow in the quicksand of Alexi Pavlov's long-winded polemics. The Russians had little interest in moving quickly on the covenant. The result was that the commission's final report for 1949 simply forwarded the incomplete draft of the covenant on to member governments for comment, and asked the secretariat to seek and compile advice on the contentious and unresolved issues of economic, social, and cultural rights, and methods of implementation.[74] "The real truth of the matter is that at this session the commission has not only failed to take any action towards the promotion of human rights," John Humphrey concluded in his diary, "it has actually taken a step backward."[75]

Within this backward step, Malik recognized not just a failure of U.S. leadership on the UNCHR, but the signs of a deeper problem in Western culture, a problem he addressed in his most lauded and reproduced speech in the UN. Delivered to the GA's First Committee on November 23, 1949, the address was part of the debate over the Soviet-sponsored "Pact for Peace" resolution, which, in addition to condemning the United States and the UK for "making preparations for war," would have called for a new nonaggression treaty between the five major powers. Malik's intervention—titled "War and Peace" when it was published in pamphlet form a few months later by a CIA front organization, the National Committee for Free Europe—described the rise of communism as a symptom of a more profound crisis in the West. At the root of the malevolent revolutionary ethos of Marxist dogma lay the false idol of materialism, of which capitalism was but the mirror image. "The spirit of business and gain, the maddening variety of things exciting your concupiscence, the utter selfishness of uncoordinated activity," all were evidence, Malik told the Political Committee, of "a general weakening of moral fibre" in the West. The communist menace had been visited on the West as a judgment and a test, but so far, Malik lamented, "The leadership of the West in general does not seem to be adequate to the unprecedented challenge of the age." The West seemed unsure of itself, unwilling to challenge communism head-on in the world of ideas and too ready to ally itself with "dark regimes" or withdraw into a fantasy of self-sufficient isolationism.[76]

The challenge presented by communism had to be met with more than the negative response of anti-communism. What was needed, Malik proposed, was a constructive program that could match the positive Soviet accomplishments in economic development and social justice, but "without the loss of the higher values which constitute the very soul of the West." These values were "rooted in the glorious Greco-Roman-Hebrew-Christian-Western-European-humane outlook," and maintained the priority of the mind and spirit over the material world. The true West saw that the state and society are "for the sake of the human person," and recognized that "there is a whole dimension of transcendent norms fully accessible to the mind and heart." Exactly what norms Malik was referring to was clear: "The deepest traditions of the West conceived of man as the subject of basic and inalienable and universal rights, rights which are based upon his very nature and which are embodied in natural law." If the West was not only going to win the Cold War, but also redeem itself and the rest of the world from the scourge of materialism of which communism was but a symptom, it needed to embrace and share this heritage.[77]

By invoking the "Greco-Roman-Hebrew-Christian-Western-European-humane outlook," Malik was deploying the authority of his Harvard education in an attempt to goad the West into action. He had, of course, been working on a "synthesis" of the Western tradition since his graduation in 1937, and his use of it here signaled the continuity between his prewar and postwar modes of activism. During the late 1930s and early 1940s, Malik had achieved some prominence as a philosopher of Arab Christianity—in 1943 Albert Hourani called him "perhaps the greatest intellectual figure in the Arab world today"[78]—and key to his philosophy was an articulation of the West as rooted not only in a post-Enlightenment rational technocratic mastery of the material world, but in a more ancient, eastern Mediterranean interaction between "Greco-Roman" philosophy and "Hebrew-Christian" theology. This meant, among other things, that his Western partisanship in the Cold War should be understood in terms of a much longer historical trajectory. Moreover, his genealogy of the West implied that in taking up this commitment to human rights and pressing the United States and other powerful European allies to lead in this field, Malik was not simply parroting a Westernized perspective he had imbibed as a student of American educational institutions, but reenacting an original conversion *of* the West *by* the East. In this respect, Malik's hybridity was not exclusive of his identification as Western: by tying together the "Greco-Roman-Hebrew-Christian-Western-European-humane" tradition, he was implying that the most compelling values of the West were themselves the result of cross-fertilization.[79]

Malik's framing of the conflict with the Soviet Union in grandiose terms of the survival of civilization was echoed a little less than six months later in the seminal U.S. National Security Council assessment, NSC-68. "The issues that face us are momentous," it read, "involving the fulfillment or destruction not only of this Republic but of civilization itself."[80] Submitted to President Truman in April 1950, NSC-68 solidified its place at the center of American security policy when, on the morning of June 25, North Korean forces attacked across the 38th parallel. A carnal house of destruction that consumed upward of 2.5 million civilian lives, the war proved the most compelling argument—both within the Truman administration and the American public at large—for a dramatic military build-up to roll back "the Soviet design" of global domination.[81] Significantly, NSC-68 also acknowledged that the United States had "the responsibility of world leadership . . . to bring about order and justice by means consistent with the principles of freedom and democracy."[82] And yet, as John Lewis Gaddis pointed out, the authors of NSC-68 almost immediately pivoted from this statement of principled leadership to a blanket authorization of "any measures, covert or overt, violent or non-violent, which serve the purpose of frustrating the Kremlin design."[83] Under these marching orders, human rights, particularly if they were seen as weakening the "moral and material strength" of the U.S. position against the Soviets, were not likely to fit into the U.S. strategy.

NSC-68 remained secret until the late 1970s, but the fact that the United States was going to emphasize a military response to the threat of communism was evident at the 1950 UN session. After having nearly all its aims frustrated at the Fourth General Assembly, the Soviet Union effectively walked out of the UN in January, the final insult being the refusal of the UN member states to seat the People's Republic of China as the rightful representative of the Chinese nation. The strategy was to be reversed in late July, but not before the U.S. had taken advantage of the situation by authorizing its action in Korea through the Security Council resolutions 83 and 84, allowing the Korean War to be prosecuted as a peace enforcement action under Article 7 of the charter—a situation not to be repeated until the First Gulf War of 1991.[84] In the General Assembly, the U.S. led the effort to pass the "Uniting for Peace" resolution. Prompted by the Soviet return to the Security Council, this resolution gave the Assembly the power, in the event of a deadlock among the permanent members of the Security Council, to recommend collective action up to and including the use of force.[85]

This assertive U.S. leadership in the realm of collective security was matched in the realm of human rights. But because it was aimed at limiting rather than expanding the effectiveness of the UN program, it only served to deepen Malik's concern over the Western soul. As in the Security Council, the Soviet boycott opened the door for the United States to have a number of their positions adopted, including a general limitations clause spelling out under what circumstances derogation from the covenant's provisions was acceptable, the rejection of proposals to allow individuals and NGOs to submit complaints, and the severance of economic, social, and cultural rights from the civil and political rights that had heretofore made up the bulk of the draft covenant.[86] With the Soviet seat empty for the sixth session, it was all too clear to Malik that the West in general and the United States in particular lacked the requisite nerve to see a progressive, binding covenant enacted. In a rare moment of praise for the Soviet delegation, Malik confided to his deputy George Hakim that the UN was of little worth without Soviet participation. "Their keenness and vigor and opposition are necessary," he wrote just a few weeks after the last UNCHR meeting, "although I do not at all agree with their point of view."[87] Elsewhere he concluded, "[The Soviet] absence this time has not helped the cause of human rights."[88]

Since his widely circulated "War and Peace" speech in the First Committee the previous fall, Malik had been besieged with invitations to give a speech or write an article for this or that college, organization, or magazine, and he now took advantage of this fame to try to develop public support for a more progressive human rights policy. He told the New England Council that the "real issue of our times" was whether the United States could rediscover its own "intellectual and spiritual foundations" and "share them with the whole world."[89] Speaking at the convocation at the University of Dubuque, he insisted that "America can help build the new temple of freedom, and not only for herself, but for the whole world."[90] Writing in the Catholic periodical *Commonweal*, Malik noted that "the United States has played a leading role in this business of human rights. The needs of the world are such that you must continue to play this leading role."[91] And speaking as "an Asian who knows something of the highest values which have characterized the Western positive tradition," Malik, in another widely hailed speech at the UN, said to the West in general and the U.S. in particular, "You can do much better also."[92]

Malik was more blunt in private discussions with Eleanor Roosevelt, which she reported to her State Department contacts the week after the UNCHR adopted its final report for the seventh session. "Dr. Malik," she said, had "stressed heavily and at length the needs and aspirations of the under-developed countries." The articles on social, economic, and cultural rights had come to symbolize those needs and aspirations, and those countries deeply resented the U.S. reluctance to state these as rights, Roosevelt explained. This was a particular tragedy, Malik had told Roosevelt, because in his estimation U.S. leadership and technical assistance were key to realizing their goals in this field. As it was reported, Malik said "that the United States must both tell these countries what to do and how to do it." Malik concluded by appealing to Roosevelt on the grounds that economic, social, and cultural rights, specifically elaborated at the international level, would be potent weapons in the hands of opposition leaders throughout the underdeveloped world to "prod their own governments" toward social reform. As will be discussed in the next chapter, given the damning African American petitions and the cries from the American Bar Association about creeping socialism, however, the U.S. government was unlikely to relish the idea of fashioning additional prods for activists, from "under-developed countries" or otherwise.[93]

Ironically, in his efforts to cultivate U.S. leadership in the development of the human rights covenants, Malik took on even more responsibility for shepherding the drafts through the UNCHR. After six years, Malik was elected chairman for the seventh session when Roosevelt stepped down, in part because she found her effectiveness had been compromised by a growing skepticism of U.S. motives among underdeveloped nations. Roosevelt told Harry Truman, "The mere fact that we spoke for something would be enough to make them suspicious."[94] As chair, Malik attempted to be independent and impartial, meaning that his interventions were less argumentative and strident than they had been in previous sessions. Instead, he partnered closely with John Humphrey to guide the UNCHR through reviewing and adopting a series of economic, social, and cultural rights—a task the Third Committee, in a direct rebuke of U.S. efforts the previous spring, had expressly designated to the commission.[95]

Malik was also the sponsor of a proposal on implementation of these rights authored by Humphrey. Unlike the civil and political rights, which many thought should be subject to some sort of complaint procedure if violations occurred, economic, social, and cultural rights were generally regarded as nonjusticiable in the same manner. Historian of the covenants Daniel J. Whelan has gone so far as to suggest that not a single delegation proposed making these rights subject to an individual, NGO, or even interstate complaint procedure, even among the most ardent supporters of the priority of economic, social, and cultural rights.[96] Malik and Humphrey instead proposed a system of periodic reporting on the "progressive" realization of these rights, with international implementation coming through the provision of technical assistance rather than penalization. The adoption of a version of this plan brought the covenants to the verge of completion. It was, in the opinion of John Humphrey, perhaps the most productive UNCHR session to date, in large part because, "we have a good chairman."[97]

Despite this progress, Malik remained frustrated because it was achieved despite, not because of, the United States. On economic, social, and cultural rights, the Americans had sought a general "umbrella clause" that would call for the "promotion of economic, social and cultural progress and development" as opposed to an elaboration of concrete rights. The United States had also been insisting that the covenant include a clause specifying that in the case of a federal state, articles dealing with matters that were normally handled at the state or provincial level could not be strictly guaranteed, but only brought "to the notice of the appropriate authorities" at the subnational level. On the right of petition for violations of civil and political rights, while not inclined to oppose allowing such petitions from individuals or NGOs, the United States wanted such a provision placed in an "optional protocol"—and added that it would not be interested in opting in. With regard to the right to self-determination, the United States opposed it outright, believing that the UNCHR and the covenant was the wrong place to address the issue.[98] In a synopsis of the commission's work for 1951 written for the *UN Bulletin*, Malik, after recounting in measured and neutral language the various debates and decisions of the session, concluded with a rather cryptic apostrophe: "Who will inherit the earth? Only the people and the country that overcoming its own internal difficulties, steps forth with courage and humor and responsibility to lead the rest of the world in the effective affirmation of what essentially belongs to man."[99] It would have been hard to argue that a country committing nearly a half-million troops to a war 5,000 miles from its shores was meek, but Malik believed, when it came to "ultimate things," the U.S. was at the least hiding its light under a basket.

Malik chaired the UNCHR for one more session, during which the commission wrapped up much of its work on what became—following a General Assembly directive to split the single treaty—the International Covenant on Civil and Political Rights and the International Covenant on Economic, Social, and Cultural Rights. As Malik described it, the work was deeply polarized, with "two more or less solid and equal blocs" voting against each other "on practically every important issue."[100] The two sides consisted of Chile, Egypt,

Pakistan, Poland, Ukraine, Uruguay, the U.S.S.R, and Yugoslavia on the one hand, and the U.S., UK, Sweden, Greece, France, China, Belgium, and Australia on the other. The final two members, Lebanon and India, divided their votes between the two blocs, siding sometimes with one group and sometimes with the other.[101] Thanks to these two swing votes, the eighth UNCHR produced two relatively progressive draft covenants. The two covenants were given identical preambles taken almost verbatim from the UDHR, and were revised to include umbrella nondiscrimination clauses as well as language in support of establishing equal rights for men and women. Not much change was made to most of the substantive civil and political rights handed down from the sixth session, although the rights to freedom of thought, conscience, and religion were slightly revised, much to the satisfaction of Malik, to clarify the right to change beliefs as well as the prohibition against coercion in matters of conscience. The UNCHR revised and augmented the fourteen articles drafted on economic, social, and cultural rights during the 1951 session, adding special protections for maternity, children, and the family, the right to form and join trade unions, and the right to science and culture—again, all Malik priorities. As to the implementation of these rights, a majority turned back a Soviet effort to require governments to strictly guarantee these rights, instead calling on each state to "take steps, individually and through international cooperation, to the maximum of its available resources, with a view to achieving progressively the full realization of the rights recognized in this covenant by legislation as well as by other means."[102]

Despite the progress made on the covenants, the conclusion of the eighth session left Malik more despondent than ever about the future prospects for human rights. Within the debates over economic, social, and cultural rights and especially over self-determination, Malik recognized a "quiet revolution" in the outlook of the commission. The priority had shifted from "freedom from discrimination and from arbitrary arrest, and freedom of religion and speech" to an emphasis on guaranteeing "an adequate standard of living." It was "an overwhelming of the ends by the means, the personal and intellectual by the social," and demonstrated the ascendancy of materialism that Malik had been trying to stem since his days at the American University of Beirut. Although he credited both the dogged consistency of the Soviets as well as the rise of the underdeveloped nations as contributing to this "revolution," the decisive factor was "the apparent unimaginative helplessness of the Western world in the face of these two impacts." In particular, it was the United States that had failed to express its authentic "spiritual message" of human rights—a message that Malik had been encouraging this "waking giant" to articulate to the world. Thus, despite having succeeded in guiding the UNCHR toward the fulfillment of its instructions, Malik completed his tenure as chair convinced that the UN's human rights program was headed in the wrong direction.[103]

As the United States continued to withdraw from participating in the UN human rights program, the UNCHR finalized the covenants during its ninth and tenth sessions, sending versions of both treaties to the ECOSOC in spring 1954. After ECOSOC approval, the drafts entered a bureaucratic purgatory in the Third Committee, where they were debated, revised, and amended for over a decade before finally being adopted by the General Assembly without dissent in 1966. An indication of both the acrimonious political climate that had come to define the UN as well as the low priority accorded to human rights, the fate of the human rights covenants seems to bear out Malik's lament, written in his diary in December 1954:

> People do not talk about human rights now as they did seven years ago when we were in the midst of working on the Universal Declaration of Human Rights. . . . The political issues of the cold war, of war or peace, of what mode of coexistence, if any, can be envisaged and should be worked for between the communist bloc and the rest of the world, and of the liberation of the still dependent peoples of Asia and Africa; these political issues, as well as the economic and material issue of the vast social revolution raging in every country in the world, and the issues of how to control and turn to beneficial uses the released energy of the atom—it is these problems today, and not the question of human rights, that seem to occupy the minds of men.

Whatever hope there was for human rights, Malik concluded, it no longer rested with the United Nations.[104]

Conclusion

Malik's sense of the prospects for the International Bill of Rights was, over the next twenty years, borne out. Finally opened for signature in 1966, neither of the two human rights covenants entered into force until another decade had passed, when each received the requisite thirty-five ratifications to become binding international law. Far from inspiring the kinds of global transformations or reform movements that early supporters like Malik hoped for, the covenants instead found themselves first sidelined by Cold War and postcolonial politics, then riding the coattails of a human rights revival led not by the UN but by NGOs like Amnesty International and Human Rights Watch (originally Helsinki Watch).[105] Clearly, the United States was not alone in its lack of enthusiasm for making human rights into international law but, as the next chapter demonstrates, the role the UN human rights program played in both international and domestic U.S. politics reveals with particular clarity just how consequential such a program could (or could not) be.

Malik's failure to overcome U.S. ambivalence about the International Bill of Rights did not diminish his enthusiasm for the West nor his efforts to influence U.S. policy more broadly. In the late 1950s, he was appointed foreign minister in the government of Camille Chamoun in large part because of his reputation for being, as British ambassador to Lebanon George Middleton put it, "persona gratissima in Washington."[106] According to Caroline Attié, this reputation proved accurate enough in 1958 when Malik helped to convince John Foster Dulles and Dwight Eisenhower to intervene in what was essentially a fairly low-level civil conflict, sending some 14,000 U.S. troops into Lebanon.[107] When the bloody and destructive Lebanese Civil War broke out in 1976, Malik helped organize the Lebanese Front for Freedom and Man (later the Lebanese Forces), an umbrella organization of primarily Christian factions,[108] and was a prominent voice representing their cause in the U.S.—although in this case, U.S. intervention had more to do with the influence of U.S. ambassador Philip Habib than Malik.[109] This kind of influence—over political, economic, or even military support—was always less important to Malik than his effort to awaken the U.S. to what he called its "radical moral responsibility."[110] Like the right to have rights that the declaration and covenants were intended to establish, Malik took responsibility for that responsibility, and in the process helped lay the foundation of the modern international human rights regime.

Chapter 5

The NAACP, the ABA, and the Logic of Containment

Shortly before the start of the 1948 General Assembly session that would see the adoption of the Universal Declaration of Human Rights, U.S. secretary of state George Marshall received a memorandum from his newly established Policy Planning Staff. Intended to offer broad, strategic analysis and advice in developing postwar foreign policies, the office was short-lived but sufficient to allow the staff's director, George F. Kennan, a position from which he could establish the early Cold War policy of containment. As a strategic Cold War policy, containment originated with Kennan's "long tele-gram" of February 22, 1946, and his subsequent "X" article in *Foreign Affairs* in which he argued that the United States need not actively seek to under-mine or destroy the Soviet Union, only check its advance in Europe and wait for the "seeds of . . . decay" to sprout from within Russian society.[1] In a 1948 memo, however, Kennan reflected on the need to contain not just commu-nism but the emerging UN human rights program as well. He acknowledged that given the very public work of the government in this field, the United States had "no choice" but to press for the adoption of the declaration, but he questioned the wisdom of negotiating statements "of this nature" in the future. The idea of making commitments, even just "moral" ones, to human rights standards "which we are not today able to observe in our own country, which we cannot be sure of being able to observe in the future, and which are in any case of dubious universal validity," struck Kennan as an invitation to damaging accusations of hypocrisy and a cause for increasing contempt for UN pronouncements.[2] Although Kennan's personal ascendancy was soon checked by the appointment of Dean Acheson as secretary of state in 1949, his "realist" assessment of the limited utility of human rights to advance U.S. interests abroad would dominate the U.S. foreign policy establishment for years to come.

If the international human rights program needed to be contained, it was because it had the potential, as Charles Malik, Carlos Romulo, and others suggested, to transform not just the outside world but the United States as well. Kennan insisted that any international bill of rights must be carefully evaluated to ensure its "consistency with our own practice and world realities."[3] Such an approach missed the point many supporters of international human rights law repeatedly emphasized. Existing practices and realities were fundamentally unjust and in need of dramatic reform. African American activists made this abundantly clear immediately following the establishment of the UN. In the span of less than eighteen months, two African American organizations petitioned the UN for vindication of their human rights. While these efforts led to no direct action on the part of the UN, they had a double effect on U.S. officials. On the one side, State Department officials responded to the challenge of the petitions by working to ensure the emerging UN human rights system was constructed in a way that prevented U.S. domestic human rights conditions from being examined under it. On the other, State Department officials and others in the Truman administration began actively supporting African American efforts to achieve redress through the U.S. court system. Through both gestures, the U.S. government sought to contain the problem of African American human rights within national boundaries.

Like the CSOP before it, the NAACP had a dramatic impact on U.S. human rights policy. A third organization had perhaps the most lasting influence, demonstrating once again the importance of civil society in early human rights politics. Among the most prominent professional organizations in the country, the ABA had in 1943 evidenced support for the development of international human rights standards, but in the years after the war it became a powerful voice of opposition against the UN in general and its human rights activities in particular. Under the leadership of Frank Holman, the ABA challenged the legitimacy of the UN human rights program and protested U.S. participation in it. Casting international human rights instruments as threats to American tradition and jurisprudence, the ABA was among the first to allege that the provisions of the International Bill of Rights were compromised by communist influence and that ratification of any human rights treaties would infect American law with socialistic principles. This effort directly affected the willingness of U.S. officials to engage in constructive dialogue on the covenant and eventually led to a Constitutional crisis over the president's treaty-making powers in the form of the notorious Bricker Amendment. Under pressure from the ABA and its allies, the last vestiges of U.S. leadership in the arena of international human rights were forfeited. Like the NAACP, the ABA saw the UN human rights program not as an extension of the American rights tradition, but as a powerful—even revolutionary—challenge to it. Unlike the NAACP, the ABA believed that meant it needed to be contained and kept from infecting American institutions and practices.

The final section of this chapter returns to the anti-Soviet origins of "containment" and considers a brief but significant U.S. government-led human rights crusade aimed at fashioning the principle of international human rights into an effective Cold War weapon. Over several months in 1949 and 1950, the Truman administration intervened in the violation of human rights in the Eastern European countries of Hungary, Bulgaria, and Rumania. The violations involved the persecution of a number of religious figures in the three countries, most notably Hungarian Cardinal Joseph Mindszenty who had been charged with spying for the West. The U.S. pursued the matter as a violation of the 1947 peace treaties, which like most World War II treaties included human rights guarantees, rather than as a violation of the UN Charter or the UDHR. Doing so recalled an older model of international human rights enforcement, one in which obligations were not reciprocal and the only parties with standing were states. Predictably, the effort failed to improve conditions in the targeted countries, and the quixotic campaign demonstrates the limited utility of pursuing human rights during the Cold War containment effort at the same time as the U.S. sought to contain those same rights.

"Appeal to the World": Containing African American Human Rights Claims

Chapter 1 notes that the NAACP was among the organizations granted consultant status for the San Francisco conference, and the work of Walter White, W. E. B. Du Bois, and Ralph Bunche contributed to a significant liberalization of the U.S. position on the charter's provisions dealing with colonialism. White and Du Bois also added their voices to the chorus of consultants who pressed Secretary of State Stettinius to make human rights a priority for the new organization. In the wake of the San Francisco gathering, however, while many of the consulting organizations continued to be involved in the process of developing a robust UN human rights regime, the NAACP moved from an advisory to activist role. Du Bois in particular reasoned that the charter was sufficiently clear on the point that member states were expected to protect and promote the human rights of all their citizens, and began making plans to have the NAACP petition the UN for redress of the legion human rights violations suffered by African Americans on a daily basis.[4] The move reinforced fears within the American political establishment that the UN human rights program dangerously blurred the border between domestic and international affairs. Those fears, rather than the hopes for a transformed global community, came to dictate U.S. human rights policy in the late 1940s.

Historian Carol Anderson has chronicled in compelling detail the work of the NAACP and other black activists on behalf of human rights during this period. An attempt to resituate the post-*Brown* civil rights movement as an impoverished and circumscribed version of a broader and "infinitely more important" struggle for human rights, Anderson's scholarship emphasizes the hypocrisy and conservatism of U.S. human rights policy as well as the enormous political pressure brought to bear on the leadership of the NAACP to reorient their efforts toward more moderate goals.[5] By placing the NAACP's contributions in the context of both the wider policy of containment and the conflicting work of the ABA, this chapter seeks to highlight once again the decisive influence of NGOs on international human rights. Such a perspective, while acknowledging the structural limitations faced by activists struggling against entrenched interests, emphasizes the agency of civil society in the formation of both specific policies and the larger discursive frame of human rights. Whether policy makers react by accommodating or resisting the demands of activists, the nature of human rights politics demands response.

For many African Americans, including the leaders of the NAACP, the American political system had time and time again proved itself incapable or unwilling to fulfill the promise of its own founding in the inalienable and equal rights of all human beings. Perhaps the most egregious case in point was the perennial failure of the U.S. Senate to pass antilynching legislation even though a majority of senators, along with the House of Representatives and the executive branch, might favor it.[6] Yet, despite the aversion of the national government to protecting even the lives and bodily integrity of black Americans, not to mention the higher-order rights of political participation and equality before the law, the NAACP had not, at least as late as June 1946, considered the nascent international law of human rights as anything other than moral support for their cause.

Instead, the initiative was seized by another important, but long forgotten, African American political organization, the National Negro Congress (NNC). Founded in 1936 by A. Philip Randolph, Ralph Bunche, and John P. Davis, the NNC was overtly socialist in ideology and actively sought closer ties to the Soviet Union. By the end of the Second World War, the NNC had become more or less an extension of the Communist Party, U.S.A (CPUSA), and many of its former supporters, including Randolf, Bunche, and Davis, had broken with the organization or been purged by the authoritarian president, Max Yergan. A complex and conflicted individual who swung from Christian missionary to militant communist to outspoken anti-communist, Yergan was nonetheless critical to the cultivation of a global outlook on the part of African Americans during the interwar period. Yergan spent his early career working for the YMCA in India, East Africa, and, most extensively, South Africa—experiences that not only radicalized him politically but helped him identify the experiences of nonwhite peoples under colonialism with those of African Americans in Jim Crow America.[7]

Yergan's decision to take the African American case to the UN was rooted in this transnational outlook and in the hope that the move would be dramatic enough to raise his and the NNC profile. Written by historian Herbert Aptheker in the spring of 1946, the petition was adopted at the June convention of the NNC and delivered to the UN Secretariat later that month by Yergan, Aptheker, Vice President Charles Collins, and Executive Secretary Revels Clayton.[8] The report detailed the social discrimination, economic privation, and political disenfranchisement suffered by African Americans, and called on the UN to undertake a fact-finding mission to the U.S. and make recommendations "to the end that higher standards in the field of human rights may be achieved in the United States of America." Aptheker also took care to note the various provisions of the charter under which the UN was authorized, or even required, to act.[9] Of course, the litany of references to human rights contained in the charter and cited by the petition were there largely because of the efforts of NGOs, but, the NNC reasoned, they were binding international law nonetheless.

While the Cold War was still new in June 1946, red-baiting was not. The taint of the CPUSA meant that the NNC was increasingly marginalized even among African American organizations, and its petition found little sympathy in the U.S. or among other UN delegations. The document was politely if coolly received by P. J. Schmidt and Lyman White of the Secretariat, and filed with the thousands of "communications" the UN was receiving from around the world regarding human rights. Even the Soviets, who, as the ideological confrontation intensified, took every opportunity to raise the issue of American racial discrimination, were wary of getting behind a petition calling for international investigation of and intervention in the domestic rights conditions of a member country. Nevertheless, the NNC petition was sufficiently compelling to inspire increased concern on the part of U.S. officials.[10] Of course, American officials did not need the NNC petition to tell them either that African Americans were deprived of basic human rights, or that this deprivation significantly complicated U.S. participation in the development of international human rights law. But the NNC petition did spur the State Department, now headed by former senator and future governor of South Carolina James F. Byrnes, to take more concrete steps to shore up the firewall between domestic racial politics and international human rights, including, as noted in the previous chapter, preventing the Commission on Human Rights from considering communications that complained of specific rights violations.[11]

By the time Eleanor Roosevelt was helping to bury the communications in the UNCHR, the potentially more incendiary NAACP document was taking shape. After observing the impact of the modest effort of a marginal organization like the NNC, NAACP director of special research W. E. B. Du Bois embarked on an effort to prepare an "impressive and definitive" report on "the situation of American Negroes" for presentation to the General Assembly. During the San Francisco conference, Du Bois had focused on the plight of the colonial peoples to the exclusion of everything else, including the proposed international bill of rights. The qualified success of the charter's trusteeship provisions led Du Bois to conclude, much as Romulo had, that the San Francisco conference was "a beginning, not an accomplishment" in regard to colonialism, but he remained unconvinced that the charter's human rights commitments were anything more than pious words.[12] Following the NNC petition—which he called "too short and not sufficiently documented"—Du Bois began to see the UN human rights program as a forum where the African American cause could be connected to the global struggle against colonialism. Proposing the project to executive secretary Walter White in August 1946, Du Bois noted that "the Indians of South Africa, the Jews of Palestine, the Indonesians and others" were planning similar petitions. "It would be," he told White, "an omission not easily to be explained if the NAACP did not make a petition and statement of this sort."[13]

While his analysis may not have been as sharp and his politics were certainly not as strident, White shared Du Bois's sense that the time had come to move the fight for African American human rights from "the local and national setting" to "the realm of the international." The NAACP leader had gained prominence as a community organizer and for his incredibly courageous reporting on dozens of lynchings, and White had recently turned his attention to the global dimensions of racism.[14] During the war, White was one of the most vocal critics of colonialism, lobbying the Roosevelt administration, as had Carlos Romulo and others, to make sure the Atlantic Charter applied to all subject peoples and not just white Europeans under the German thumb. In his widely read *A Rising Wind* (1945), White detailed how the war was proving a watershed in the history of race relations worldwide. Presciently, he concluded that after fighting for freedom abroad, returning African American soldiers would rebel against the constraints of a segregated society and bring a new, global perspective to their struggle.

> World War II has given to the Negro a sense of kinship with the other colored—and also oppressed—peoples of the world. Where he has not thought through or informed himself on the racial angles of colonial policy and master-race theories, he senses that the struggle of the Negro in the United States is part and parcel of the struggle against imperialism and exploitation in India, China, Burma, Africa, the Philippines, Malaya, the West Indies, and South America. The Negro soldier is convinced that as time proceeds that identification of interests will spread even among some brown and yellow peoples who today refuse to see the connection between their exploitation by white nations and discrimination against the Negro in the United States.[15]

Such sentiments were increasingly common among much of the black intellectual elite in the United States.

Despite a deteriorating personal and professional relationship, White supported Du Bois's plan and, along with the rest of the NAACP board of directors, approved the project. Du Bois's original intent was to have the petition ready for the first General Assembly session in September 1946, but once work began it quickly became apparent that the project would require more time to complete. In order to research and draft the petition, Du Bois assembled a team of scholars and lawyers including Earl Dickerson, Milton Konvitz, Robert Ming, Jr., and Leslie S. Perry.[16] The final member of the group was historian and internationalist Rayford W. Logan. Labeled admiringly by the *Chicago Defender* "a bad Negro with a Ph.D.," Logan had taken Du Bois as his model in activism, scholarship, and dignity. Logan attended the San Francisco conference and, as a longtime student of colonial administration, advocated for a universal, international trusteeship system. For the petition project, Logan's task was perhaps the most difficult. He was to make the case that the UN Charter had established the protection of human rights as an obligation under international law, and that it provided some potential remedy for those denied their rights by national governments. The trick, Logan quickly realized, was to overcome that hobgoblin of international human rights, the domestic jurisdiction clause of Article 2(7), which was even then being reaffirmed by John Foster Dulles in opposition to Romulo's proposed colonial people's conference.[17]

Given the scope and complexity of the project, it is no surprise that by the time delegates began to gather in New York for the meetings of the General Assembly, Du Bois and his team were still hard at work compiling and organizing their materials. An early version of the petition was available at the start of the first UNCHR session in January 1947. At that time, Du Bois, accompanied by Ralph Bunche, spoke briefly with John Humphrey, giving him a draft of the petition and asking him to place it on the agenda for the General Assembly. The decision taken by the UNCHR regarding communications meant that the NAACP petition was filed, along with all other communications, with the secretariat where it was sealed from all but a few sets of eyes. Du Bois, whose tenacity was legendary among friend and foe alike, regrouped with his team to revise the petition once again and make plans to work around the barrier of the commission's communications policy.[18]

By the middle of the summer, the petition was finally ready and Du Bois began contacting UN officials in the Secretariat and among the delegations to line up support for placing it on the fall agenda. Against his better judgment, Du Bois acceded to Walter White's request that he first contact the U.S. mission to the UN, specifically American UNHCR representative Eleanor Roosevelt. White had cause to be optimistic about U.S. reaction to the NAACP effort, given that Roosevelt had long been among the most prominent white proponents of black rights and that she had taken a seat on the NAACP board of directors at the same time she agreed to represent the Truman administration at the UN. Du Bois, who had never been impressed by Roosevelt or her husband, was unsurprised by the "vague and meager advice" she returned.[19] He had better luck with the Indian delegate, V. L. Pandit, who was still basking in her victory over Jan Smuts (see Chapter 3) and told Du Bois she would do what she could to have the petition placed before the General Assembly or the Economic and Social Council.[20] Du Bois then contacted Humphrey at the secretariat in order to set up a formal and pubic meeting whereby the NAACP could submit its petition to the UN in front of a gathering of invited guests and press.[21] This time, Du Bois hedged his bets against having his work quietly filed away and gave a copy of the petition to George Streator of the *New York Times*, who published a piece in the Sunday, October 12, edition entitled "Negroes to Bring Cause Before U.N."[22] With the public's interest piqued, Humphrey agreed to an October 23 meeting in the New York offices of Henri Laugier, assistant secretary general for social affairs.

As finally presented to the UN, the NAACP petition was titled *Appeal to the World: A Statement on the Denial of Human Rights to Minorities in the Case of Citizens of Negro Descent in the United States of America and an Appeal to the United Nations for Redress*. In his statement at the presentation ceremony, Walter White recalled the racial roots of the Second World War and warned that any future peace was contingent on the resolution of the problem of discrimination. In a move that foreshadowed rhetorical strategies of contemporary activists, White emphasized the common interests and interconnections of people around the world. "Injustice against black men in America," White said, "has repercussions upon the status and future of brown men in India, yellow men in China, and black men in Africa."[23] In his brief statement, Du Bois also anticipated contemporary NGO practice when he declared that this "documented statement of grievances" was intended "to induce the nations of the world to persuade this nation to be just to its own people."[24] In response, Humphrey offered the only thing he was authorized to: a statement of UN policy on human rights communications and a reiteration of the self-affirmed powerlessness of the UNCHR to act on any such petition. In a telling addition, however, he pledged that members of the commission would be able to review the work as part of their effort to draft the international bill of rights.[25]

As Humphrey's remarks indicated, work on the international bill of rights could serve to deflect and channel discussion of specific human rights abuses into the formulation of general principles. This was precisely what the State Department intended when, in November, Roosevelt requested NAACP input on the prospective human rights declaration. "I have no suggestions for Mrs. Roosevelt," was all Du Bois scrawled at the bottom of a memo from Walter White.[26] In a longer, if no more conciliatory, response, Du Bois described his complete lack of interest in a "World Charter of Human Rights."

Citizen of a country that had proclaimed "all men are created equal" nearly 200 years earlier and provided a Constitutional guarantee of the rights of African Americans 100 years after that, Du Bois was deeply skeptical of legal statements—let alone nonbinding "declarations"—on human rights. "What is wrong about human rights is not the lack of pious statements," he fumed, "but the question as to what application is made of them and what is to be done when human rights are denied in the face of laws and declarations." Du Bois was fast concluding that the UN was no more effective an ally than the U.S. federal government in pursuing his goal of racial justice.[27]

The more moderate and pragmatic White was willing to engage Roosevelt and the State Department on their terms. Of the input requested by Roosevelt, White told Du Bois it "may well be one of the most important documents which the Association has ever produced."[28] Du Bois could be forgiven for taking such a comment as a slight against *Appeal to the World*, on which the ink was not yet dry, but White had clearly moved on from the petition to emphasizing what he hoped would be a more constructive dialogue with the State Department. This rapprochement had begun a few weeks before Du Bois and White handed Humphrey their appeal, when the NAACP's Legal Defense Fund had asked the State Department for assistance in preparing arguments for an upcoming Supreme Court case, *Shelley v. Kraemer*, challenging race-based restrictive covenants.[29] The official response was to point the NAACP to the Department of Justice as the primary coordinator of the government's positions on such matters, but State Department lawyer John Maktos did suggest that State make available the background memo it had prepared for Justice, as well as relevant public statements by prominent department officials.[30] The State Department went even farther the week after *Appeal to the World* was submitted, with legal advisor Ernest A. Gross telling Attorney General Tom Clark that discriminatory restrictive covenants such as those challenged in *Shelley v. Kraemer* were detrimental to the U.S. internationally. "The United States has been embarrassed in the conduct of foreign relations by acts of discrimination taking place in this country."[31]

Although their petition had been quickly shepherded toward an uncertain fate at the UN, the NAACP's efforts had succeeded in making racial conditions in the United States an international issue, and had prodded the State Department to make an unprecedented foray into a deeply contested domestic issue on the side of expanded equality for African Americans. But while department officials admitted that domestic rights issues could not be kept separate from global politics, Maktos and Gross both took the opportunity of the NAACP Supreme Court work to affirm and reiterate the government's position that adjudication and remediation of domestic rights issues *must* be kept separate from international institutions and laws.[32] As Gross told Clark in his letter putatively supporting the NAACP case in *Shelley v. Kraemer*, the U.S. was under no international legal obligation "to guarantee observance of specific human rights and fundamental freedoms without distinction to race, sex, language or religion," even if it was good policy and public relations to do so.[33] Thus the sword of the NAACP petition effort was double-edged: on the one hand, by appealing to the world through the UN, the organization demonstrated what a liability U.S. racial injustice was for the aspiration of American global power, and made an ally of what had traditionally been one of the most conservative factions in the federal government. On the other, if the NAACP and State Department made for strange bedfellows before the Supreme Court, it was because State was determined to keep such issues contained to domestic institutions—a fact that would animate much of the U.S. participation in the effort to develop international human rights law.

When in December 1947 the UN convened in Geneva at the old home of the League of Nations, the Palais des Nations, *Appeal to the World* became, as an NAACP internal memo put it, a "political football." In the Sub-Commission on the Prevention of Discrimination and Protection of Minorities, the Soviet delegation savored the opportunity to go on the offensive and sought to place the petition on the agenda. The United States countered with a proposal to allow all petitions—including those from the Soviet sphere—to be considered by the sub-commission. Given the previous American position on communications in the UNCHR, the sincerity of the move was doubtful and the ultimate outcome—the skirmish ended with no petitions being heard and the Russians appearing hypocritical (and the Americans only slightly less so)—was likely what the Truman administration had hoped for. It was an inglorious end to a provocative experiment, but the more subtle and lasting impact of the NAACP petition came in the UNCHR. There the American position, which had been more open and flexible the previous spring, began to congeal around several more cautious positions: emphasize the nonbinding declaration over the convention, limit the language on nondiscrimination within both documents, and include a so-called "federal clause" in any eventual human rights treaties.[34]

The NAACP would take the fight for black rights to other venues, particularly the courts, and deploy a discourse other than human rights, particularly Constitutional law—a strategic shift that would have its benefits as well as its limitations. Led by Thurgood Marshall, the NAACP Legal Defense Fund pursued a brilliant campaign of legal challenges to segregation that would culminate in *Brown v. Board of Education*, but did so squarely within the limits of domestic legal institutions, practices, and concepts. It was precisely the historical failure of those domestic rights resources—a history that makes Marshall's accomplishments all the more impressive—that had led Du Bois, and for a brief time White, to pursue the African American cause at the international level. The UN's developing international human rights regime offered hope not as an extension of American traditions, but as a critical corrective and supplement. The idea that the U.S. would itself be transformed by a potential international law of human rights was also at the heart of another organization's activism during this period.

Backlash: The American Bar Association and the End of American Human Rights

If, by the end of 1948, the NAACP had conceded to containing the "American dilemma" of racial injustice within the discourse and political institutions of the United States, another more influential American NGO was just beginning to examine the domestic implications of the new international ideology of universal human rights. Beginning that year, the ABA launched a coordinated campaign to undermine public and official support for both the UN generally and international human rights standards in particular—a campaign that culminated in the effective withdrawal of U.S. participation from the UN human rights program. Perhaps even more than either the CSOP or the NAACP, the ABA demonstrated the paramount influence of civil society in the formation of U.S. human rights policy during the mid-twentieth century.

As an organization, the ABA had long been active in opposing progressive and liberal reforms—including the initiative, referendum, and recall movement of the early twentieth century, the nomination of Louis A. Brandeis to the Supreme Court in 1916, and much of the New Deal.[35] Since the Russian Revolution, the ABA had also promoted a rather virulent strain of American nationalism, through its Committee on American Citizenship, against what committee chairman R. E. L. Saner called "various forms of Bolsheviki doctrines."[36] In a 1918 speech before the Louisiana State Bar Association and reprinted in the *American Bar Association Journal*, Rome G. Brown asserted that while the U.S. had little to fear from the external threats "of Mexican banditti, or of the yellow peril of the Orient, or of Spanish tyranny, or of the yet barbarous and inhuman militarism of the Hun," the nation was vulnerable to a creeping socialism from within. As a manifestation of "a direct and pure democracy in government," socialism threatened the American tradition of liberty. Brown defined this American tradition of rights in the following terms:

> Freedom from unauthorized search and imprisonment, freedom of religion, and, *above all*, the right to acquire and hold property, and the right of individual liberty in all social and business relations—the efficient protection of these individual rights was, more than anything else, the purpose, and the accomplishment, of our constitutional government. [emphasis added][37]

These same principles would guide the ABA opposition to the UN human rights program.

In the mid-1940s these more reactionary inclinations were muted, thanks in large part to the wartime abeyance of both isolationism and—once the U.S.S.R. was an official U.S. ally—anti-communism. At a 1943 meeting the ABA House of Delegates adopted a series of resolutions drafted by the Comparative and International Law Section (CILS), in which the ABA endorsed the establishment of a future international organization and initiated studies of "an adequate post-war judicial system of permanent international courts" and "the fundamental principles, including a bill of rights, which are constitutional in character and which should be generally acceptable as a minimum for the preservation of international order and justice under law."[38] The CILS contained, unsurprisingly, most of the internationalist members of the ABA, including John W. Davis, George A. Finch, Green Hackworth, Manley O. Hudson, Philip Jessup, William Draper Lewis, and Hans J. Morgenthau. Debate in the general House of Delegates, however, indicated that a good portion of the lawyers outside the section worried about, as board of governors member Robert Maguire put it, "invad[ing] and occupy[ing] fields in which they have no right to speak for lawyers of the United States." The board of governors opposed both the endorsement of a new international organization and the call to study an international bill of rights, but the majority seemed swayed by Iowa Supreme Court Justice Frederic M. Miller who recalled his own service in World War I and then invoking his son in the Army Air Corps: "We must see to it that our boys are not let down as we were. This time we must not only win the war, but win the peace. The American Bar Association owes a duty of leadership."[39]

Such leadership was relatively short-lived, however. The following year, the CILS offered a six-part resolution outlining the "constitutional principles" for a "permanent organization of the nations . . . for the purpose of maintaining peace by legal sanctions and the suppression of aggressive war." The resolution recommended that member states should "enjoy equal rights and equal representation in the general assembly," that the organization should include a council empowered to maintain the peace and a permanent court of international justice within a wider international judicial system, and that the United States should be a member of the organization. Once again, the board of governors came out against the resolution, seeking to limit the ABA statement to one expressing support for recent congressional resolutions in favor of some new postwar international peace machinery. Section member Thomas B. Gay expressed surprise that the governors were unwilling even to adopt the part that essentially restated the 1943 resolution specifically endorsing the creation of a new organization, but apparently the year had brought with it a change of heart as former supporters of bold leadership now favored taking more time to "think about the details and work out all the various ramifications and features." This time the House of Delegates sided with the board of governors and the section's resolution was deferred.[40]

Instead of sending it back to the CILS for further study, however, the House referred it to a new committee created at the suggestion of the board of governors that would coordinate any further ABA statements on international organization. This move effectively took the mandate away from the section and ensured that future recommendations would be less progressive and more in keeping with the conservative nature of the general leadership of the ABA. The committee, which after the war would be renamed the Committee on Peace and Law Through the United Nations (CPLUN), included two members of the CILS, Frederic Miller and former ABA president William Ransom, and five others, including a Seattle corporate lawyer named Frank E. Holman. Over the next several years, the section would be relegated to dealing with questions of international law narrowly defined, particularly with regard to the reorganization and operation of the world court, while the committee served as the primary forum for formulating ABA positions on UN activities, including human rights.[41]

By the beginning of 1948, with the war over and the UN firmly established, the ABA, led by the CPLUN, began to push back against the developing UN human rights system. At its February meeting, the House of Delegates adopted a resolution written by the committee—and opposed by the CILS—that expressed opposition to the creation of an international human rights court or a standing committee within the UN to hear complaints of human rights violations, as well as the right of "individuals, associations or groups" to petition the UN. "A Pandora's box of international friction and provocations through UN interventions in the internal policies and member states," the CPLUN argued, "might be opened by the adoption of these correlated proposals."[42] By September, the association came out against the declaration and covenant more generally, and ensured that the full weight of the ABA's political clout would be mobilized against the UN human rights program by unanimously electing Frank Holman president for the coming year.[43]

Born in Utah in 1886, Holman graduated from the University of Utah in 1906 and studied law at Oxford University on a Rhodes scholarship. Chafing at the authority of the Mormon Church, Holman relocated to Seattle in 1924 where he became a pillar of the local community until his death in 1967. During the war, his chronic allergy condition kept him out of the armed forces and he instead served on the state and federal Alien Enemy Hearing Boards, the administrative bodies established by attorney general Francis Biddle as a "courtesy" to enemy aliens threatened with internment.[44] Although a member of the CPLUN, Holman was never much of an internationalist, even if he could appreciate the importance of some amount of international order during the war. In 1946, after the CILS endorsed the principle of "limited world government," Holman published a longwinded response entitled, "World Government: No Answer for America's Desire for Peace," in which he warned that "our way of life, our civilization, our standards, would be put in jeopardy" under world government. Recalling some of the racial paranoia of Rome Brown, Holman declared, "to live in a world dominated politically, . . . socially, economically, and culturally, by the masses of India, China and Indonesia, or by such a combination as Russia might control—for men with an Anglo-Saxon and a Christian background this would be an intolerable world."[45]

Seeking the ABA presidency in 1948 primarily to defend "our kind of government and its institutions," Holman targeted the developing UN human rights program as both "revolutionary" and "dangerous."[46] The UNCHR, he told the California Bar Association shortly after his election, was a veiled attempt to "promote state socialism, if not Communism throughout the world," and thus it was incumbent upon American lawyers to sound the alarm for an "oblivious" press and public before it was too late. Again employing a racial logic that was prevalent in the writings of ABA spokesmen three decades earlier but fast becoming anachronistic, Holman lamented the fact that the "Anglo-Saxon" members of the UNCHR—Roosevelt, Hodgson of Australia, and Dukes of the UK—had little legal training and were compromised by overabundant sympathy for socialist ideals. The covenant and declaration drafts, Holman claimed, represented grave threats to the American way of life and government and needed to be thoroughly rewritten or abandoned.[47] Such arguments would gain traction in the coming years, but Holman was too late to derail the declaration—the U.S. was firmly behind it and, thanks in large part to the stewardship of Charles Malik, it would become a defining achievement of the UN in less than three months.

The ABA attack on the UN human rights program intensified in the wake of the UDHR, with Frank Holman making headlines and garnering increased support in large part because of his repeated emphasis on the threat of communist subversion lurking in the documents' provisions. An article entitled "Human Rights on Pink Paper" appeared in a number of publications in early 1949 and purported to expose the "communistic" content of the just-adopted UDHR. The ABA president pointed to Declaration Articles 22 (social security), 23 (protection against unemployment and fair pay), 24 (rest and leisure), 25 (food, clothing, housing, and medical care), and 26 (education) as the foundation of a "collectivist society" that might well be imposed on the U.S. if "the internationalists" were not stopped. Ignoring the pains the U.S. delegation went through to ensure that the UDHR was *not* considered a legally binding treaty, Holman warned darkly, "You have by a few pages of treaty language transformed the government of the United States into a socialistic state." A great admirer of Wisconsin Senator Joseph McCarthy, who earlier that year had explosively and disingenuously claimed to have a list of 205 current and former Communist Party members working with the Truman State Department, Holman placed the human rights treaties at the center of a multipronged conspiracy of Communist subversion aimed at world domination.[48]

Holman's pyrotechnics attracted the attention of the U.S. State Department, which sent Roosevelt's principal advisor James Simsarian to attend a number of regional conferences organized by the CPLUN during the first several months of 1949. At a February meeting in Boston, he observed an "aggressive" defense of the UN human rights program by CILS members Roscoe Pound, Zechariah Chafee, and Louis B. Sohn.[49] This was heartening, but more significant was that the vocal opposition of the CPLUN group seemed to be drawing more support from many of the "practicing lawyers" in the audience, "who held official positions in the American Bar Association or in local Bar associations."[50] By the spring, Simsarian's boss Durward Sandifer had given up on talking to Holman and his circle of hardcore opponents, but as work continued on the remaining components of the international bill of rights, the State Department could hardly ignore the fact that the Holman line was becoming more and more widely held within the ABA and, more ominously, beyond.[51]

Some of the effects of the lawyers' criticisms can be seen in the U.S. agenda for the 1950 UNCHR session. The general limitations clause, the denial of the right of petition for individuals and groups, and the exclusion of economic, social, and cultural rights all seemed tailored to counter the effectiveness of Holman's argument that the covenant would impose a socialistic world government. None of these accommodations mattered when in April a California Appellate Court ruling confirmed the worst fears of Holman and the others worried that the UN human rights program was infecting American legal institutions. Handed down on April 24, 1950, the decision in *Sei Fujii v. State of California* invalidated the state's discriminatory Alien Land Law, which barred land ownership by "aliens ineligible for citizenship" and was targeted specifically at disadvantaging Japanese immigrant farmers.[52] Sei Fujii, a first-generation immigrant and graduate of the University of Southern California Law School, attempted to purchase a small parcel on the outskirts of Los Angeles in 1948 and, when the state moved to seize the property, he worked with the American Civil Liberties Union to bring suit challenging the validity of the statute.[53] Fujii and his lawyers argued not only that the Alien Land Law violated the Fourteenth Amendment due process and equal protection clause but that it contravened the explicit commitments in the UN Charter to promote "universal respect for, and observance of, human rights and fundamental freedoms for all without distinction as to race, sex, language, or religion." The court based its decision exclusively on the latter contention, stating "such a discrimination against a people of one race is contrary to both the letter and to the spirit of the charter which, as a treaty, is paramount to every law of every State in conflict with it."[54]

The argument had been made before, first by Rayford Logan in *Appeal to the World* and then again by the NAACP legal team in front of the U.S. Supreme Court in *Shelley v. Kraemer*. A similar contention had been made by both Charles Malik and Carlos Romulo in the UNCHR. In every forum beginning with the San Francisco conference, however, the Truman administration insisted that the charter created no legally binding human rights commitments, and the U.S. Supreme Court ignored the argument from the charter in finding against restrictive covenants in *Shelley*, relying exclusively on the Constitution. The California ruling breached this barrier and reaction was swift, with most agreeing with the editors of the *Stanford Law Review*, who thought the court had made a mistake: "The Charter," they said, "does not impose an obligation on the United States to strike down inconsistent state legislation."[55] The legal rationale was advanced by Manley Hudson in an influential article published in July 1950, which argued that the charter's human rights provisions were addressed "to the political, not the judicial departments" of the government and therefore required an act of Congress to become law within the United States. The provisions were, as it came to be known, "non-self-executing," and the courts could not use them as the legal basis for decisions invalidating domestic laws.[56] This was precisely the reasoning the California Supreme Court used two years later when it upheld the invalidation of the Alien Land Law, but reversed the appellate court's finding on the applicability of the UN Charter. Reinscribing American jurisprudence within the borders of the nation, this court ruled that the charter's human rights provisions had no legal effect domestically, but that the discriminatory statute still violated the Fourteenth Amendment.

With the *Fujii* case, Holman had his smoking gun, and what appeared shrill alarmism to some in 1949 now looked like a prescient analysis of things to come. Among those who were increasingly receptive to the ABA perspective on international human rights law was the U.S. Senate, which in early 1950 began debating the Convention on the Prevention and Punishment of the Crime of Genocide. Ratification of the treaty was a priority of the Truman administration, and when the Foreign Relations Committee began hearings in January the sentiment was trending decidedly toward ratification. Of the parade of witnesses testifying before members of the committee, the vast majority favored swift ratification—including a number of administration officials, as well as labor, civil rights, and religious leaders.[57] New chairman of the CPLUN Alfred T. Schweppe, a colleague of Holman's from Seattle, and former ABA President Carl B. Rix were nearly alone in testifying against ratification, with Charles W. Tillett, the head of the CILS, urging senators to adopt the convention.[58] A logjam in the Foreign Relations Committee, however, meant that by the time they were ready to send the convention to the Senate floor for a vote, it was late summer and, in the wake of the *Fujii* ruling, a wave of letters in opposition to ratification had reached the Senate.[59] Committee chairman Tom Connally, a Democrat from Texas who had been one of the U.S. delegates to the United National Conference on International Organization, balked at bringing the treaty forward by citing the ABA opposition as the primary reason for tabling the convention for this session.[60] It was a tremendous victory for the Holman faction of the ABA and emboldened them to continue their assault on U.S. participation in the development and implementation of international human rights law.

The success of the ABA in thwarting ratification of the Genocide Convention should have indicated to State Department officials that the ABA was not about to be appeased by excluding economic, social, and cultural rights from the covenant, or ensuring the document had an iron-clad non-self-execution clause. In his reaction to the *Fujii* ruling, Holman revealed that what concerned him was not so much that a panel of California judges had mistakenly attempted to apply the UN Charter as "supreme law of the land," but that the entire judicial and executive structure of the U.S. government was increasingly infected with the "un-American" ideology of "so-called human rights." While the California Supreme Court, taking its cue from Manley Hudson, successfully "corrected" the lower court's mistaken reading of the charter, Holman recognized in the application of the Fourteenth Amendment not a recuperation of the rightful basis of American law in the U.S. Constitution, but a regrettable innovation in American jurisprudence.

> Some will say that the final decision in the *Fujii* case is merely based on a new and more modern construction of the Fourteenth Amendment, but this new construction was clearly brought about in the face of a well settled construction that had stood the test of years, and obviously because of the internationalist concept of the United Nations Charter, a ratified treaty.[61]

In many ways, Holman was correct. This "new and modern construction" of the post-Civil War Fourteenth Amendment *was* an abandonment of sixty years of "well settled construction," enshrined by the Supreme Court's 1896 decision in *Plessy v. Ferguson*, that allowed for racial discrimination to permeate all levels of American society and law. And while much of the credit was due to the legal strategy of the NAACP's Thurgood Marshall and Charles Hamilton Houston, there is no doubt that the rise of human rights ideals during and after the Second World War was deeply influential in making judges—including those of the U.S. Supreme Court—receptive to these arguments.[62] For Holman and the reactionary forces he represented, it was precisely the broader social and political, rather than strictly legal trends, he found most offensive.

In paranoid style, Holman saw the explicit rejection of the theory that the UN Charter could invalidate discriminatory laws as proof that the problem was much deeper than any specific treaty. What the *Fujii* case had revealed was the danger new developments in international law posed to the balance of powers in the United States. Given the exclusive authority of the executive branch of the federal government to set and pursue foreign policy, local representatives were essentially frozen out of the diplomatic process through which international treaties were negotiated. Furthermore, once ratified, the federal government had the responsibility to see that the terms of the treaty were fulfilled. Given that the proposed human rights treaties covered "the whole gamut of so-called human rights and human relations," such an obligation would require the extension of federal regulation and oversight into every facet of American life. Under these conditions, Holman warned, "the doctrine of states rights and local self-government can become as nonexistent in the United States as in the highly centralized governments of Europe and Asia." With the emergence of human rights as a new field of international law, the treaty-making authority of the Executive became a "blank check" through which "our whole concept and theory of government" might be sold out from under the American people.[63]

In response to this threat to long-standing American values, the ABA decided to invent a new tradition. After their campaign against the Genocide Convention had proven that the Senate might be particularly responsive to arguments about the dangers of treaty making to the American system of government, Holman and his supporters were emboldened to press not only for the abandonment of the UN human rights program, but for a Constitutional amendment barring *any* future treaties involving human rights from entering into domestic force in the United States. The idea had first arisen at the regional seminars organized by the CPLUN in 1949, where participants suggested that the dangers posed by a potential international human rights covenant might be mitigated "through reservations attached by the Senate to its consent to ratification, and possibly through amendment of the Constitution of the United States." Dismissed as far-fetched at the time, with the *Fujii* ruling and the rise of a more assertive "third concept" in the UN pushing for a broadly inclusive human rights covenant, revision of the fundamental law of the United States became a viable option in a short span of time.[64]

During the summer of 1951, the idea found a political patron in the conservative Republican senator from Ohio, John W. Bricker. Bricker began his political career as a vocal opponent of the expansion of federal authority under the New Deal, and ran as Thomas Dewey's vice-presidential candidate against Roosevelt and Truman in 1944. Elected to the Senate in 1946, Bricker was undistinguished as a legislator until he recognized in the ABA proposal for a Constitutional amendment a vehicle to simultaneously advance his isolationist, states rights, small government, and anti-communist agendas. He introduced the amendment in September 1951 and made the issue a centerpiece of his 1952 reelection campaign. Democratic presidential candidate Adlai Stevenson thought Bricker's views were sufficiently out of the mainstream to try and tie Dwight Eisenhower to him as a reactionary isolationist, but it was Stevenson who appeared out of touch.[65] The results were a landslide victory for Eisenhower, reelection for Senator Bricker and, during the 1953 Senate session sixty-four cosponsors for what had become known as the Bricker Amendment.[66]

Eisenhower had long been a political cipher, but the contention that he was a closet isolationist was never very plausible and was definitively laid to rest when, a few weeks after the election, he named John Foster Dulles his secretary of state. Few in the Republican establishment had the foreign affairs credentials of Dulles, but for watchers of American human rights policy, he was a mixed blessing. On the one hand, Dulles had been one of the earliest supporters of the international promotion of human rights, having cochaired the Commission to Study the Bases of a Just and Durable Peace during the war. On the other, as a member of the American delegation at San Francisco, Dulles had been the intellectual force behind the drafting and adoption of charter Article 2(7), which he conceived in order to keep most human rights issues within the purview of domestic jurisdiction. After the war, Dulles was key to the development of the so-called "bipartisan" foreign policy under Truman, helping to ensure widespread support for continued U.S. leadership in the UN generally, and little Republican opposition to the UN human rights program in particular. In the wake of Thomas Dewey's surprising loss to Truman, Dulles, who had been Dewey's presumed choice for secretary of state, worked with the Acheson State Department to counter the early criticisms from the ABA.[67] He was, however, skeptical of the transformative potential of international law in general, and by the time he was preparing to take control of U.S. foreign policy he was emphasizing that "the one indispensible sanction is [national] community opinion" rather than legal compulsion.[68]

But if the development of U.S. human rights policy over the previous thirteen years had demonstrated anything, it was that the personal views of American policy makers counted for less than did the pressure from "outside," whether from domestic civil society organizations or "friends" abroad. Taking office in January 1953, it was the former that the Eisenhower administration was most attentive to. Preparing for their first session of the UNCHR, the Eisenhower State Department decided to fully reverse the policy of support for the human rights covenants, even at the risk of alienating those countries that strongly supported the treaties, "especially those of Latin America and the Middle and Far East." There were several reasons, including the fear that they could serve as "a source of propaganda" about domestic conditions or "disadvantage" U.S. interests abroad, but the most specific reason was that the covenants were "under attack by large and important groups in this country such as the American Bar Association," and that further work on the covenants "would tend to keep alive and strengthen support for the Bricker amendments to the Constitution." Of the domestic support for the covenants, department analysts noted only that there was "a considerable body of organized opinion" in favor of continued engagement, but apparently it was neither large nor important.[69]

That the primary motivation for the change in policy was the threat to the president's ability to conduct foreign policy posed by the ABA assault on treaty-making powers was made clear by the venue in which it was announced. Testifying during the Senate Judiciary Committee's hearings on the Bricker Amendment, Dulles dubiously conceded that while past administrations may have tried "to use the treaty-making power to effect internal social changes," the Eisenhower administration could be trusted to be more responsible. To amend the Constitution would be an overreaction, and "embarrass" and "detract from the authority" of the president to conduct international affairs. As a sign of the newfound responsibility with which such affairs would be pursued, Dulles told the senators that the U.S. would not "become party to any [human rights] covenant or present it as a treaty for consideration by the Senate." With such immediate dangers averted, the secretary of state asked the Senate not to adopt the Bricker Amendment or any similar provision, suggesting instead that the area "be kept under constant observation and study" and the executive's powers remain intact.[70]

Dulles's statement before the Senate came on the eve of the ninth session of the UN Commission on Human Rights, and the change in U.S. policy was perhaps best symbolized by the figure now occupying the seat which, for the previous eight sessions had been held by the imposing, endearing, and impressive Eleanor Roosevelt. Mary Pillsbury Lord, descendant of the Pillsbury Flour Mills founder and wife of New York textiles magnate Oswald B. Lord, was appointed to the post by Eisenhower after serving as cochair of the National Citizens for Eisenhower-Nixon during the 1952 campaign.[71] Just in case the significance of the replacement of one of the world's most famous and admired people by a Manhattan socialite-cum-political fundraiser was lost on the commission members, Mrs. Lord promptly echoed Dulles's line that the United States was no longer interested in the development of the human rights covenant. Instead, she proposed that they now shift their work to studying "various aspects of human rights throughout the world," perhaps developing a plan for annual reports on human rights from member countries, or even establishing a system of "advisory services." Such services, as a U.S. position paper described them, were "to be in the form of experts going to countries requesting the services, scholarship and fellowships being provided for training abroad and arrangements for seminars." Other UNHCR members, eager to complete the two covenants, were not impressed.[72]

Like the CSOP before it, the ABA succeeded in transforming U.S. human rights policy through a combined strategy of engaging the public sphere and lobbying officials. With less direct access to the executive branch and the foreign policy makers at the State Department, the ABA instead leveraged their influence with the legislative branch, particularly the Senate, to force disengagement from the UN human rights efforts. Apart from their political success, the ABA also succeeded in articulating the idea of human rights as essentially foreign to the American tradition of rights, an idea that would hold sway for at least two decades. Foreign or not, the idea of human rights was sufficiently powerful that the U.S. tried at least one more time after the adoption of the UDHR to make it a dynamic force in international affairs. Ultimately, however, the pursuit of the Eastern European Cases, as they came to be called, demonstrated the limits, much more than the possibilities, of American international human rights activism.

Human Rights and the Cold War:
The Eastern European Cases

If the actions of the ABA on the one side and the NAACP on the other left officials at the State Department feeling caught between, as one memo put it, "complaints that we are going too far" and the criticism that "we are not prepared to go far enough," prior to 1953, the U.S. government was still not prepared to cede its image as the leading defender of human rights around the globe.[73] That image was increasingly untenable in the UNCHR where, as Charles Malik and Carlos Romulo could attest, the United States was surpassed only by the Soviet Union in foot-dragging and reservations. In early 1949, however, events conspired to provide the United States with an opportunity to unabashedly champion international commitments to human rights standards at the same time it satisfied a number of otherwise competing foreign policy interests. Over a few short months in 1949 and 1950, the so-called Eastern European Cases allowed the U.S. to use the new principles of universal human rights as weapons in the nascent Cold War, without fear that doing so might compromise their more cautious positions on other human rights matters. By highlighting the violations of freedom of religion and speech, by emphasizing the authority of the peace treaties rather than the UN Charter and the UDHR, and by limiting both the venue of adjudication and the potential remedial actions, the Truman administration hoped to simultaneously contain and champion human rights.

The General Assembly's third session is known as the "Human Rights Assembly" for more than its two most famous accomplishments, the Genocide Convention and the UDHR. Resolutions were also introduced and adopted on subjects such as the treatment of Indians in South Africa, trade union rights, and freedom of information. Near the end of the session, caught up in the spirit of the season, two delegations placed another new human rights issue on the agenda. In separate proposals, Bolivia and Australia requested that the GA investigate and, if circumstances required, take action in the increasingly dire human rights situation in the Eastern European republics of Hungary and Bulgaria (Rumania was later added to the list of countries of concern).[74] Prompted to action by the arrest and subsequent show trial of Hungarian Cardinal József Mindszenty, who in February had been sentenced to life in prison on the fabricated charge of conspiring with the U.S. government to overthrow the socialist regime, the Bolivian and Australian proposals were designed to highlight the rapidly deteriorating rights conditions in these countries. As hostilities grew between the East and West and the need for discretion evaporated, the Soviet-backed governments in Hungary, Bulgaria, and other Eastern European countries moved to liquidate internal opposition in both political and civil society. Mass arrests, expulsions, and even the occasional defenestration were coupled with policies designed to bring all aspects of the national society under state control.[75]

In Hungary, where there had been a secularization and nationalization of religious schools, one of the few voices of dissent left free in the country by late 1948 was Cardinal Mindszenty. Uncompromising and fearless, Mindszenty was a jealous and vociferous guardian of the privileges of the Church, and regarded the Communist state as an illegitimate Soviet puppet regime. He spent most of 1948 stirring up resistance to the proposed school nationalization, even threatening excommunication for any Catholic member of Parliament who voted for the plan. With the eyes of the world focused on Berlin and the dramatic airlift operations underway by the West, the Hungarian authorities moved against Mindszenty, arresting him the day after Christmas.[76] The cardinal's arrest provoked widespread international condemnation, with Pope Pius XII calling the seizure an attack on the "holy rights of religion."[77] Meeting in Paris, the members of the UN, almost all of whom had just voted to approve the Universal Declaration, found it hard to ignore these developments.

The U.S. State Department was delighted that the Bolivians and Australians had taken the lead in bringing the issue before the Assembly. Shielded from accusations of ideologically motivated posturing, the Truman administration's foreign policy team was more than willing to see a new diplomatic front opened in the increasingly heated Cold War. But while they were happy to see those away from the frontlines of the East-West confrontation offer indictments of the political practices behind the Iron Curtain, the stakes were too high for the United States to relinquish control of the matter. Australia was a solid ally in the Cold War, but the head of its delegation, foreign secretary Herbert Evatt, who had led the small powers against the Big Four at the San Francisco conference and was now president of the Assembly, might show too much independence. Bolivian delegate Victor Andrade Uzquiano had also spoken of the special mission of small nations to enhance UN commitment to justice in a way that worried some in the State Department. Secretary of state Dean Acheson quickly told the U.S. delegation at the UN to coordinate and contain the matter.[78] Whatever the origins of the initiative, therefore, what unfolded over the next eighteen months was orchestrated almost entirely from Washington.

When the Assembly took up the draft resolutions, the Soviet Union and its allies challenged the right of the UN even to discuss the matter (not yet members of the UN, Hungary and Bulgaria had been invited to send representatives, but declined). In doing so, the Soviet delegation invoked the old workhorse, Article 2(7). Their objection was countered by Australia's claim that under Article 10 of the charter, the assembly's right of discussion was universal, Article 2(7) notwithstanding. Evatt was adamant that the drafters had intended to give the GA as broad a mandate as possible in regards to matters that could be discussed. The GA president was on firm ground when he spoke of the intent of the drafters, as it was Evatt himself who had been the most important advocate of a broad right of discussion for the assembly. Charles Malik went beyond the Australian claim and asserted that, given the fact that the charter was replete with references to human rights and fundamental freedoms, the GA had a positive duty, and not simply the discretionary right, to discuss violations of human rights anywhere in the world.[79]

The Soviet bloc was joined in its objections by an unlikely ally. The Union of South Africa also opposed placing the discussion of the human rights violations in Eastern Europe on the GA agenda, despite its decidedly Western orientation in the Cold War. The South African delegate asserted that the principle of noninterference in cases involving matters of a domestic nature was a "basic and cardinal principle of the Charter" and the insertion of the UN into the domestic affairs of states would set a dangerous precedent. This was the same precedent South Africa had fought when V. L. Pandit had introduced her resolution condemning the treatment of Indians in South Africa during the first GA session. Consistency and self-interest, if not sympathy for the Communist regimes in Eastern Europe, required a principled stance in the name of domestic jurisdiction.[80]

The United States had backed the South African position in 1946 and had deployed much the same argument in squelching the NAACP petition. But the opportunity to expose the deteriorating conditions in the Soviet sphere led Washington to a more nuanced position than their friends in Pretoria. The key was to distinguish between the assembly's right of discussion, which the Americans affirmed, and the UN right to intervene in domestic matters, which they denied. The United States delegation was prepared to support in the main the Australian and Lebanese line that, given the numerous references to human rights in the Charter, the General Assembly was well within its rights to consider the matter. But the U.S. also went on record with the opinion that Article 2(7) prevented the UN from interference in domestic matters, even in cases of gross human rights abuse, with "interference" understood to mean any UN official resolution or statement.[81]

The position of discussion-but-no-action was generally consistent with those taken in the South African and NAACP cases, but the State Department was quick to differentiate the Eastern European issue from those two. Critical to the U.S. decision to pursue this matter vigorously was the fact that Hungary, Bulgaria, and Rumania, as former allies of Germany, had recently signed peace treaties with the Allies in Paris that, among other things, contained articles pledging the new governments to respect human rights and fundamental freedoms.[82] As with the human rights provisions of the UN Charter, the United States was the first to propose the inclusion of human rights guarantees in the peace treaties and managed to secure the assent of the other Great Powers. All five peace treaties (Finland and Italy also negotiated settlements at Paris) included provisions similar to Article 1 of the Hungarian treaty, which held that:

> Hungary shall take all measures necessary to secure to all persons under Hungarian jurisdiction, without distinction as to race, sex, language or religion, the enjoyment of human rights and of the fundamental freedoms including freedom of expression, of press and publication, of religious worship, of political opinion and of public meeting.[83]

For the three countries concerned, it was familiar language. After the First World War, all three, along with Poland and many of the successor states to the Hapsburg and Ottoman empires, signed either separate "Minorities Treaties" or general peace treaties with "Minorities Clauses" in which they pledged to uphold the rights of "racial, religious, or linguistic minorities." Although better known for the protections of minority group rights, including the rights to establish schools, use their native language, and preserve cultural traditions, the treaties also required equality before the law and nondiscrimination in civil and political rights.[84] The treaties were marred, however, by the unequal obligations they imposed (none of the victors had to guarantee such rights), and to the extent that they continued the traditions of "the old structure of a Great-Power condominium that controlled Eastern Europe," as Carole Fink put it, there was little hope that they would improve conditions on the ground for individuals and minority groups.[85] After the Second World War, the widespread sense among many observers was that the Minorities

Treaties had not only failed but, with Hilter's exploitation of the issue of *Auslandsdeutschen* (Germans outside the Reich), provided a fig leaf for German aggression against its neighbors.[86] In this sense, by invoking the treaty mechanisms rather than working through the UN, the U.S. was returning to an older model of international rights protection that was discredited among most proponents of human rights, as well as many of the local inhabitants they purported to be concerned about.

Invoking the treaties did have its benefits. The existence of the human rights articles in the Paris Peace Treaties gave added weight to the argument that the human rights situations in Hungary, Bulgaria, and Rumania were of international concern. The treaties effectively distinguished the cases from the situation of African Americans or Indian South Africans, and also provided specific mechanisms for response that went beyond just "discussion." The American government was willing to risk increased involvement by the UN, in part because they believed the peace treaties allowed the United States to control the scope and direction of UN involvement in this particular human rights issue much more thoroughly.[87] Acheson set the tone in March 1949, when he told the U.S. delegation to the UN that the United States could fully support the idea of discussing the matter in the Assembly, giving the widest possible airing of Communist dirty laundry, but could also head off any attempt to directly intervene in the matter by pointing to the treaty mechanisms as the appropriate venue to address the human rights violations in the countries concerned.[88]

In the first step toward implementing this strategy, U.S. representative Benjamin V. Cohen made a procedural move designed to limit how far UN discussions would be allowed to go. Cohen asked that the matter be taken up by the General Assembly First Committee, which dealt with political matters, as opposed to the Third Committee, which had purview over human rights. Discussion in the Third Committee carried the danger that the matter might be referred to the Economic and Social Council, an outcome—given how hostile ECOSOC was becoming to U.S. interests—that the State Department instructed the U.S. delegation to avoid at all costs.[89]

The substantive rights violations alleged against the Eastern European governments were numerous. They included the complete abridgement of the freedoms of speech, of the press, and of association. Both the U.S. and Australia also alleged that the independence of the judiciary in these countries had been irreparably compromised, and that opposition political parties had been summarily liquidated. Finally, the same delegates also claimed that the Communist authorities, through a deliberate process of intimidation and falsified criminal charges, had completely obliterated freedom of religion in their countries and attempted to bring local churches under totalitarian state control. The Polish and Soviet representatives offered a defense of the Eastern European regimes, with the Russians adding that this whole matter represented a U.S. effort to dominate the world under the cover of a UN mandate. Soviet protests notwithstanding, the indictment was fairly damning.[90]

With these allegations before the First Committee, the Bolivian delegation proposed a draft resolution in which the GA expressed its "deep concern" regarding the apparent human rights violations in Eastern Europe, as well as its support for the efforts on the part of certain signatories to the peace treaties to see the human rights provisions of the treaties implemented. In the period between the assembly's initial debate on the issue and when the First Committee discussed the matter, the U.S. State Department and the British Foreign Office had each sent official communications to the governments of Hungary, Bulgaria, and Rumania accusing them of violating the human rights provisions of their respective treaties and demanding that they take action to ensure their compliance. The Bolivian draft resolution also asked the Eastern European governments to take note of their obligations under the peace treaties, particularly their obligations to work with treaty signatories in the settlement of disputes. Finally, the resolution left the door open to possible further UN action by placing the issue on the agenda for the assembly's fourth session the following fall.[91]

In addition to the Bolivian proposal, a draft resolution was submitted by Cuba and Australia calling for a special UN commission to investigate these alleged human rights violations, and Chile submitted a proposal that the GA formally "condemn" the actions of the Eastern European governments in regard to the suppression of human rights and fundamental freedoms. These proliferating amendments to the Bolivian draft resolution were exactly what State Department officials had feared in bringing the issue before the UN. The idea that the UN would appoint an international commission to investigate the human rights conditions inside any sovereign state, even those behind the Iron Curtain, was beyond the pale of what the United States could accept. Even the relatively toothless condemnation of the Chilean proposal was too much, opening up the possibility of the UN routinely passing judgment on the domestic affairs of member states. The U.S. delegation succeeded in pressing the Chileans to withdraw their amendment, but the Australian-Cuban proposal was brought to a vote in the committee. The State Department correctly read their ability to manage the debate in the First Committee, as the amendment only garnered four votes (Lebanon and New Zealand joining the sponsors). After that the First Committee voted 34–6 with 11 abstentions to send the Bolivian draft to the General Assembly, where it was adopted by the same margin.[92]

The Truman administration emerged from the Third General Assembly with what it hoped for: a general discussion of the human rights violations in the Soviet sphere in Eastern Europe, and a resolution supporting its efforts to secure adherence to the provisions of the peace treaties. The United States managed to contain the whole affair, highlighting the issue of religious persecution and heading off all efforts to bring the matter before the ECOSOC or establish a special investigatory commission. Over the next six months, the United States in conjunction with the United Kingdom moved forward with the treaty mechanisms, aiming not to resolve the dispute but to compile a record of obstinacy on the part of the Communist regimes. At the same time the First Committee was considering the various draft resolutions, the governments of Hungary, Bulgaria, and Rumania issued responses to the initial communiqués from the U.S. and UK. Each rejected both the allegations of human rights violations and the demand for remedy. On May 31, the U.S. legations in Budapest, Bucharest, and Sofia delivered a second round of notes to the three governments, stating that the United States intended to invoke the treaty mechanisms for the settlement of disputes. Following the treaty provisions, the United States also delivered letters to the other two chiefs of mission in the Eastern European capitols, the British and Soviets. The three former allies were required to consult on any dispute in order to facilitate a coordinated resolution. Unsurprisingly, the Soviets rejected the premise of the letter and refused to meet their British and American counterparts. After waiting the prescribed two months, the U.S. and UK then moved forward without Soviet cooperation, sending yet another round of diplomatic notes to the various governments asking that all parties appoint representatives to a special committee—as called for in the treaties—charged with substantiating any alleged treaty violation and deciding a binding resolution of the dispute. These letters, sent on August 1, were answered with yet another round of denials and refusals to cooperate on September 1, just in time for the convening of the fourth GA session.[93]

The General Assembly for a second time took up the matter of human rights in Eastern Europe in September 1949. Benjamin V. Cohen revisited the litany of alleged human rights abuses in the three Soviet Satellites, as they were now called by the State Department, and submitted into the UN record the entire diplomatic correspondence of the previous six months. The Soviet representative again rose to defend the Hungarian, Bulgarian, and Rumanian governments and again charged the United States with attempting to dominate the world through the UN. Their protests against discussing the cases proved no more effective than they had the previous spring, and, in conjunction with Bolivia and Canada the U.S. then proposed a new resolution in which the Assembly would refer the matter to the International Court of Justice (ICJ) for an advisory opinion. After beating back yet another attempt by the Australians to have a special UN committee set up in the event of a stalemate in the treaty proceedings, the U.S. garnered broad support for the draft resolution even among members, such as South Africa, who had hesitated to discuss the matter in the first place. The resolution was adopted by the General Assembly on October 23 by a vote of 47 to 5 with 7 abstentions.[94]

In seeking a referral of the matter to the ICJ, the United States was careful to ask the world court to consider only a narrow set of questions regarding the implementation of the treaty mechanisms. It was vitally important, from the State Department's perspective, that the ICJ *not* be asked to rule on the substantive matter of whether or not the governments of Hungary, Bulgaria, and Rumania were violating the human rights of their citizens. Officials in Washington reminded the U.S. delegation at the UN, "Our reason for this has been that it is unlikely that this country is prepared to have the International Court of Justice given compulsory jurisdiction to render decisions with respect to human rights in the United States."[95] The adopted resolution asked the ICJ to consider a series of four questions, none of them in regards to the observance of human rights and fundamental freedoms. The first was whether a dispute existed between parties to the treaty as defined by the treaty's provisions. If the court decided a dispute did in fact exist, it was also asked whether the parties were obliged to settle it through the mechanisms provided for in the treaty and appoint members to a commission with the power to render binding decisions. If this answer was also yes, and in the event that certain parties refused to appoint a representative to the commission, the court was asked whether the secretary-general of the UN could appoint a representative for that party. And finally, if the third question was answered in the affirmative, the court was asked if the commission thus composed could in fact render binding decisions. In moving from the UN to the ICJ, the U.S. hoped to paint the Soviet Union and its satellites not only as human rights violators, but as treaty breakers as well.[96]

The International Court of Justice heard the case in March. For the first time in its history, the United States sent an official representative to argue before the court. Although it was given a new name with the establishment of the UN in 1945, the ICJ was the direct descendant of the Permanent Court of Arbitration set up in the Hague in 1899. Under the League of Nations covenant, the world court was given a broader mandate and rechristened the Permanent Court of International Justice, only to be renamed and reorganized again in the wake of the Second World War. The ICJ adjudicated disputes between states on matters of international law, and although its decisions were in some cases regarded as binding, the court possessed no independent enforcement apparatus beyond the measures states or the UN might choose to implement on their own. Until the Eastern European Cases, the U.S. submitted only written briefs to the court and was generally reluctant to have disputes to which it was a party brought before the court. Benjamin V. Cohen made oral arguments on behalf of the United States. A protégé of Felix Frankfurter, Cohen was among the most competent and experienced lawyers in international law and had been involved with questions of human rights at the State Department since 1944. In his arguments before the ICJ, however, Cohen focused exclusively on the dispute resolution obligations of the treaties, heeding well Acheson's admonition not to allow the question of human rights violations to come before the court.[97]

The ICJ took up the case in two parts, initially dealing with questions one and two and deferring questions three and four until such time as it was necessary to answer them. The court delivered its first advisory opinion on March 30, 1950. By an 11 to 3 majority, it found that indeed there existed a dispute under the terms of the peace treaties (Question 1) and that the parties were obliged by the terms of the treaties to appoint representatives to the commissions mandated in the relevant articles (Question 2). Not surprisingly, however, the Eastern European states refused to comply with the ICJ ruling and, after a period of sixty days the court considered the latter two questions put to it in the General Assembly resolution. On July 18 the court delivered its second advisory opinion in the case, finding that none of the treaties authorized the UN secretary-general to make appointments to the treaty commissions. Given the court's negative finding on Question 3, Question 4 as to whether a commission containing members appointed by the secretary-general could issue binding decisions was rendered moot.[98]

In the wake of this ruling, and with the opening of the General Assembly's fifth session fast approaching, the State Department weighed its options. The refusal of the Soviet bloc countries to participate in the treaty proceedings and their defiance of the court's advisory opinion opened the door to the UN beginning its own investigation into the allegations and even perhaps providing some remedy, up to and including sanctions. Some in the State Department were tempted to pursue such a course of action, given the utter lack of sympathy for the behavior of the Eastern European satellites outside the Soviet circle. But although there appeared little doubt in the minds of U.S. officials that a General Assembly inquiry would find grave human rights violations in Hungary, Bulgaria, and Rumania, the precedent of such an investigation carried serious risks. Relying on the treaties had until now allowed the U.S. to contain both the definition of human rights and the manner of their enforcement. Shifting the matter to the UN opened the possibility not only of expanding the definition to include all those listed in the UDHR, but of a proliferation of investigations into violations around the globe. Given the fact that the UN human rights work was increasingly unpopular domestically, as evidenced by the ABA's successful campaign to scuttle the Genocide Convention (see above), American officials found such an eventuality decidedly unappealing. Ultimately, and in consultation with the British Foreign Office, the State Department concluded that the risks were too great to back a special investigatory commission, believing that further efforts would do little to improve conditions in the three countries and that there was not much more propaganda value to be had by publicizing the violations. The instructions to the U.S. delegation were to seek a general resolution condemning the Eastern European countries for abrogating their international obligations under the peace treaties, and inviting member-states to send any information they had on human rights violations in these countries to the secretary-general for compilation.[99]

There appeared to be little stomach for pursuing the matter when it came up for discussion in the General Assembly. With the outbreak of war on the Korean peninsula in June and the boycott of the Security Council proceedings by the Soviet Union over the issue of Chinese representation, the United States was mobilizing its diplomatic resources toward other ends. Even the Australians, who had been the most vocal supporters for the establishment of a UN special commission, were now preoccupied with events in Asia and were willing only to sponsor a draft resolution that offered a harsh condemnation of the Eastern European governments, but made no mention of any further investigation by the UN. The resolution was adopted by the Assembly on November 3 by 40-5 with 12 abstentions, bringing the episode to an anticlimactic, if entirely predictable, end.[100]

In pursuing its case against Hungary, Bulgaria, and Rumania, the Truman administration attempted to turn human rights into an anti-Soviet weapon to be wielded in international institutions. It was a decidedly risky strategy, given the fact that the ongoing American system of racial discrimination was an increasingly prominent issue in international human rights fora and a conservative domestic backlash against international human rights protections had already begun. Nevertheless, the administration hoped that by focusing on the issue of freedom of religion and by utilizing the peace treaty mechanisms rather than the UN machinery—particularly the ECOSOC and the UNCHR—they could limit their exposure to charges of hypocrisy. Ultimately, while it did place a spotlight on the dire situation in the Soviet satellite states, the policy failed to either deflect criticism from U.S. domestic affairs or provide relief for the persecuted religious figures.

Conclusion

Abandoning any further effort to intervene in the violations of human rights in the Eastern European republics, the Truman administration was not only marshaling its diplomatic resources toward other ends, but also acceding to the ascendant policy of containment. For if containment meant defending South Korea from Northern aggression, or maintaining the economic and political stability of Western Europe, it also meant conceding those lands behind the Iron Curtain to Moscow. As an enduring basis for Cold War foreign policy, containment precluded the possibility of a zealous promotion of global human rights standards by the U.S. Further, by emphasizing the need to prevent the emergence of more Communist, or even leftist, governments, containment pushed the United States toward supporting, strengthening, and installing authoritarian regimes the world over.

Only with the end of the Vietnam War and the emergence of détente as a new rationale did the promotion of human rights return as a significant factor in U.S. foreign policy. Ironically, Congressional pressure on the Executive once again led the way: Representative Don Fraser (D-Minn.) organized and chaired the House Subcommittee on Human Rights and International Organization in 1971, Tom Harkin (D-Iowa) introduced legislation tying U.S. foreign aid to human rights performance in certain fields in 1974 and 1975, and the passage of the Jackson-Vanik Amendment denied "most favored nation" trade status to certain countries that restricted immigration.[101] By the late 1970s, the discourse of human rights had returned to Washington to such an extent that Jimmy Carter, in his inaugural address, could declare, "Our commitment to human rights must be absolute."[102] From the early 1970s to the present, human rights have remained a significant rhetorical, if not always real, component of U.S. foreign policy.

Containment also describes the response of the U.S. political establishment to the human rights activism of both the NAACP and the ABA. As African Americans brought their case to the UN, the Truman administration began a concerted effort not only to head off consideration of their petition by the international community, but also to contain the struggle for black rights within the boundaries of a specifically American discourse of rights. At the same moment Du Bois and his team were preparing to unveil their indictment of the American political system's ability to deal justly with its nonwhite citizens, the president's Committee on Civil Rights issued its seminal report, *To Secure These Rights*, outlining a decidedly national program of reform. Taking its title from the Declaration of Independence, the report posed the question of African American rights in terms of the American commitment to freedom and equality. This strategy also informed Truman's executive orders desegregating the armed forces and the federal government, as well as the Justice Department's decision to file amicus briefs in support of the challenge to restrictive covenants and school segregation led by the NAACP Legal Defense Fund. This approach, aimed at demonstrating the capacity of the American system to deliver on the American promise, was continued by Eisenhower and achieved its definitive expression with the deployment of National Guard troops to enforce the desegregation of Little Rock's Central High School in the fall of 1957. Ever conscious of the international audience, U.S. policy makers were nonetheless careful to keep their legal and political arguments confined to the national level. This was true of most activists as well. When the young Rev. Dr. Martin Luther King, Jr., took to the podium on that hot August afternoon in 1963, he spoke of "a great America," of "the magnificent words of the Constitution and the Declaration of Independence," of "citizenship rights," and of America's "promissory note" to "life, liberty, and the pursuit of happiness." When he told of his dream, it was a dream "deeply rooted in the American dream," and although King dreamt of freedom ringing, it was hemmed in by the "hilltops of New Hampshire, . . . the mighty mountains of New York, . . . the heightening Alleghenies of Pennsylvania, . . . the snowcapped Rockies of Colorado, . . . the curvaceous peaks of California, . . . Stone Mountain of Georgia, Lookout Mountain of Tennessee, . . . [and] every hill and every molehill of Mississippi."

Of course, it was the singular triumph of King and the civil rights movement to articulate the true meaning of America's creed with the proposition that racial discrimination was unacceptable as public policy or private practice. Such had never been the case, save perhaps for a brief period following the Civil War, and the array of forces working against this reading of American nationalism were powerful and entrenched. Among them was the ABA, for whom the American creed was states rights and property rights, not equal rights or human rights. But while the civil rights movement made the ABA views seem not merely conservative but wholly reactionary, the national limits of King's speech bear the mark of Holman's crusade to reclaim the discourse of rights and freedoms from the United Nations. It was, in the end, not just the communist menace that needed to be contained, but the menace of a diverse cosmopolis, as the 1949 report by Holman's Committee on Peace and Law through the UN indicates:

> Peoples who do not know the meaning of freedom are to be metamorphosed into judges of the freedom of others. A common pattern is to be set for billions of people of different languages, religions, standards of living, culture, education, and mental and physical capacity. A few people, with beliefs utterly foreign to each other, meet, debate, and by majority vote seek to determine how the people of the world shall live on a common pattern. To bring some people to a higher standard, those far above those standards, under the guise of precarious sacrifice to the common good, are to accept the mediocrity of the average. Are the people of the United States ready for such sweeping changes?[103]

Frank Holman, John Bricker, and eventually John Foster Dulles knew they were not. Isolated from the international conversations about—let alone attempts to guarantee—human rights, the American conversation nonetheless continued, if in an impoverished idiom.

Conclusion: Toward Universal Human Rights

"History flows" or "moves on" means that history has not "yet" delivered all that with which "it" is pregnant, that history has not "come to an end," that "it" continues to be in labor and will deliver still more, that the last word, not only about the past that is "finished and done away with," but especially of the past as "its" place in the determination of the present and the future, has not "yet" been said.
—Charles Malik, "Will the Future Redeem the Past?" June 11, 1960

On June 11, 1960, Charles Malik took the stage before a small audience in Williamsburg, Virginia. After fifteen years of diplomatic and government service, he had just returned to the academic life that he regarded as his true calling, teaching philosophy as a visiting professor at Dartmouth during the spring semester. In Williamsburg, however, he was billed as a former president of the United Nations General Assembly, a position he had occupied during the 1958–1959 session. His presidency coincided with the ten-year anniversary of the Universal Declaration of Human Rights, but the coincidence of the GA being led by one of the principal architects of that document went entirely unnoticed by nearly all observers, reflecting how little the UDHR figured into UN politics, and how much perceptions of Malik had come to be defined by his role in the 1958 Lebanese crisis.[1] Less a victory lap than a consolation prize, Malik's tenure as GA president concluded a political career that ended in bitterness and controversy—a bitterness and controversy that affects Malik's reputation in the Arab world to this day. On that lovely spring afternoon in eastern Virginia, refreshed by his months in bucolic Hanover, New Hampshire, Malik offered a blunt, challenging, and impassioned assessment—one member of the audience called it "the greatest speech I ever heard"[2]—of the American role in the world over the past twenty years. This speech, given at the nadir of post-World War II human rights politics, also presented a view of history and of universality, which, while it went largely unremarked at the time, constitutes a fitting coda for this book.

The former foreign minister of Lebanon had been invited as part of Colonial Williamsburg's annual "Prelude to Independence" program, which ran between May 15 and July 4 to commemorate the seven-week period between the Virginia Assembly's adoption of the Virginia Resolution for American Independence and Continental Congress approval of the Declaration of Independence. This celebration of "the first steps toward our freedom" was established in 1950 by John D. Rockefeller, III, after he had taken over leadership of Colonial Williamsburg from his father. Beginning in the late 1920s, John D. Rockefeller, Jr., bankrolled and promoted the restoration of the capitol of colonial Virginia to reconstruct, preserve, and endorse an idealized view of the American experiment—a view Rockefeller and his partner W. A. R. Goodwin feared had become obscure in modern America. Historian Anders Greenspan argues that the younger Rockefeller wanted to go beyond genteel preservation to full-throated proselytization and, with the onset of the Cold War, began to transform Colonial Williamsburg into a national and international showcase for American ideals of individual liberty, democracy, and self-government.[3] This weekend was dedicated to precisely this kind of global boosterism, as the re-created capital hosted the Williamsburg International Assembly, a gathering of nearly sixty graduate students from forty-two countries to discuss "the American Image."

Malik was deeply sympathetic to this more assertive mission, and certainly believed the Enlightenment ideals that helped to animate the American Revolution were critically important to share with the world. Yet he took the opportunity of this invitation to reinterpret and redirect Colonial Williamsburg's motto—*that the future may learn from the past*—away from the distant to the immediate past, and thereby authorize a more critical, connected, and engaged relationship with history than was typically found among the costumed "interpreters" of Williamsburg. Posed in the form of a question, the title of Malik's talk, "Will the Future Redeem the Past?" suggested a level of contingency and doubt that more sanguine believers in American providence might not be prepared to countenance. Further, by asking whether the future would redeem rather than learn from the past, Malik's premise reversed the relationship, locating both agency and responsibility among those who had to live in the world created by the past. Malik's speech, greeted with "a continuous roar which lasted for what seemed five minutes and which subsided only when he arose to acknowledge the tribute,"[4] called for those in the present not simply to sit at the feet of and learn from the "great men" of history, but to take "upon ourselves the whole moral guilt of the past" in order to move into a better future.[5]

Malik's overt concern was with the "over-all advance" of international communism, and the question of redemption was, in this instance, one that hinged on making up for the mistakes of the previous twenty years. He was, he said, not interested in identifying those mistakes in any specific way, but he insisted on the fact that there *were* mistakes, that "this act or decision or person *could have been different*."[6] From his perspective, the struggle against communism begins with a view of history in which mistakes are possible, the course of events is not determined by the mechanisms of impersonal force, and people can take moral responsibility for their actions. Redeeming the past also implies an ongoing, unbroken connection with that past. If history is sealed and completed, even if it appears alive as in an ancient mosquito frozen in amber or an interpreter in breeches and tricorne on Duke of Gloucester Street, what one does in the present can have no effect on that past. But if "at no moment 'in history' does history come to an end," then past, present, and future remain in dynamic tension, and the meaning of history and the lessons it may or may not hold for us are determined as much by what we do today as by what was done yesterday and will be done tomorrow.

Undoubtedly, among the mistakes Malik left unstated was the U.S. failure to vigorously pursue and promote a robust international human rights system at the UN. During and immediately after the Second World War, many people recognized the potential of human rights to serve as a singular concept around which a reorientation of the international order could occur. The members of the CSOP believed international human rights law could provide a basis for an emerging global citizenship and civil society, coupling peace with progressive change in a way that could lead to a more rational and just world order. Carlos Romulo hoped international protections for human rights could inspire and provide the space for a more ordered and less contentious process of decolonization—one that followed "the Philippine Pattern." For Malik, the international human rights system could, if properly constituted, do this and more. In Malik's grandiose vision, human rights were the key not simply to rolling back communism, but to the apotheosis of the "human person" as both a subject on the world stage and the supreme value of all political systems. In each case, the success of human rights depended on the "waking giant" of the United States, and when the giant failed to take up human rights, these hopes dissolved.

And yet, the 1940s were not without accomplishment, and among the possibilities of the future redeeming the past is the possibility that some of the potential of history might still be realized—that the past, in Malik's words, "continues to be in labor and will deliver still more."[7] The UDHR—which Malik had to remind his audience existed—was among those historical possibilities about which "the last word" had not yet been spoken. In 1960, the International Covenants still languished in the Third Committee, and while the UDHR was occasionally invoked to protest the Chinese occupation of Tibet, South African apartheid, or the arrest of Patrice Lumumba in the Congo,[8] international human rights, as Samuel Moyn never tires of insisting, had become largely irrelevant as a political discourse or practice.[9] But Moyn is more correct in his assertion that "human rights are best understood as survivors" than in his contradictory conclusion that human rights were "stillborn" in the 1940s, precisely because the significance of the postwar human rights efforts was not determined by the jaundiced eye cast on the UDHR by realist Cold Warriors or radical anticolonialists of the 1950s and 1960s.[10] What Malik knew, and what many of those who participated in the revival of human rights in the 1970s and 1990s knew, was that the shadow of World War II is long, that the potential of the Universal Declaration unfolds across decades not years, and that even if, like Walter Benjamin's Angel of History, we too see the twentieth century as a towering pile of wreckage, progress may yet be marked by a return to rather than flight from this difficult past.

Viewing the postwar human rights system as defined and bounded by the shortcomings, biases, and reservations of some of its authors not only forecloses the possibilities of a more connected and fluid history; it also limits the potential universality of these principles. At Williamsburg, Malik insisted that the true key to redeeming past failures and reclaiming past accomplishments lay in knowing, affirming, and championing the "ultimate values" of the West. The values of human rights, to the extent that they embodied these ultimate values, were the highest achievement of Western civilization precisely because they were offered as universal values. Communism was of course not shy about claiming that its view of human nature and the human being was true everywhere and always. This willingness to proclaim universality was among the features that made Marxism so attractive to many in the Third World. Malik implored his audience to be equally as bold, to reject those Western voices who repeated "that their ideas, their way of life, their civilization, is 'not for export,' but only their industrial products."[11] No matter how much aid or how many "gadgets" the West offered, if you withhold your ultimate values, Malik said, "Asia and Africa will turn on [you] and spit in [your] face." From here, force alone is the only recourse. In 1960, one year before then vice president Lyndon Johnson headed to Saigon with promises of US$30 million in military aid,[12] Malik warned that a "civilization in which the human and the universal has atrophied can relate itself to others only through force, and force is not an enduring mode of relation, and it can always be broken by force."[13]

Malik's insistence on the universality of "ultimate values" of Western civilization makes many today, as in 1960, blush if not bristle. The fear, as Judith Butler once put it, is "that 'universalizability' is indissociable from imperialist expansion."[14] Such a sense of the universal as "the parochial property of the dominant culture"[15] maps neatly onto the static view of history in which paternity is all that matters and the determination of the meaning of a principle or of the past is fixed by its origins. Malik presented a more dynamic view of universality in which the process of sharing constituted both the test of and the truth of universal values. This is close to the conception of universality advanced, in conversation with Butler, by Ernesto Laclau, when he argues that universality "is neither formal nor abstract" but adheres in the process of articulating a broader and broader range of specific experiences and demands in a single representative discourse. For Laclau, universalization is the "articulation" of particular demands in an "equivalential chain" under a "tendentially empty signifier."[16] For Malik, this means there is "a profound part of your being that you honestly feel you must share with others."[17] If the future could, and would, redeem the past, overcoming a relativist view that insists universality is at best an error in logic and at worst a mask for domination, then the UDHR would be the first and not last word in the universalization of human rights, with the process of articulation opening human rights discourse to more and more particular demands.[18]

The availability of the international human rights system to just such a process of articulation depends in part on an orientation, shared by many advocates for human rights, that insists on human rights not only for themselves but more especially for others. "Only he therefore who feels with humanity," Malik said near the end of his speech, "who is at one with all conditions of men, *who is insufficient and incomplete without them,* who is not protected and separated from them, can help them and lead them and love them and be loved by them." Well before his works became widely popular in the late

1950s, Malik had read and been influenced by the Jewish philosopher Martin Buber, who was among the very few contemporary intellectuals Malik would admit to being "profoundly influenced" by.[19] Buber's dialogic principle of the "I-Thou" relationship described exactly the kind of moral responsibility Malik imagined at the heart of the Western relationship with Asia and Africa.[20] Certainly, it was a form of responsibility that could slide into paternalism, even neocolonial paternalism, particularly given Malik's chauvinistic insistence on the singular accomplishments of Western civilization. But if the universality of human rights, both because of and in spite of their Western genealogy, can be understood as a Buberian gesture of universal responsibility, then Malik's own limitations and biases, no less than those of Eleanor Roosevelt, Carlos Romulo, or Quincy Wright, do not determine the applicability of the discourses, structures, and practices of human rights.

The "gigantic world struggle" with international communism around which Malik oriented his meditation on history and universality is now part of the past and as such in need of redemption as much as anything else—indeed many of Malik's own decisions and actions in the cause cannot be justified. But if his framing of the possibilities of an engaged historical consciousness and a dialogic universal morality can be themselves reinterpreted and redirected toward the present and future of the international human rights system, we may be able to conclude with this final point: human rights remain unexhausted in their global emancipatory potential. This is not only because human rights laws—including the International Bill of Rights—at both the national and international levels continue to provide crucial leverage to those resisting the undiminished coercive capacities of state and economic structures. Equally important, no other concept, terminology, or mechanism has shown the same capacity to be at once productively empty—in terms of being available for appropriation and rearticulation—and practically specific—in terms of enumerating particular legal obligations and remedies. Finally, and perhaps most important, the structures and practices of the contemporary human rights movement constitute the richest, most extensive, and most densely bundled network through which the world is constituted as a moral community: a community increasingly aware of its past and present inequities and exclusions, but determined in its responsibility—renewed, reiterated, and reconceived across an increasingly transnational civil society—to justice at the level of humanity and the human.

Notes

Introduction: Human Rights Hegemony in the American Century

Charles Malik, "A Foreigner Looks at the United States," in *Man's Loyalties and the American Ideal: Proceedings of the Second Annual Symposium Sponsored by the State University of New York* (Albany, N.Y.: SUNY Press, 1951), 131.

1. New York-based Human Rights Watch had been warning for years that the Human Rights Commission was in "serious decline" and had been co-opted by an "abusers club" who used seats on the commission to block any effective action. See Human Rights Watch, "U.N. Rights Body in Serious Decline," April 25, 2003.

2. UN General Assembly [UNGA], *In Larger Freedom: Toward Development, Security, and Human Rights for All: Report by the Secretary General*, 21 March 2005, A/59/2005, 45–46.

3. UNGA, 60th Session, 72nd Plenary Meeting, Official Record. 15 March 2006, A/60/PV.72.

4. Michael Ignatieff, "Introduction: American Exceptionalism and Human Rights," in *American Exceptionalism and Human Rights*, ed. Michael Ignatieff (Princeton, N.J.: Princeton University Press, 2005), 1.

5. Tzvetan Todorov, "Right to Intervene or Duty to Assist?" in *Human Rights, Human Wrongs*, ed. Nicholas Owen (Oxford: Oxford University Press, 2003), 35–36. On hypocrisy and human rights, also see Costas Douzinas, *The End of Human Rights* (Oxford: Hart, 2000), 122–28.

6. Andrew Moravcsik, "The Paradox of U.S. Human Rights Policy," in Ignatieff, *American Exceptionalism*, 149–50.

7. Sameul Moyn, *The Last Utopia: Human Rights in History* (Cambridge, Mass.: Harvard University Press, 2010), 46.

8. Ibid., 6–9.

9. Ibid.; Kirstin Sellars, *The Rise and Rise of Human Rights* (New York: Sutton, 2002).

10. For example, from the Rothermere conference (unpublished), see Richard Siegel, "The Death Penalty and American Human Rights Policy," and Mortimer Sellers, "The United States and the International Criminal Court"; and from the Carr Center conference (published in Ignatieff, *American Exceptionalism*), see Carol Steiker, "Capital

Punishment and American Exceptionalism" and Harold Hongju Koh, "America's Jekyll-and-Hyde Exceptionalism."

11. Ignatieff, "Introduction," 4–8.

12. Ibid., 25.

13. On the eighteenth-century American roots of human rights, see Michael Zuckert, "Natural Rights in the American Revolution: The American Amalgam," in *Human Rights and Revolutions*, ed. Jeffrey N. Wasserstrom, Lynn Hunt, and Marilyn B. Young (Lanham, Md.: Rowman and Littlefield, 2000).

14. Ignatieff, "Introduction," 1.

15. Mary Ann Glendon, *A World Made New: Eleanor Roosevelt and the Universal Declaration of Human Rights* (New York: Random House, 2001), xvii and passim.

16. Elizabeth Borgwardt, *A New Deal for the World: America's Vision for Human Rights* (Cambridge, Mass.: Belknap Press of Harvard University Press, 2005), 9 and passim.

17. Rowland Brucken, "A Most Uncertain Crusade: The United States, Human Rights and the United Nations, 1941–1954" (Ph.D. dissertation, Ohio State University, 1999).

18. Carol Anderson, *Eyes Off the Prize: The United Nations and the African American Struggle for Human Rights, 1944–1955* (New York: Cambridge University Press, 2003), 4 and passim.

19. In many respects, this was a "hegemonic" struggle, in the sense that American postwar dominion was established not only through projection of coercive force, but also through construction of a shared set of ethico-political values. As pointed out long ago by Antonio Gramsci, such values are never simply imposed from above but negotiated—contentiously, continuously, and often inconclusively—in the public spheres. See Antonio Gramsci, *Selections from the Prison Notebooks*, trans. and ed. Quintin Hoare and Geoffrey Nowell Smith (London: Lawrence and Wishart, 1971), 53, 57–58, 80n; Chantal Mouffe, "Hegemony and Ideology in Gramsci," in *Gramsci and Marxist Theory*, ed. Chantal Mouffe (Boston: Routledge & Kegan Paul, 1979), 193–94; and Ernesto Laclau and Chantal Mouffe, *Hegemony and Socialist Strategy: Towards a Radical Democratic Politics*, 2nd ed. (New York: Verso, 2001), 159–65.

20. See, for example, William Korey, *NGOs and the Universal Declaration of Human Rights: A Curious Grapevine* (New York: St. Martin's, 1998); Ann Marie Clark, *Diplomacy of Conscience: Amnesty International and Changing Human Rights Norms* (Princeton, N.J.: Princeton University Press, 2001); Margaret E. Keck and Kathryn Sikkink, *Activists Beyond Borders: Advocacy Networks in International Politics* (Ithaca, N.Y.: Cornell University Press, 1998); Claude E. Welch, Jr., ed., *NGOs and Human Rights: Promise and Performance* (Philadelphia: University of Pennsylvania Press, 2001).

21. Anderson, *Eyes Off the Prize*; Brucken, "A Most Uncertain Crusade."

22. Korey begins his book with a brief account of the consultant group (25–50); see also Dorothy B. Robins, *Experiment in Democracy: The Story of U.S. Citizen Organization in Forging the Charter of the United Nations* (New York: Parkside, 1971), 129–32;

Paul Gordon Lauren, *The Evolution of International Human Rights: Visions Seen* (Philadelphia: University of Pennsylvania Press, 1998), 188–89; Micheline R. Ishay, *The History of Human Rights: From Ancient Times to the Globalization Era* (Berkeley: University of California Press, 2004), 214–15; A. W. Brian Simpson, *Human Rights and the End of Empire: Britain and the Genesis of the European Convention* (Oxford: Oxford University Press, 2001), 261; Stephen C. Schlesinger, *Act of Creation: The Founding of the United Nations* (Boulder, Colo.: Westview, 2003), 122–25; Glendon, *A World Made New*, 17.

23. Moyn, *The Last Utopia*, 61–62.

24. Jürgen Habermas, *The Structural Transformation of the Public Sphere: An Inquiry into a Category of Bourgeois Society*, trans. Thomas Burger (Cambridge, Mass.: MIT Press, 1991), 26–27. Translated into English in 1989 at the same moment the velvet revolutions began taking hold in Eastern Europe, Habermas's work helped inspire renewed interest in the role of civil society in modern political life. Most analyses of civil society have remained decidedly national, or subnational, in scope, in part due to the symbiotic relationship between civil societies and the self-conscious "imagined communities" of modern nationalism. This study suggests the possibility that a global civil society is constituted both by and through an engagement with international human rights. On human rights and civil society more generally, see Jean L. Cohen and Andrew Arato, *Civil Society and Political Theory* (Cambridge, Mass.: MIT Press, 1992), 142–59.

25. Glendon, *A World Made New*; Susan Waltz, "Universalizing Human Rights: The Role of Small States in the Construction of the Universal Declaration of Human Rights," *Human Rights Quarterly* 23 (2001): 44–72; Susan Waltz, "Reclaiming and Rebuilding the History of the Universal Declaration of Human Rights," *Third World Quarterly* 23, 3 (2002): 437–38.

26. Michael Ignatieff, *Human Rights as Politics and Idolatry*, ed. Amy Gutmann (Princeton, N.J.: Princeton University Press, 2001), 92–95.

27. Lauren, *The Evolution of International Human Rights*, 241–80.

28. This is the approach taken by arguably the most ardent defender of universality, Jack Donnelly. A Lockean political philosopher, Donnelly readily acknowledges the Western origins of rights theory and even denies the possibility of a non-Western philosophical basis for human rights. Nevertheless, Donnelly argues that they are universal precisely because they are designed to protect the "minimum requirements of a life of dignity," that is to say, a life that is fully human. Donnelly's notion of the "moral universality" of human rights offers an analytic avenue to universalism that owes much to the Enlightenment, even if it allows more indeterminacy as to what specific rights are enumerated in particular times and places. Jack Donnelly, *Universal Human Rights in Theory and Practice* (Ithaca, N.Y.: Cornell University Press, 1989), 16–23.

29. Adamantia Pollis and Peter Schwab, "Human Rights: A Western Construct with Limited Applicability," in *Human Rights: Cultural and Ideological Perspectives*, ed. Pollis and Schwab (New York: Praeger, 1979). The relativist thesis is actually a constellation of related arguments, all of which cast doubt on the premise that human rights are valid for all human beings everywhere. Typologies of relativism abound in the literature,

with Jack Donnelly identifying three categories (radical, strong, and weak cultural rel-ativisms), R. G. Peffer offering four (descriptive, normative, meta-ethical, and meta-evaluative relativisms), while Alison Dundes Renteln limits herself to two (normative and descriptive). At a minimum, the argument from relativism acknowledges that norms and values emerge from and are rooted in particular cultural contexts, and cau-tions that the language of universalism can, and often does, mask particular ideological interests. At its most strident, the relativist position claims that cultures must be wholly autonomous in determining their ultimate values and that any attempt to implement or enforce human rights standards beyond the West constitutes a new and dangerous form of imperialism aimed at destroying the cultural integrity and national sovereignty of non-Western peoples. Donnelly, *Universal Human Rights*, 109–10; R. G. Peffer, *Marx-ism, Morality, and Social Justice* (Princeton, N.J.: Princeton University Press, 1990), 272–74; Alison Dundes Renteln, *International Human Rights: Universalism Versus Relativism* (Newbury Park, Calif.: Sage, 1990).

30. This account of the relativist position is given in Arvind Sharma, *Are Human Rights Western? A Contribution to the Dialogue of Civilizations* (New York: Oxford Uni-versity Press, 2006), 248–53.

31. Makau Mutua, *Human Rights: A Political and Cultural Critique* (Philadelphia: University of Pennsylvania Press, 2002), 155. Continuing in a similar vein, Mutua writes: "Human rights reject the cross-fertilization of cultures and instead seek the transforma-tion of non-Western cultures by Western cultures. . . . What the guardians and custo-dians [of human rights] seek is the remaking of non-Europeans into little dark, brown, and yellow Europeans—in effect dumb copies of the original. This view of human rights retrenches and revitalizes the international hierarchy of race and color in which whites, who are privileged globally as a race, are the models and saviors of nonwhites, who are victims and savages."

32. Serious cultural concerns were raised at the outset of the UN human rights proj-ect by the American Anthropological Association. In 1947, the AAA sent a "Statement on Human Rights" to the Human Rights Commission, then drafting the UDHR, warn-ing that the proposed declaration was likely to reflect "the values prevalent in the coun-tries of Western Europe and America." AAA, "Statement on Human Rights," *American Anthropologist* 49, 4 (Oct./Dec. 1947): 539–43.

33. Harvard colleagues Glendon and Mutua offer just such conflicting views of the contributions of Malik and Romulo.

34. Diane F. Orentlicher, "Relativism and Religion," Comment in Ignatieff, *Human Rights as Politics and Idolatry*, 151–53; Ignatieff, *Human Rights as Politics and Idolatry*, 171–72. Jean L. Cohen and Andrew Arato, and Carlos Santiago Niño likewise emphasize the importance of discursive ethics to the formation of legitimate, and broadly universal, human rights regimes. See Cohen and Arato, *Civil Society and Political Theory*, 413–14; Carlos Santiago Niño, *The Constitution of Deliberative Democracy* (New Haven, Conn.: Yale University Press, 1996), 43–66.

35. Two studies that shed considerable light on this emerging field are Bonny

Ibhawoh, *Imperialism and Human Rights: Colonial Discourses of Rights and Liberties in African History* (Albany, N.Y.: SUNY Press, 2008); and Roland Burke, *Decolonization and the Evolution of International Human Rights* (Philadelphia: University of Pennsylvania Press, 2010).

36. Clark Eichelberger, "Loyalty to the United States and the United Nations," in *Man's Loyalties and the American Ideal: Proceedings of the Second Annual Symposium Sponsored by the State University of New York* (Albany, N.Y.: SUNY Press, 1951), 35.

37. Ibid., 34–35.

38. Malik, "A Foreigner Looks at the United States," 131.

39. Ibid., 129–31.

40. Charles Malik, *War and Peace* (Stamford, Conn.: Overbrook, 1950), 34.

41. Malik, "A Foreigner Looks at the United States," 127.

Chapter 1. The Study of Peace, Human Rights, and International Organization

1. Mark Mazower, *No Enchanted Palace: The End of Empire and the Ideological Origins of the United Nations* (Princeton, N.J.: Princeton University Press, 2009). This point has been made early and often. See, for instance, Herbert W. Briggs, "Power Politics and the International Organization," *American Journal of International Law* 39, 4 (October 1945): 668–70; Lawrence S. Finkelstein, "Reviewing the United Nations Charter," *International Organization* 9, 2 (May 1955): 213; Andrew Boyd, "The Role of the Great Powers in the United Nations System," *International Journal* 25, 2 (Spring 1970): 356; Georg Shild, "The Roosevelt Administration and the United Nations: Re-Creation or Rejection of the League Experience?" *World Affairs* 158, 1 (Summer 1995): 29–30; Gerry Simpson, *Great Powers and Outlaw States: Unequal Sovereigns in the International Legal Order* (Cambridge: Cambridge University Press, 2005), 165–66.

2. This point was immediately apparent to Leland Goodrich; see his "From League of Nations to United Nations," *International Organization* 1, 1 (February 1947): 3–21.

3. Mazower, *No Enchanted Palace*, 25.

4. Ruth B. Russell, *A History of the United Nations Charter: The Role of the United States 1940-1945* (Washington, D.C.: Brookings Institution, 1958).

5. Stephen C. Schlesinger, *Act of Creation: The Founding of the United Nations* (Boulder, Colo.: Westview, 2003).

6. Dorothy B. Robins, *Experiment in Democracy: The Story of U.S. Citizen Organization in Forging the Charter of the United Nations* (New York: Parkside, 1971).

7. Paul Gordon Lauren, *The Evolution of International Human Rights: Visions Seen* (Philadelphia: University of Pennsylvania Press, 1998), 188–89; William Korey, *NGOs and the Universal Declaration of Human Rights: "A Curious Grapevine"* (New York: St. Martin's, 1998), 29–50.

8. M. Glen Johnson, "The Contributions of Eleanor and Franklin Roosevelt to the Development of International Protection for Human Rights," *Human Rights Quarterly* 9, 1 (February 1987): 25–27; Elizabeth Borgwardt, *A New Deal for the World: America's Vision for Human Rights* (Cambridge, Mass.: Harvard University Press, 2005), 5–6.

9. Ruth B. Henig, ed., *The League of Nations* (New York: Barnes & Noble, 1973), 146–52.

10. "Smuts Urges a Return to a 'Reformed League,'" *New York Times*, November 7, 1938, 14; *Tribuna* editors quoted in "Rome Press Hails Axis Arbitration," *New York Times*, November 4, 1938, 8.

11. Clark M. Eichelberger, *Organizing for Peace: A Personal History of the Founding of the United Nations* (New York: Harper & Row, 1977), 111–12; "Munich Concession Termed Betrayal," *New York Times*, October 14, 1938, 17.

12. Warren F. Kuehl and Lynne K. Dunne, *Keeping the Covenant: American Internationalists and the League of Nations, 1920–1939* (Kent, Oh.: Kent State University Press, 1997), 43, 165–70; Robert D. Accinelli, "Militant Internationalists: The League of Nations Association, the Peace Movement, and U.S. Foreign Policy, 1934–38," *Diplomatic History* 4, 1 (Winter 1980): 19–38; Alfred E. Clark, "Clark M. Eichelberger Dies at 83; Led American UN Association," *New York Times*, January 27, 1980, 20.

13. Eichelberger quoted in Harold Josephson, *James T. Shotwell and the Rise of Internationalism in America* (London: Associated University Press, 1975), 237.

14. Eichelberger, *Organizing for Peace*, 114. Beginning in January 1940, he would make regular and adept use of radio as a means of promoting his agenda, culminating in his syndicated NBC program, *The UN Is My Beat*, broadcast weekly from 1949 to 1953.

15. Ibid., 114–15.

16. Josephson, *James T. Shotwell*, 18–19.

17. Charles Benedetti, "James T. Shotwell and the Science of International Politics," *Political Science Quarterly* 89, 2 (June 1974): 381.

18. James T. Shotwell, *The Autobiography of James T. Shotwell* (Indianapolis: Bobbs-Merrill, 1961), 207–19; Benedetti, "James T. Shotwell," 390; Josephson, *James T. Shotwell*, 160–76. The notion of "outlawing" war was coined by local lawyer-turned-international-crusader Salomon O. Levinson and supported by Wilson's old nemesis in the League fight, Idaho Senator William Borah. Shotwell was always careful to distinguish his position from the so-called "Outlawry" movement, which saw the Pact as an adequate substitute for further American participation in international organizations. He was thus disappointed when Levinson, a supremely adroit publicist, claimed and received credit for the origin and completion of the Kellogg-Briand Pact. See Robert H. Ferrell, *Peace in Their Time: The Origins of the Kellogg-Briand Pact* (New Haven, Conn.: Yale University Press, 1952).

19. Eichelberger, *Organizing for Peace*, 106, 109.

20. Ibid., 116. Eichelberger was particularly concerned about Coughlin's demagogic radio broadcasts and established his relationship with CBS precisely to counter their effects. The CSOP director also enlisted prominent religious figures Daniel Poling, an evangelical minister with a weekly radio program of his own, and Monsignor John A. Ryan, a Roman Catholic priest and social reformer.

21. Commission to Study the Organization of Peace (hereafter CSOP), "Preliminary Report," *Building Peace: Reports of the Commission to Study the Organization of Peace, 1939–1972* (Metuchen, N.J.: Scarecrow, 1973), 1: 2, 4, 6–7. CSOP, "For Release Tuesday

A.M. November 12, 1940," Box 151, Folder "CSOP 1940," Papers of Clark M. Eichelberger, Rare Books and Manuscripts Division, New York Public Library.

22. Lauren, *The Evolution of International Human Rights*, 152–53.

23. "Mrs. Catt Decries Armament Drive," *New York Times*, October 20, 1938, 9.

24. Robert Hillmann, "Quincy Wright and the Commission to Study the Organization of Peace," *Global Governance* 4, 4 (October–December 1998).

25. The fourth key organizer of the CSOP was Clyde Eagleton, NYU professor of international law and executive committee member of the LNA.

26. William T. R. Fox, "The Truth Shall Make You Free: One Student's Appreciation of Quincy Wright," *Journal of Conflict Resolution* 14, 4 (December 1970): 450.

27. William Ballis, "Quincy Wright: An Appreciation," *Journal of Conflict Resolution* 14, 4 (December 1970): 454. Although Shotwell was a considerable intellectual presence on the CSOP, the younger and more energetic Wright was far more deeply involved with nearly all aspects of the work.

28. League of Nations Covenant (1920), Art. 22.

29. Steven J. Bucklin, "The Wilsonian Legacy in Political Science: Denna F. Fleming, Frederick L. Schuman, and Quincy Wright" (Ph.D. dissertation, University of Iowa, 1993), 33–34. Bucklin notes that in his assessment of the League Mandate in Iraq, Wright characterized the Iraqi people as "adolescent" beneficiaries of benevolent British rule. This was a relative assessment compared to the French Mandatory in Syria, but Wright's thinking reflects how even those who regarded themselves as anti-imperialists shared the chauvinistic view of the non-European and North American world as uncivilized.

30. Ibid., 36–37.

31. Ibid., 53–54.

32. Quincy Wright, *A Study of War*, 2nd ed. (Chicago: University of Chicago Press, 1965), 909.

33. Ibid., 351.

34. Quincy Wright, *Human Rights and World Order* (New York: Commission to Study the Organization of Peace, 1942), 5–11, 18–19.

35. Quincy Wright, "Suggested Outline of Topics for the Third Phase of the Studies of the Commission to Study the Organization of Peace," March 27, 1942, Box 152, Folder "CSOP Mtgs 1942," Papers of Clark M. Eichelberger.

36. Clark Eichelberger, "Confidential notes on Interview with the President," 7 September 1939, Box 151, Folder "Pre-CSOP '39," Papers of Clark M. Eichelberger; Shotwell, *Autobiography*, 312.

37. Rowland Brucken, "A Most Uncertain Crusade: The United States, Human Rights and the United Nations, 1941–1954" (Ph.D. dissertation, Ohio State University, 1999), 25–26.

38. Franklin Roosevelt, "Address of 6 January 1941," in *The Public Papers and Address of Franklin D. Roosevelt*, 13 vols., ed. Samuel Rosenman (New York: Random House, 1938–1950), 9: 672. Although most of the speech was drafted by aides, the Four Freedoms formulation was devised by the president. As early as July 1940, he spoke of

"five freedoms" (freedom of information separated from freedom of expression) essential to reestablishment of world peace. See "Roosevelt Names 5 Basic Freedoms of Any Just Peace," *New York Times*, July 6, 1940, 1.

39. Cass Sunstein has argued that there were greater domestic, rather than international, implications of the Four Freedoms speech, as it set the stage for Roosevelt's attempt to establish a "Second Bill of Rights" inclusive of the kinds of economic and social rights many later critics would regard as alien to the American rights tradition. See Cass R. Sunstein, *The Second Bill of Rights: FDR's Unfinished Revolution and Why We Need It More Than Ever* (New York: Basic Books, 2004).

40. Declaration by United Nations, *Foreign Relations of the United States* (*FRUS*) 1942, 1: 25–26. Churchill credits Roosevelt with inventing the term "United Nations" at the last minute, a name that became the most common wartime designation for the anti-Axis alliance. Winston S. Churchill, *The Grand Alliance* (Boston: Houghton Mifflin, 1950), 685.

41. Lauren, *The Evolution of International Human Rights*, 145, 327 n.16.

42. "President's Bill of Rights Speech," *New York Times*, December 16, 1941, 30.

43. Cordell Hull, Secretary of State to President Roosevelt, December 19, 1941, *FRUS* 1942, 1: 3–4; Franklin Roosevelt, President Roosevelt to the Secretary of State, December 27, 1941, *FRUS* 1942, 1: 13–14.

44. James Shotwell, "America After the War," address delivered over Columbia Broadcasting System, December 13, 1941, Box 152, Folder "CSOP—1941–42," Papers of Clark M. Eichelberger.

45. Leo Pasvolsky to Clark Eichelberger, July 8, 1942, Box 152, Folder "Welles Committee," Papers of Clark M. Eichelberger.

46. Clark M. Eichelberger, Personal Meeting Minutes, October 30, 1942; Department of State, "Draft Constitution of the International Organization," n.d. [1942], both Box 152, Folder "Welles Committee," Papers of Clark M. Eichelberger.

47. Eichelberger, *Organizing for Peace*, 196–201; Russell, *A History of the United Nations Charter*, 215–17, 323–39.

48. Brucken, "A Most Uncertain Crusade," 39–40, 45–57. Well aware of Wilson's disastrous failure to bring the U.S. into the League of Nations, the State Department was determined to maintain control over the process of postwar planning as much as to ensure the political feasibility of the postwar organization. Thus, while Welles and Hull brought representatives from private organizations into the process, they squelched any other attempt to pursue official inquiries outside State Department efforts. They also asked members of Congress to participate in and comment on the process.

49. Eichelberger, *Organizing for Peace*, 206–8.

50. Brucken, "A Most Uncertain Crusade," 52–54; Russell, *A History of the United Nations Charter*, 220-22.

51. Lloyd C. Gardner, "The Atlantic Charter: Idea and Reality, 1942–1944," in *The Atlantic Charter*, ed. Douglas Brinkley and David R. Facey-Crowther (New York: St. Martin's, 1994), 46. The most pertinent internal factor influencing de-emphasis of

protection of human rights as a cornerstone of postwar American policy was undoubtedly the ascendancy of secretary of state Cordell Hull over his longtime nemesis, the more liberal undersecretary Sumner Welles.

52. Brucken, "A Most Uncertain Crusade," 81–82.

53. Historian of the Dumbarton Oaks conferences Robert C. Hilderbrand notes that Churchill was unwilling "to take the issue of postwar organization very seriously." Working prior to the opening of the Soviet archives, Hilderbrand nonetheless concludes that "no working plans or proposals had been formulated by the Kremlin by the end of 1943." Robert C. Hilderbrand, *Dumbarton Oaks: The Origins of the United Nations and the Search for Postwar Security* (Chapel Hill: University of North Carolina Press, 1990), 38, 44.

54. Ibid., 2–3.

55. Ibid., 173, 207–8.

56. Memo from Edward Stettinius to Cordell Hull, September 9, 1944, Box 5, Folder "International Organizations, Progress Reports on Dumbarton Oaks Conversations, AG-OC 1944," Papers of Leo Pasvolsky, Manuscripts Division, Library of Congress.

57. "Additional Paragraphs Suggested by Mr. Ben Cohen for Inclusion in Section II, Principles, of the Draft Proposals," Box 5, Folder "International Organizations."

58. Memo from Stettinius to Hull, September 9, 1944.

59. A. W. Brian Simpson, *Human Rights and the End of Empire: Britain and the Genesis of the European Convention* (London: Oxford University Press, 2001), 244.

60. Memo from Stettinius to Hull, September 9, 1944.

61. Hilderbrand, *Dumbarton Oaks*, 86–87.

62. Memo from Stettinius to Hull, September 20, 1944, Box 5, Folder "International Organizations."

63. Ibid.

64. "Dumbarton Plan Assailed by Group," *New York Times*, October 20, 1944, 4.

65. Carl Berendsen quoted in Lauren, *The Evolution of International Human Rights*, 174.

66. Manley O. Hudson, "Weight of Meetings of October 29, November 12, and November 25–26, 1944," December 9, 1944, Papers of Clark M. Eichelberger.

67. Eichelberger, *Organizing for Peace*, 252–54; for an account of this remarkable public relations effort on the part of the CSOP and others, see Robins, *Experiment in Democracy*, 31–99.

68. Clark Eichelberger, "Fundamentals of a Continuing Organization of the United Nations," October 12, 1943, Box 153, Folder "CSOP Mtgs, drafts, etc., 1943," Papers of Clark M. Eichelberger.

69. CSOP, *Fourth Report, Part III. International Safeguard of Human Rights* (New York, CSOP, 1944), 8–9, 22–23.

70. William A. Neilson to Clark M. Eichelberger, October 20, 1944, Box 154, Folder "Human Rights-Report 1944," Papers of Clark M. Eichelberger.

71. Margaret Olson to Carl Van Doren, December 17, 1944, Box 154, Folder "Human Rights, JWD Statement 2/45, 1944," Papers of Clark M. Eichelberger.

72. Quincy Wright to Clark Eichelberger, February 15, 1945, Box 155, Folder "Human Rights Committee, Mtgs. February–March 1, 1945," Papers of Clark M. Eichelberger.

73. CSOP, "Speech by John W. Davis," February 5, 1945, Box 155, Folder "Human Rights-CSOP-Letters to American Delegation, March 31, 1945," Papers of Clark M. Eichelberger.

74. Wright to Eichelberger, February 15, 1945. In his influential treatise published nearly simultaneously with the San Francisco conference, Hersch Lauterpacht called for a "High Commission" for human rights consisting of "independent persons of the highest distinction." H. Lauterpacht, *An International Bill of the Rights of Man* (New York: Columbia University Press, 1945), 196.

75. Robins, *Experiment in Democracy*, 81–83.

76. George J. Hecht to Clark Eichelberger, May 10, 1945; *A Third World War Can Be Prevented Now!* (New York: True Comics Magazine, 1945): both in Box 155, Folder "Comic Book—1945," Papers of Clark M. Eichelberger.

77. "Telegram to the State Governors Urging Proclamation of Dumbarton Oaks Week," February 20, reprinted in Robins, *Experiment in Democracy*, 192–94.

78. Schlesinger, *Act of Creation*, 122–25; Robins, *Experiment in Democracy*, 86–90. Roosevelt's considerable political acumen was evidenced not only with the establishment of the consultants, but with the selection of the delegation itself, which included such Republican heavyweights as Senator Arthur Vandenberg as a delegate and rising GOP star John Foster Dulles as a primary advisor.

79. Clark M. Eichelberger, "Members of the Commission at the United Nations Conference," n.d. [1945], Box 155, Folder "Human Rights, 1945," Papers of Clark M. Eichelberger.

80. Schlesinger, *Act of Creation*, 62–63.

81. John P. Humphrey, *Human Rights & the United Nations: A Great Adventure* (Dobbs Ferry, N.Y.: Transnational, 1984), 12. See also Robins, *Experiment in Democracy*, 129–32; Korey, *NGOs and the Universal Declaration*, 32; B. Simpson, *Human Rights and the End of Empire*, 261; Lauren, *The Evolution of International Human Rights*, 188; Schlesinger, *Act of Creation*, 122–25; Glendon, *A World Made New*, 17; Micheline R. Ishay, *The History of Human Rights: From Ancient Times to the Globalization Era* (Berkeley: University of California Press, 2004), 214–15.

82. Naomi Wiener, "The Transatlantic Connection: The American Jewish Committee and the Joint Foreign Committee in Defense of German Jews, 1933–1937," *American Jewish History* 90, 4 (Dec. 2002): 362–64; Canon John Nurser, "The 'Ecumenical Movement' Churches, 'Global Order,' and Human Rights: 1938–1948," *Human Rights Quarterly* 25 (2003): 862.

83. "Leaders in U.S. Ask World Rights Bill," *New York Times*, December 15, 1944, 10.

84. "International Bill of Human Rights to Be Offered at World Peace Parley," *New York Times*, March 21, 1945, 13. That Proskauer was thinking about the particular importance of human rights for Jews, as well as the general potential of the new world

organization, is indicated by the fact that in addition to the human rights commission, he asked Roosevelt to support a commission on migration and on statelessness, neither of which made it into the Charter.

85. Robins, *Experiment in Democracy*, 130-31.

86. Edward R. Stettinius, "Stettinius Diary—San Francisco Conference, Vol. 1: April 23, Midnight–May 31, 1945," May 2, 1945, Records of Harley A. Notter, RG 59 Records of the Department of State, National Archives and Records Administration (NARA), College Park, Md.

87. John S. Nurser, *For All Peoples and All Nations: The Ecumenical Churches and Human Rights* (Washington, D.C.: Georgetown University Press, 2005), 28–43.

88. Clark Eichelberger to Members of the CSOP, May 5, 1945, Box 155, Folder "Human Rights, 1945," Papers of Clark Eichelberger; Eichelberger, *Organizing for Peace*, 269–71.

89. Nurser, *For All Peoples*, 114–15.

90. Eichelberger to Members of the CSOP, 5 May 1945.

91. Schlesinger, *Act of Creation*, xv–xviii, 115–16.

92. Nurser, *For All Peoples*, 116–17.

93. Russell, *A History of the United Nations Charter*, 642.

94. Nurser, *For All Peoples*, 114.

95. "Consultation of the United States, United Kingdom, Soviet Union, and China on their Amendments to the Dumbarton Oaks Proposals, Status of Consultations," May 4, 1945, Box 10, Folder "UNCIO, Minutes—Four-Power and Latin American, MY 1945," Papers of Leo Pasvolsky.

96. Minutes, "UNCIO, CONS Four Min 4, May 4, 1945, 12:15pm," May 4, 1945, Box 10, Folder "UNCIO, Minutes—Four-Power and Latin American, MY 1945."

97. Department of State, *The United Nations Conference on International Organization, San Francisco, California, April 25 to June 26, 1945, Selected Documents* (Washington, D.C.: U.S. GPO, 1946), 6: 506–7.

Chapter 2. A Pacific Charter

1. Edwin R. Embree, Pearl S. Buck, Ray Lyman Wilbur, Quincy Wright, and Walter White to Franklin D. Roosevelt, January 16, 1942, Official File, Papers of Franklin Delano Roosevelt, Franklin D. Roosevelt Presidential Library, Hyde Park, N.Y.

2. Elizabeth Borgwardt, *A New Deal for the World: America's Vision for Human Rights* (Cambridge: Belknap Press of Harvard University Press, 2005), 1–4, 22–30. Borgwardt's description of the seaborne rendezvous, which she terms the first "superpower summit," is dramatic and evocative.

3. Winston S. Churchill, *The Grand Alliance* (Boston: Houghton Mifflin, 1950), 434; Ruth B. Russell, *A History of the United Nations Charter: The Role of the United States 1940–1945* (Washington, D.C.: Brookings Institution, 1958), 34–35.

4. Sumner Welles, *Where Are We Heading?* (New York: Harper, 1946), 15; Robert A. Divine, *Roosevelt and World War II* (Baltimore: Johns Hopkins University Press, 1969),

58. For an examination of the Atlantic Charter's origins and influence, see Lloyd C. Gardner, "The Atlantic Charter: Idea and Reality, 1942–1944" in *The Atlantic Charter*, ed. Douglas Brinkley and David R. Facey-Crowther (New York: St. Martin's, 1994); and Borgwardt, *A New Deal for the World*, whose excellent book traces the intellectual impact of the Atlantic Charter in the postwar institutions of the Nuremberg Tribunals, the UN, and the Bretton Woods financial organizations.

5. "Joint Statement by President Roosevelt and Prime Minister Winston Churchill, August 14, 1941," *FRUS* 1941, 1: 367–68.

6. The original British draft also called for an "effective international organization" as opposed to the more vague "wider and permanent system of general security." Again, Roosevelt objected to such strong and specific language, preferring to emphasize a bilateral effort on the part of the U.S. and UK to ensure peace and stability throughout the world unhampered by "a new Assembly of the League of Nations" or other international organization. Until his death on the eve of the San Francisco conference, Roosevelt continued to believe the true key to a lasting international peace lay not with a broad-based international organization, but with the ongoing cooperation of the Great Powers, a plan he referred to as the "Four Policemen" (U.S. and UK, plus the Soviet Union and China). See A. W. Brian Simpson, *Human Rights and the End of Empire: Britain and the Genesis of the European Convention* (London: Oxford University Press, 2001), 174–79.

7. Gardner, "The Atlantic Charter: Idea and Reality," 57.

8. Winston Churchill, September 9, 1941, 374 House of Commons Debates, Fifth Series (London: HMSO, 1941), cols. 68–69.

9. Raymond Daniell, "Churchill Credits Plan to Roosevelt," *New York Times*, November 11, 1942, 1. Much as their postwar efforts in support of international human rights would be confined to the attempt to establish the European Convention on Human Rights, the British government was willing to see principles they themselves had declared universal enforced only within Europe. See Simpson, *Human Rights and the End of Empire*.

10. Ruth B. Russell, *A History of the United Nations Charter: The Role of The United States, 1940–1945* (Washington, D.C.: Brookings Institution, 1958)

11. Margaret E. Keck and Kathryn Sikkink have labeled this dynamic the "Boomerang Pattern" in their prominent analysis of contemporary NGO politics. Margaret E. Keck and Kathryn Sikkink, *Activists Beyond Borders: Advocacy Networks in International Politics* (Ithaca, N.Y.: Cornell University Press, 1998), 12–13.

12. "Statement by Dr. Quo Tai-Chi, Minister of Foreign Affairs, Chungking, August 18, 1941," *FRUS* 1941, 4: 337.

13. Telegram from The Ambassador in China (Clarence Gauss) to the Secretary of State, 19 August 1941, *FRUS* 1941, 4: 383–84.

14. Chiang Kai-shek to Franklin Delano Roosevelt, 7 Jan. 1942, *FRUS* 1942, China, 2–3.

15. Carlos Romulo, "Billion Oriental Look to America for Aid in Crisis," *Philippines Herald*, September 15, 1941, 1, 4.

16. On American rule in the Philippines, see Paul A. Kramer, *The Blood of Government: Race, Empire, the United States, and the Philippines* (Chapel Hill: University of North Carolina Press, 2006); Stanley Karnow, *In Our Image: America's Empire in the Philippines* (New York: Random House, 1989).

17. Carlos Romulo, *I Walked with Heroes* (New York: Holt, Rinehart, 1961), 9.

18. Carlos Romulo, "The Tragedy of Our Anglo-Saxon Education," in *Encyclopedia of the Philippines*, ed. Zolio M. Galang (Manila: Exequiel Floro, 1950), 1: 342.

19. On the political significance of creative translation in the Philippine context, see Vincente L. Rafael, *The Promise of the Foreign: Nationalism and the Technics of Translation in the Spanish Philippines* (Durham, N.C.: Duke University Press, 2005).

20. Carlos Romulo, *Mother America: A Living Story of Democracy* (Garden City, N.Y.: Doubleday, Doran, 1943), 4.

21. Carlos Romulo, "Flow of American Aid on Famed Burma Road," *Philippines Herald*, September 24, 1941, 1.

22. Romulo, *I Walked with Heroes*, 213.

23. Romulo, "Billion Oriental Look to America for Aid in Crisis," 4.

24. "Memorandum of Conversation," March 20, 1942, *FRUS* 1942, 4: 273–74. The Arab world too responded to the opportunity presented by the Atlantic Charter. During the war, Syrian, Lebanese, Moroccan, and Iraqi officials all invoked the document in hopes of garnering American support for their national independence and sovereignty vis-à-vis European powers. Wadsworth to Hull, March 23, 1943, *FRUS* 1943, 4: 963–94; Wadsworth to Hull, August 18, 1943, *FRUS* 1943, 4: 985–86; C. Burke Elbrick, Memorandum, September 30, 1943, *FRUS* 1943, 4: 744–45; Gaudin to Hull, 13 November 1943, *FRUS*, 1943, 4: 1024.

25. Telegram from The Ambassador in the United Kingdom (Winant) to the Secretary of State, *FRUS*, 1941, 3: 182–85.

26. U Thant quoted in June Bingham, *U Thant: The Search for Peace* (New York: Knopf, 1966), 153.

27. Russell, *A History of the United Nations Charter*, 76–77. The trip proved to be a mistake for the Burmese prime minister. Not only was he rebuffed in both London and Washington, but his voyage home took him through Honolulu on December 7, 1941, where he went missing for several days after the Japanese attack. After finally managing to depart from Hawaii on January 4, he was seized by British authorities before being returned to Rangoon on suspicion of conspiring with the Japanese and sent to Uganda for the duration of the war. James MacDonald, "Official Detained," *New York Times*, January 19, 1942, 1.

28. The definitive treatment of the colonialism issue in the Anglo-American alliance remains William Roger Louis, *Imperialism at Bay: The United States and the Decolonization of the British Empire, 1941–1945* (New York: Oxford University Press, 1978).

29. Chiang to Roosevelt, August 11, 1942, *FRUS* 1942, 1: 714–15.

30. Roosevelt to Chiang, August 12, 1942, *FRUS* 1942, 1: 715–16.

31. Phillips to Roosevelt, Mar. 3, 1943, *FRUS* 1943, 4: 205–7.

32. Hull to Warren, Apr. 28, 1943, *FRUS* 1943, 4: 312–13. The proposed changes, which would have extended the ban from owning to leasing, and made it easier for the state to seize property held by Asian Americans, were never enacted. The bill's main sponsor, State Senator Claire Engle, was elected to the U.S. House (where he promptly offered a bill to permanently exclude Japanese and Japanese Americans from the West Coast) before the bill could be considered. After an initiative to put a similar bill on the California ballot failed to gather enough signatures, the law remained unchanged until invalidated by the California Supreme Court in 1952. The case, *Sei Fujii v. California* is described in Chapter 5. See "Japs Face Tight State Land Ban," *Los Angeles Times*, January 16, 1943, 4; "California Avoids a Japanese Issue," *New York Times*, September 10, 1944, 22; "Permanent Jap Removal Offered in Engle Bill," *Los Angeles Times*, September 1, 1944, 12.

33. I've adopted "diplomacy of conscience" from Ann Marie Clark's study, *Diplomacy of Conscience: Amnesty International and Changing Human Rights Norm* (Princeton, N.J.: Princeton University Press, 2001).

34. Robert C. Hilderbrand, *Dumbarton Oaks: The Origins of the United Nations and the Search for Postwar Security* (Chapel Hill: University of North Carolina Press, 1990), 58–59.

35. Russell, *A History of the United Nations Charter*, 52–55.

36. Hilderbrand, *Dumbarton Oaks*, 236–37.

37. Ibid., 227. Reformed or not, the church had yet to receive its full human rights dispensation.

38. "Informal Minutes of Meeting of the Joint Steering Committee of the Washington Conversations (Chinese Phase) held at 10:00 A.M., October 2, at Dumbarton Oaks," Box 9, Folder "Conference File, Dumbarton Oaks Conference, Washington Conversations—general, OC 1944," Papers of Leo Pasvolsky; Memo from Edward Stettinius to Franklin Roosevelt, October 2, 1944, Box 5, Folder "International Organizations, Progress Reports on Dumbarton Oaks Conversations, AG-OC, 1944," Papers of Leo Pasvolsky.

39. "Informal Record of Meeting of Members of the American Group at Dumbarton Oaks—12:00 Noon," Box 9, Folder "Conference File, Dumbarton Oaks Conference, Washington Conversations—general, OC 1944," Papers of Leo Pasvolsky.

40. Stephen G. Craft, *V. K. Wellington Koo and the Emergence of Modern China* (Lexington: University Press of Kentucky, 2004), 179; William C. Widenor, "Nationalism, imperialism and Sino-American relations: V. K. Wellington Koo and China's quest for international autonomy and power, 1912–1949" (Ph.D. dissertation, University of Illinois at Urbana-Champaign, 1998), 313–14.

41. Memo from Stettinius to Roosevelt, October 2, 1944.

42. Widenor, "Nationalism, Imperialism and Sino-American Relations," 318–19.

43. Hilderbrand, *Dumbarton Oaks*, 236.

44. Widenor, "Nationalism, Imperialism and Sino-American Relations," 356–58; Craft, *V. K. Wellington Koo*, xiv.

45. "Tentative Chinese Proposals for a General International Organization," Box 6, Folder "Int'l Organization, Working Books, Unidentified, (2 of 2)," Papers of Leo Pasvolsky.

46. Craft, *V. K. Wellington Koo*, 174. The role of race in the Pacific War is described definitively in John Dower, *War Without Mercy: Race and Power in the Pacific War* (New York: Pantheon, 1986). Koo was all too aware that a statement on racial equality had been firmly vetoed by American President Woodrow Wilson when the Japanese had introduced it into the League of Nations Covenant. This failure is one of the few instances where Wilson's most notorious domestic agenda—the extension of Jim Crow into the federal system—and his most important international initiative intersected. For an account of Japanese efforts to secure a statement of racial equality at the Paris Peace Conference, see Noriko Kawamura "Wilsonian Idealism and Japanese Claims at the Paris Peace Conference," *Pacific Historical Review* 66 (1997): 503–26.

47. "Conv. B, Joint Formulation Group Record 3, October 6, 1944," Box 9, Folder "Conference File, Dumbarton Oaks Conference, Washington Conversations—Conv. B, Minutes, Joint Formulation Group Records 1–4, OC 1944," Papers of Leo Pasvolsky.

48. Craft, *V. K. Wellington Koo*, 180-81. The Chinese role at Dumbarton Oaks was not all deference. Stung by both the obstinance of the Soviets and the condescension of the British, the Chinese leaked the preconference proposals of the three other delegations to James Reston of the *New York Times*, who then went on to describe them to readers in an August 23 article. Reston's work on the Conference would eventually win him a Pulitzer, but it was a source of embarrassment and aggravation for the three governments. While the leak may not have affected the conference's outcome any more than the official Chinese proposals did, it did expose the Big Three plan to public scrutiny. See Hilderbrand, *Dumbarton Oaks*, 175–76, 77–78; Craft, *V. K. Wellington Koo*, 172, 174; James B. Reston, "For Use of Forces," *New York Times*, 23 August 1944, 1, 10.

49. Russell, *A History of the United Nations Charter*, 830; "Levantines Charge French Coercion," *New York Times*, May 23, 1945.

50. Charles Malik to Mr. Thomas, February 8, 1945, Box 109, Folder 2, Papers of Charles H. Malik, Manuscripts Division, Library of Congress.

51. Department of State, *The United Nations Conference on International Organization, San Francisco, California, April 25 to June 26, 1945, Selected Documents* [*UNCIO*] (Washington, D.C.: U.S. GPO, 1946), 1: 251–53; Department of State, *Dumbarton Oaks Proposals for General International Organization*, 1945, Box 97, Folder 5, Papers of Charles H. Malik.

52. "Two Arab States Score France at Parley," *New York Times*, May 22, 1945, 4; "Levant Appeals to "Frisco Parley as Fighting Spreads," *Boston Globe*, May 29, 1945, 1.

53. O'Hare McCormick, "Abroad: San Francisco and the Crisis in the Levant," *New York Times*, May 30, 1945, 18.

54. Russell, *A History of the United Nations Charter*, 646–57, 713–50, Stephen C. Schlesinger, *Act of Creation: The Founding of The United Nations* (Boulder, Colo.: Westview, 2003),193–206, 219–22.

55. Russell, *A History of the United Nations Charter*, 750-51, 759, 761–75; Schlesinger, *Act of Creation*, 227–32; John H. Crider, "Assembly to Act as 'Town Meeting,'" *New York Times*, May 30, 1945, 15.

56. Herbert Evatt, "The General Assembly," in *Peace on Earth* (New York: Hermitage House, 1949), 28.

57. Romulo, *I Walked with Heroes*, 309.

58. Department of State, *UNCIO*, 3: 587, 529–30. Mark Mazower argues that it is more than just an irony of history that South Africa was a principal proponent of making human rights a central concern of the UN. According to his history of the founding of the UN, such support demonstrates the unbroken continuity between the reformed if still racialized form of empire represented by the British Commonwealth, and the UN system. While this is an important insight, my argument is that the UN as established at San Francisco was more equivocal and in fact contained many significant elements—human rights commitments among them—that distinguished it from the past. Nevertheless, the South African support for human rights at San Francisco demonstrates the extent to which "human rights" was as yet an empty signifier in the world, and how debating the meaning of the term would constitute one of the major political and ethical struggles of our time. Mark Mazower, *No Enchanted Palace: The End of Empire and the Ideological Origins of the United Nations* (Princeton, N.J.: Princeton University Press, 2009), 7–8, 28–65.

59. Department of State, *UNCIO*, 3: 602–3.

60. Ibid., 544–49.

61. Ibid., 494–502.

62. Paul Gordon Lauren, *The Evolution of International Human Rights: Visions Seen* (Philadelphia: University of Pennsylvania Press, 1998), 177–78.

63. "Synopsis of Essential Observations Made by the Mexican Delegation on the Dumbarton Oaks Proposals," February 1, 1945, Box 9, Folder "Conference File, Inter-American Conference on Problems of War and Peace, Mexican Resolution, FE-MR 1945," Papers of Leo Pasvolsky.

64. Department of State, "Summary Report of the Ninth Meeting of Committee 1/1," June 1, 1945, *UNCIO*, 6: 223–24.

65. "Text of Stettinius' Speech Projecting a Five-Point Foreign Policy for This Country," *New York Times*, May 29, 1945, 8.

66. Department of State, "Summary Report of the Tenth Meeting of Committee 1/1," June 2, 1945, *UNCIO*, 6: 325–26.

67. Edward Stettinius, "Diary, San Francisco Conference, Vol. I: April 23, Midnight–May 31, 1945," Records of Harley A. Notter, Records of the Department of State, RG 59, NARA; "UNCIO, CONS Four Min 4," May 4, 1945, Box 10, Folder "UNCIO, Minutes—Four-Power and Latin America, MY 1945," Papers of Leo Pasvolsky.

68. Department of State, "Summary Report of the Seventeenth Meeting of Committee 1/1," June 14, 1945, *UNCIO*, 6: 507–8.

69. Department of State, "Summary Report of the Tenth Meeting of Committee II/3," May 22, 1945, *UNCIO*, 12: 57–59.

70. Department of State, "Summary Report of the Eleventh Meeting of Committee II/3," May 24, 1945, *UNCIO*, 12: 83, 89; A. W. Brian Simpson, *Human Rights and the End of Empire: Britain and the Genesis of the European Convention* (London: Oxford University Press, 2001).

71. Russell, *A History of the United Nations Charter*, 808–9.

72. Huntington Gilchrist, "Colonial Questions at the San Francisco Conference," *American Political Science Review*, 39, 5 (1945): 982–83.

73. Department of State, *UNCIO*, 1: 164–65. The *Chicago Daily Tribune* reporter called Romulo, whose slight stature was a constant subject of commentary, a "little Filipino ball of fire." Arthur Sears Henning, "New Problems Delay Parley's End to June 23," *Chicago Daily Tribune*, June 15, 1945, 1.

74. Department of State, "Summary Report of the Second Meeting of Committee II/4," May 10, 1945, *UNCIO* 10: 428–29.

75. Department of State, "Summary Report of the Third Meeting of Committee II/4," May 11, 1945, *UNCIO* 10: 433–34.

76. Department of State, "Summary Report of the Fourth Meeting of Committee II/4," May 15, 1945, *UNCIO* 10: 440–41.

77. Department of State, "Summary Report of the Fifth Meeting of Committee II/4," May 17, 1945, *UNCIO* 10: 453–54.

78. Carlos Romulo, *Romulo: A Third World Soldier at the UN* (New York: Praeger, 1986), 39.

79. Sydney Gruson, "Britain to Renew Offer to Indians," *New York Times*, May 31, 1945, 2. The "offer" here was to form a government under the authority of the viceroy, with promises of Dominion status after the war—essentially the same as under the failed 1942 Cripps Mission.

80. "Gandhi Disowns Parley Delegation," *New York Times*, April 18, 1945, 15. V. L. Pandit, future Indian ambassador to the UN and sister of Jawaharlal Nehru, attended the conference and called the official Indian delegation "British knights, sailing under false colors." Like the other representatives, including chairman of the Indian delegation Sir A. Ramasamy Muladiar, she called for a peace based on justice; William Moore, "Indian Woman Twists the Tail of British Lion," *Chicago Daily Tribune*, April 27, 1945, 6.

81. Department of State, *UNCIO*, 1: 244–45.

82. "Summary Report of the Eleventh Meeting of Committee II/3," May 24, 1945, *UNCIO*, 83.

83. W. E. B. Du Bois, *Color and Democracy: Colonies and Peace* (New York: Harcourt, Brace, 1944), 8–9, 12.

84. Roy Wilkins to Walter White, May 24, 1945; Memorandum of Meeting of Committee on Administration, May 28, 1945: both Box A639, Folder "United Nations, the United Nations Conference on International Organization, 1945 May 11–June," Papers of the NAACP, Group II, Manuscripts Division, Library of Congress.

85. Walter White to NAACP Board of Directors, May 9, 1945; Walter White, "Memorandum for the Files from the Secretary," June 4, 1945: both Box A639, Folder "United

Nations, the United Nations Conference on International Organization, 1945 March–May 10," Papers of the NAACP, Group IV.

86. Charles Henry, *Ralph Bunche: Model Negro or American Other?* (New York: New York University Press, 1999), 137–38; Brian Urquhart, *Ralph Bunche: An American Life* (New York: Norton, 1993), 119–21.

87. Lawrence S. Finkelstein, "Bunche and the Colonial World: From Trusteeship to Decolonization," in *Ralph Bunche: The Man and His Times*, ed. Benjamin Rivlin (New York: Holmes & Meier, 1990), 124–25.

88. "Summary Report of Fifteenth Meeting of Committee II/4," *UNCIO*, 8: 561–63; Arthur Sears Henning, "Charter Holds Sway over U.S. Defense System," *Chicago Daily Tribune*, June 25, 1945, 6; Russell, *A History of the United Nations Charter*, 818.

89. Urquhart, *Ralph Bunche*, 121.

90. "Untitled [Report on Trusteeship Debates]," n.d. [1945], Box 4.9, Folder 335, Papers of Carlos Romulo, University Archives, University of the Philippines, Diliman, Quezon City, Philippines.

91. "Summary Report of Fifteenth Meeting of Committee II/4," *UNCIO*, 8: 562.

92. Henning, "New Problems Delay Parley's End to June 23," 1.

93. Marika Sherwood, "'There Is No New Deal for the Blackman in San Francisco': African Attempts to Influence the Founding Conference of the United Nations, April–July, 1945," *International Journal of African Historical Studies* 29, 1 (1996): 84–85.

94. Carlos Romulo to Sergio Osmeña, July 15, 1945, Box 1.1, Folder 15, Papers of Carlos Romulo.

95. Henning, "Charter Holds Sway over U.S. Defense System," 6.

Chapter 3. Carlos Romulo, Freedom of Information, and the Philippine Pattern

1. Verbatim Record, Final Plenary Session, June 26, 1945, *United Nations Conference on International Organization Journal* 53: 181.

2. Carlos P. Romulo to Sergio Osmeña, July 15, 1945, Box 1.1, Folder 15, Papers of Carlos P. Romulo, University Archives, University of the Philippines, Diliman, Quezon City; Carlos Romulo, *Romulo: A Third World Soldier at the UN* (New York: Praeger, 1986), 188–93.

3. Romulo to Victor Buencamino, August 27, 1945, Box 2.2, Folder 158, Papers of Carlos P. Romulo.

4. Mary Ann Glendon, *A World Made New: Eleanor Roosevelt and the Universal Declaration of Human Rights* (New York: Random House, 2001), 87–90; Johannes Morsink, *The Universal Declaration of Human Rightst: Origins, Drafting, and Intent* (Philadelphia: University of Pennsylvania Press, 1999), 32, 284–87.

5. H. Ford Wilkins, "Philippine Republic Is Born as U.S. Rule Ends in Glory," *New York Times*, July 4, 1946, 1; "U.S. Give Freedom to the Philippines," *Chicago Daily Tribune*, July 4, 1946, 1.

6. Representative C. Jasper Bell, conservative Democrat from Missouri, gave away the game when he remarked that the "whole philosophy" behind the Act was to exercise

control over the Philippines "economically even though we lost them politically." This was accomplished through a variety of measures; the most egregious, from the Filipino point of view, gave U.S. citizens "parity" with Filipinos in ownership of business enterprises in the Philippines, although Filipinos certainly were not allowed the same privileges in the U.S. Not without critics in the U.S., the Act was vehemently opposed by many in the Philippines and was ratified only after President Rojas, in a highly questionable maneuver, ejected some opposition members of Congress during the vote. In this way, both the terms and adoption of the Bell Act have been understood by scholars as exemplifying neocolonialism. See Daniel B. Schirmer and Stephen Rosskamm Shalom, *The Philippines Reader: A History of Colonialism, Neocolonialism, Dictatorship, and Resistance* (Boston: South End Press, 1987), 87–96; Stanley Karnow, *In Our Image: America's Empire in the Philippines* (New York: Random House, 1989), 333–36; Thomas C. Nowak and Kay A. Snyder, "Clientelist Politics in the Philippines: Integration or Instability?" *American Political Science Review* 68, 3 (September 1974): 1148–51; Stephen R. Shalom, "Philippine Acceptance of the Bell Trade Act of 1946: A Study of Manipulatory Democracy," *Pacific Historical Review* 49, 3 (August 1980): 499–517.

7. Augusto Fauni Espiritu, *Five Faces of Exile: The Nation and Filipino American Intellectuals* (Stanford, Calif.: Stanford University Press, 2005), 45.

8. Carlos P. Romulo, *I Saw the Philippines Fall* (New York: Doubleday, 1943), 322–23. Seated next to Romulo at Notre Dame was another recipient of an honorary degree: the president of the United States, Franklin D. Roosevelt. When it came time for Roosevelt to speak, he, like Romulo, celebrated the special relationship between the U.S. and the Philippines, grounded as it was in "the fact that both nations have the deepest respect for the inalienable rights of man." Noting that the principles of "fundamental human rights" were now firmly embedded in the new Constitution of the Philippine Commonwealth, Roosevelt slid from the specifics of the U.S.-Philippine relationship to a more general, international principle: "There can be no true national life either within a nation itself or between that nation and other nations unless there be the specific acknowledgement of and the support of organic law to the rights of man." See "Texts of the President's Speeches Before Farmers and Notre Dame Students," "Notre Dame Hails Roosevelt's Aims," *New York Times*, December 10, 1935, 12, 13.

9. Carlos P. Romulo, *I Walked with Heroes* (New York: Holt, Rinehart, 1961), 198–99, 204–7, 225–28.

10. Romulo to Douglas MacArthur, August 18, 1942, Papers of Carlos P. Romulo; Romulo, *I Saw the Philippines Fall*, 19.

11. Carlos P. Romulo, *Mother America: A Living Story of Democracy* (Garden City, N.Y.: Doubleday, 1943), xiv, 14–15, 31, 137.

12. Romulo, *I Saw the Philippines Fall*, 1–29; Romulo, *Mother America*, 137.

13. Romulo, *My Brother Americans*, 165; Romulo, *Mother America*, 93, 125; Carlos P. Romulo, "The Philippine Pattern," *Far Eastern Survey* 13, 14 (July 12, 1944): 125.

14. Office of Special Services, "Basic Plan," 19 October 1942, Papers of Carlos P. Romulo.

15. Carlos Romulo, "Human Rights as a Condition of Peace in the Far East," *Annals of the American Academy of Political and Social Sciences* 243 (January 1946): 9–10.

16. United Nations General Assembly [UNGA], *Official Records Plenary Meetings of the General Assembly, Verbatim Record, 23 October–16 December 1946* (Flushing Meadows, N.Y.: United Nations, 1947), 821; "U.N Asked to Call Dependent Lands," *New York Times*, November 4, 1946, 8.

17. UNGA, *Official Records Plenary Meetings of the General Assembly, Verbatim Record, 23 October–16 December 1946*, 821.

18. Ibid., 823.

19. UNGA, "Philippine Draft Resolution," 6 February 1946, A/BUR/24; UNGA, "Philippine Draft Resolution, Revised," 14 November 1946, A/C.3/76; UNGA, *Official Records Plenary Meetings of the General Assembly, Verbatim Record, 23 October–16 December 1946*, 819; Sydney Gruson, "UNO Sidetracks Free Press Motion," *New York Times*, January 15, 1946, 6; Arthur M. Vandenberg, Jr., ed., *The Private Papers of Senator Vandenberg* (Boston: Houghton Mifflin, 1952), 239.

20. "Politics and Personnel, General Assembly, United Nations, New York, October 23–December 16, 1946," 1946, Records of the Bureau of International Affairs and Its Predecessor, Box 13, RG 59, NARA II; SD/A/C.3/2, n.d. [1946], Records of the Bureau of International Affairs and Its Predecessors, Box 26, RG 59, NARA II.

21. ASNE quoted in Carroll Binder, "Freedom of Information and the United Nations," *International Organization* 6, 2 (May 1952): 221.

22. Nicholas Owen, *The British Left and India: Metropolitan Anti-Imperialism, 1885–1947* (Oxford: Oxford University Press, 2007), 284.

23. In 1944, Frances Guther described the Indian independence movement as "a gigantic struggle of heroic proportions between two powerful wills—the English will to rule versus the Indian will to freedom." Frances Gunther, *Revolution in India* (New York: Island Press, 1944), 3.

24. "Politics and Personnel, General Assembly, United Nations, New York, October 23–December 16, 1946"; Paul Gordon Lauren, *The Evolution of International Human Rights : Visions Seen* (Philadelphia : University of Pennsylvania Press, 1998), 212–13.

25. Mark Mazower, *No Enchanted Palace: The End of Empire and the Ideological Origins of the United Nations* (Princeton, N.J.: Princeton University Press, 2009), 28–65.

26. Romulo, *I Walked with Heroes*, 31–36.

27. M. L. Dockrill and John Fisher call Smuts, with no small contempt for his idealism, the "leading appeaser" at Paris for favoring a less punitive peace settlement. M. L. Dockrill and John Fisher, *Paris Peace Conference, 1919: Peace Without Victory?* (New York: Palgrave, 2001), 56. More generously, George Curry credits Smuts with seeding Woodrow Wilson's League of Nations plan and providing the American president with a critical interlocutor and ally at the Paris Peace Conference. George Curry, "Woodrow Wilson, Jan Smuts, and the Versailles Settlement," *American Historical Review* 66, 4 (July 1961): 968–69.

28. Paul Gordon Lauren argues that the Second World War "forced people to

examine themselves, their moral values, their attitudes about race, and the consequences of extreme racial prejudice in ways that nothing else had ever been able to do before in history." While by no means the end of racial discrimination, the war marked "the turning point" in global public opinion on race. Paul Gordon Lauren, *Power and Prejudice: The Politics and Diplomacy of Racial Discrimination*, 2nd ed. (Boulder, Colo.: Westview, 1996), 177.

29. UNGA, *Official Records Plenary Meetings of the General Assembly, Verbatim Record, 23 October–16 December 1946*, 1007–18, 1028–30; A/C.1&6/92.

30. On U.S. defense of South African racism, see Thomas Borstelmann, *Apartheid's Reluctant Uncle: The United States and Southern Africa in the Early Cold War* (New York: Oxford University Press, 1993); Roland W. Brucken, "A Most Uncertain Crusade: The United States, Human Rights and the United Nations, 1941–1954" (Ph.D. dissertation, Ohio State University, 1999), 144; Carol Anderson, *Eyes Off the Prize: The United Nations and the African American Struggle for Human Rights, 1944–1955* (New York: Cambridge University Press, 2003). Romulo himself was aware, at least since his days as a student at Columbia University, that the problem of African American discrimination was the biggest mote in the eye of American democracy. *I Walked with Heroes*, 136–38.

31. Lauren, *The Evolution of International Human Rights*, 205.

32. UNGA, *Official Records Plenary Meetings of the General Assembly, Verbatim Record, 23 October–16 December 1946*, 820–21.

33. United Nations Commission on Human Rights [UNCHR], Working Group on the Declaration on Human Rights, "Summary Record of the Second Meeting. Held at the Palais des Nations, Geneva, on Friday, 5 December 1947, at 3 p.m.," E/CN.4/AC.2/SR.2.

34. UNCHR,, "Summary Record of the Ninth Meeting. Held at Lake Success, New York, on Saturday, 1 February 1947, At 11 a.m.," E/CN.4/SR.9.

35. UNCHR,, "Summary Record of the Fifteenth Meeting. Held at Lake Success, New York, on Tuesday, 5 February 1947, at 11 a.m.," E/CN.4/SR.15.

36. Roland Burke, *Decolonization and the Evolution of International Human Rights* (Philadelphia: University of Pennsylvania Press, 2010), 62–63, 82–83.

37. UNCHR, "Summary Record of the Fifth Meeting. Held at Lake Success, New York, on Wednesday, 29 January 1947, at 11 a.m.," E/CN.4/SR.5.

38. Romulo, *I Walked with Heroes*, 287, 322.

39. E. San Juan, Jr., *The Philippine Temptation: Dialectics of Philippines-U.S. Literary Relations* (Philadelphia: Temple University Press, 1996), 219; Philippine Writers League, "Objectives," in *Literature Under the Commonwealth* (Manila: A.S. Florentino, 1973), 56.

40. John P. Humphrey, "The Memoirs of John P. Humphrey, the First Directory of the United Nations Division of Human Rights," *Human Rights Quarterly* 5, 4 (November 1983): 410.

41. G. Edward White, "The First Amendment Comes of Age: The Emergence of Free Speech in Twentieth-Century America," *Michigan Law Review* 95, 2 (November 1996): 302, 310-16.

42. See generally Paul L. Murphy, *World War I and the Origin of Civil Liberties in the*

United States (New York: Norton, 1979); Samuel Walker, *In Defense of American Liberties: A History of the ACLU* (New York: Oxford University Press, 1990); Mark A. Graber, *Transforming Free Speech: The Ambiguous Legacy of Civil Libertarianism* (Berkeley: University of California Press, 1991); Eric Foner, *The Story of American Freedom* (New York: Norton, 1998), 163–94.

43. Commission on Freedom of the Press, *A Free and Responsible Press: A General Report on Mass Communication: Newspapers, Radio, Motion Pictures, Magazines, and Books* (Chicago: University of Chicago Press, 1944), 126–28.

44. Stephen Bates, *Realigning Journalism with Democracy: The Hutchins Commission, Its Times, and Ours* (Washington, D.C.: Annenberg Washington Program in Communications Policy Studies of Northwestern University, 1995).

45. UNCHR, "Report to the Economic and Social Council on the First Session of the Commission, Held at Lake Success, New York, from 27 January to 10 February 1947," E/259; UNCHR, Sub-Commission on Freedom of Information [SCFOI], "Draft Agenda for the Conference on Freedom of Information," E/CN.4/Sub.1/9; UNCHR, SCFOI, "Draft Agenda for the Conference on Freedom of Information: Proposal of the French Delegation," E/355; R. J. Cruikshank, "Paper Submitted by Mr. R. J. Cruikshank, United Kingdom Member of Sub-Commission on Freedom of Information and of the Press," E/CN.4/Sub.1/12. On Chafee, see John Wertheimer, "Freedom of Speech: Zechariah Chafee and Free-Speech History," *Reviews in American History* 22, 2 (June 1994): 365–77.

46. UNCHR, SCFOI, "Summary Record of the Ninth Meeting. Held at Lake Success, New York,on Friday, 23 May 1947, at 11 a.m.," E/CN.4/Sub.1/SR.9; UNCHR, SCFOI, "Summary Record of the Fourteenth Meeting. Held at Lake Success, New York, on Tuesday, 27 May 1947, at 3 p.m.," E/CN.4/Sub.1/SR.14; John P. Humphrey, *Human Rights and the United Nations: A Great Adventure* (Dobbs Ferry, N.Y.: Transnational, 1984), 35–36.

47. UNGA, "Philippine Draft Resolution, Revised," November 14, 1946, A/C.3/76. The language of the Filipino draft proposal for a freedom of information conference corresponds to a more general sentiment shared by many in Asia that rights could not be decoupled from responsibilities in the pursuit of justice. Responding to a circular letter from the newly formed UN Educational Scientific and Cultural Organization, no less a figure than Mohandas Gandhi had written that in the effort to establish human rights, the priority of responsibility must not be forgotten. See Mahatma Gandhi, "Letter to the Director-General of UNESCO," in *Human Rights: Comments and Interpretations*, ed. UNESCO (New York: Allan Wingate, 1948), 18. Over the years, responsibility and its connection to a unique "Asian tradition" (Gandhi credited his "illiterate mother" with forming his ideas regarding human rights and responsibilities) would gain potency from India to the Philippines, achieving its most notorious expression in the Asian Values debate of the 1990s.

48. Salvador Lopez, "Text of Statement Made at Thirteenth Meeting of First Session of Sub-Commission on Freedom of Information and of the Press by Mr. Salvador Lopez," E/CN.1/Sub.1/30.

49. Zechariah Chafee, "Text of Statement Made at Second Meeting of First Session

of Sub-Commission on Freedom of Information and of the Press by Mr. Zechariah Chafee," E/CN.4/Sub.1/14.

50. San Juan, Jr., *The Philippine Temptation*, 219.

51. Philippine Writers League, "Manifesto," in *Literature Under the Commonwealth*, 57–58.

52. Lauren, *The Evolution of International Human Rights* 151–52; R. A. Wilford, "The PEN Club, 1930-50," *Journal of Contemporary History* 14, 1 (January 1979): 99–116. On the introduction of freedom of the press to the Philippines, see Alindogan Ables Higino, *Mass Communication and Philippine Society* (Diliman, Quezon City: University of the Philippines Press, 2003), 17–24.

53. Theodore Schoeder, founder of the Free Speech League, noted in 1905 that a newspaper editor in the Philippines was arrested for reprinting the Declaration of Independence. David M. Rabban, "The Free Speech League, the ACLU, and the Changing Conceptions of Free Speech in American History," *Stanford Law Review* 45, 1 (Nov. 1992): 86.

54. Romulo, *I Walked with Heroes*, 123–25, 182.

55. Ibid., 140

56. Ibid., 105–6. The *Times* editorial reflected the paper's outspoken opposition to Governor-General Francis B. Harrison's policy of swift "Filipinization" of many colonial institutions, including the University of the Philippines. A 1914 editorial declared that giving Filipinos more authority meant a return to a time "when justice halted—when the masses of people were sunk in ignorance—when disease was rampant and unchecked—when roads were trails and bridges were few—when the seven devils of discontent bred revolution, and progress was a word unknown—when the intolerant few rode roughshod over many—when the weak staggered and fell, with none to raise them up and help them on." Dire warnings like this reflected a racially coded assessment of the Filipino capacity not only for self-government, but for basic administrative competence. See Paul A. Kramer, *The Blood of Government: Race, Empire, the United States, and the Philippines* (Chapel Hill: University of North Carolina Press, 2006), 363–69.

57. Vincente L. Rafael, *The Promise of the Foreign: Nationalism and the Technics of Translation in the Spanish Philippines* (Durham, N.C.: Duke University Press, 2005), 14–15.

58. Carlos Romulo, "The Tragedy of Our Anglo-Saxon Education," in *Encyclopedia of the Philippines*, ed. Zolio M. Galang (Manila: Exequiel Floro, 1950), vol. 1, 337–43.

59. Stuart Hall, *The Hard Road to Renewal* (London: Verso, 1988), 273.

60. While exactly when, why, and how the Cold War began remains a subject of continuing investigation, most historians date its inception to the last half of 1947 and the first half of 1948. See, for example, Gordon S. Barrass, *The Great Cold War: A Journey Through the Hall of Mirrors* (Stanford, Calif.: Stanford Security Studies, 2009), 50-56; Tony Judt, *Postwar: A History of Europe Since 1945* (New York: Penguin, 2005), 129–54; David Reynolds, "The European Dimensions of the Cold War," in *Origins of the Cold War: An International History*, ed. Melvyn P. Leffler and David S. Painter, 3rd ed. (New

York: Routledge, 2005), 173–75; John Lewis Gaddis, *We Now Know: Rethinking Cold War History* (New York: Oxford University Press, 1997), 26–53; Pierre de Senarclens, *From Yalta to the Iron Curtain: The Great Powers and the Origins of the Cold War*, trans. Amanda Pingree (Washington, D.C.: Berg, 1995) 212–38; James L. Gormly, *The Collapse of the Grand Alliance, 1945–1948* (Baton Rouge: Louisiana University Press, 1987), 154–73.

61. Quoted in David Holloway, "Stalin and the Bomb," in Leffler and Painter, *Origins of the Cold War*, 74.

62. E/CONF.6/SR.1. On the final collapse of the alliance, see Judt, *Postwar*, 123–26; Gaddis, *We Now Know*, 46–48.

63. Memorandum from Walter Kotschnig to Sandifer, et al., 1 March 1948, Box 10, Folder: "Mr. Kotschnig," Subject File, 1941–1951, Bureau of United Nations Affairs, RG 59, NARA.

64. E/CONF.6/SR.6; SD/E/Conf.6/19, April 1948, Box 46, Position Papers Maintained by the Executive Director, 1945–1974, Records of the Bureau of International Organization Affairs and Its Predecessors, RG 59, NARA.

65. E/CONF.6/C.1/SR.3.

66. A. W. Brian Simpson, *Human Rights and the End of Empire: Britain and the Genesis of the European Convention* (Oxford: Oxford University Press, 2001), 593–95.

67. International Conference on Freedom of Information, "Summary Record, Committee I," E/CONF.6/C.1/SR.6.

68. Michael L. Hoffman, "Free Press Parley Opens with Clash," *New York Times*, March 24, 1948, 13; ibid., E/CONF.6/SR.1.

69. Ibid., E/CONF.6/C.1/SR.14.

70. Ibid., E/CONF.6/C.1/SR.3.

71. Humphrey, *Human Rights and the United Nations*, 53; William Benton, "Report to Secretary Marshall," 1 May 1948, SD/E/Conf.6/19, Box 46, Position Papers Maintained by the Executive Director, 1945–1974, Records of the Bureau of International Organization Affairs and Its Predecessors, RG 59, General Records of the Department of State, NARA.

72. Ibid.; "Press Conference Lauded by Romulo," *New York Times*, May 4, 1948, 22; International Conference on Freedom of Information, "Summary Record, Committee I," E/CONF.6/SR.13.

73. Kenneth Cmiel, "Human Rights, Freedom of Information, and the Origins of Third World Solidarity," in *Truth Claims: Representations and Human Rights* (Piscataway, N.J.: Rutgers University Press, 2002), 107–30.

74. Alfred Sauvy, "Trois mondes, une planète," *L'Observateur*, August 14, 1952, 14. "We speak freely of two existing worlds," Sauvy wrote, "of their possible confrontation, of their coexistence, etc., forgetting all too often that a third one exists, the most important and indeed the first in chronological order. . . . For this Third World, ignored, exploited, scorned, like the Third Estate, also wants to be something." Significantly, he posited the *tiers monde* as heir of the *tiers état*, the "ignored, exploited, scorned" class

of eighteenth-century France in whose name the Declaration of the Rights of Man and of the Citizen was composed and proclaimed. Trans. from Robert Malley, "The Third Worldist Movement," *Current History* 98, 631 (1999): 360.

75. UNGA, *Official Records of the Third Session of the General Assembly, Part 2, Plenary Meetings of the General Assembly, Summary Records of Meetings April–May 1949* (hereafter *Third GA Session*) (New York: UN, 1950), 362–63. Noriega was a member of Mexico's long-ruling Institutional Revolutionary Party (PRI) and, like Romulo, had served as editor for one of the party's organs, *El Nacional*. See Cmiel, "Human Rights, Freedom of Information," 117.

76. *Third GA Session*, 372–73. A Maronite Christian from Lebanon, Baroody was employed by the Saudi monarchy to represent the kingdom at the UN until the late 1970s. Despite his "great charm," Humphrey noted that "he made many enemies" and he considered him a major impediment to the development of the UN human rights program (*Human Rights and the United Nations*, 135). Ralph Bunche apparently found Baroody's loquaciousness insufferable. On one occasion, Bunche found this attitude difficult to hide, provoking a concerted effort by Baroody to have him fired from the Secretariat. Brian Urquhart, *Ralph Bunche: An American Life* (New York: Norton, 1993), 410-11.

77. *Third GA Session*, 376.

78. Ibid., 386.

79. Cmiel, "Human Rights, Freedom of Information," 121.

80. *Third GA Session*, 369–70.

81. Ibid., 370.

82. Ibid., 423–27.

83. Thomas J. Hamilton, "Vishinsky Finds Going Rough at U.N. Assembly," *New York Times*, October 23, 1949.

84. Kathleen Teltsch, "U.N. Committee Votes to Shelve Pact on Freedom of Information," *New York Times*, September 28, 1949, 4.

85. SD/A/C.3/122, 29 August 1949, Box 26, Position Papers Maintained by the Executive Director, 1945–1974, Records of the Bureau of International Organization Affairs and Its Predecessors, RG 59, NARA.

86. UN, *Yearbook on Human Rights for 1950* (New York: UN, 1952), 475–82.

87. Romulo, "Statement by H. E. Ambassador Carlos P. Romulo," December 10, 1949, Papers of Carlos P. Romulo.

88. Carlos Romulo, "The Battle for Asia," *New York Times*, September 11, 1949, 68.

89. Richard H. Parke, "Acheson Stresses Self-Help by Lands We Have Assisted," *New York Times*, October 21, 1949, 1.

90. "U.N. Body Brings News Code Draft," *New York Times*, May 20, 1950, 4; Milton Bracker, "U.N. Group Assails Soviet's Jamming," *New York Times*, May 17, 1950, 3; Humphrey, *Human Rights and the United Nations,* 119–20.

91. Kathleen Teltsch, "U.N. Unit Proposes a New Press Group," *New York Times*, March 20, 1952, 13; Humphrey, *Human Rights and the United Nations*, 152.

92. "Informed World Urged," *New York Times*, October 27, 1953, 11; Humphrey, *Human Rights and the United Nations*, 190.

93. Salvador P. Lopez quoted in Roger J. Bresnahan, *Angles of Vision: Conversations on Philippines Literature* (Quezon City, Philippines: New Day, 1992), 110-11.

94. Carlos P. Romulo, *Crusade in Asia: Philippine Victory* (New York: John Day, 1955), 259–60, 272–73.

95. Romulo, "Cultural Changes of the Present," August 17, 1962, Box 4.4, Folder 301, "Carlos P. Romulo Papers—Speeches, Addresses, Messages, Etc. 1962 (AP-AG)," Papers of Carlos P. Romulo. Whether or not he was reading Ernest Renan, Romulo captured much of his most famous sentiment: "For, the essential element of a nation is that all its individuals must have many things in common but it must also have forgotten many things." See Ernst Renan, "What Is a Nation?" in *Becoming National: A Reader*, ed. Geoff Eley and Grigor Suny (New York: Oxford University Press, 1996), 41–55.

96. Romulo, "Our Cultural Identity in Asia," January 27, 1967, Papers of Carlos P. Romulo.

Chapter 4. Charles Malik, the International Bill of Rights, and Ultimate Things

1. "Politics and Personnel, General Assembly, United Nations, New York, October 23–December 16, 1946," 1947, Records of the Bureau of International Affairs and Its Predecessors, Box 13, Records of the Department of State [RG 59], NARA.

2. Kamal S. Salibi calls Malik's appointment as foreign minister in 1956 by Camille Chamoun "a declaration of policy" because of his strident "pro-western inclinations." See Kamal S. Salibi, *The Modern History of Lebanon* (Delmar, N.Y.: Caravan, 1977), 199. On Malik's Western orientation in outlook and policy, see also Caroline Attié, *Struggle in the Levant: Lebanon in the 1950s* (New York: Tauris, 2004) 106–8; Irene L. Gendzier, *Notes from the Minefield: United States Intervention in Lebanon and the Middle East, 1945–1958* (New York: Columbia University Press, 1997), 123–25; David C. Gordon, *Lebanon: The Fragmented Nation* (Stanford: Hoover Institute Press, 1980), 226–28.

3. Quoted in John P. Humphrey, *Human Rights & the United Nations: A Great Adventure* (Dobbs Ferry, N.Y.: Transnational, 1984), 18.

4. Charles Malik, "Lebanon and Human Rights: The Centrality of Freedom," in *The Challenge of Human Rights: Charles Malik and the Universal Declaration*, ed. Habib C. Malik (Oxford: Centre for Lebanese Studies, 2000), 16–18.

5. Humphrey, *Human Rights & the United Nations*, 17.

6. The notion of a "novel" human rights subject is brilliantly explored in Joseph R. Slaughter, *Human Rights, Inc.: The World Novel, Narrative Form, and International Law* (New York: Fordham University Press, 2007), especially chap. 1.

7. Charles Malik, "The Lebanon and the International Life," *Sommaire* (Beirut: Joseph and Aurore Oughourlian, 1948), 14–15, in Folder 5, Box 231, Papers of Charles H. Malik.

8. Memorandum of Conversation, 22 October 1946, Box 11, Folder: "Memoranda of Conversations, L–O," Subject File, 1941–1951, Bureau of United Nations Affairs, RG 59, General Records of the Department of State, NARA.

9. Malik corresponded regularly with Chiha until the latter's death in 1954. See Eyal Zisser, *Lebanon: The Challenge of Independence* (New York: Tauris, 2000), 13; and, more generally, Michelle Hartman and Alessandro Olsaretti, "'The First Boat and the First Oar': Inventions of Lebanon in the Writings of Michel Chiha," *Radical History Review* 86 (Spring 2003): 37–65; Kais M. Firro, "Lebanese Nationalism Versus Arabism: From Bulus Nujaym to Michel Chiha," *Middle Eastern Studies* 40, 5 (2004): 1–27; Ashur Kaufman, "Phoenicianism: The Formation of an Identity in Lebanon in 1920," *Middle Eastern Studies* 37, 1 (2001): 173–94.

10. Hartman and Olsaretti, "'The First Boat and the First Oar,'" 51–55.

11. Malik, "The Lebanon and the International Life," 13.

12. Ibid., 15.

13. Glenn Mitoma, "Charles H. Malik and Human Rights: Notes on a Biography," *Biography* 33, 1 (2010): 220–39.

14. Charles Malik, "The *Idea* of the School of Arts and Sciences of the American University of Beirut," June 20, 1942, Folder 4, Box 124, Papers of Charles H. Malik, 24–26.

15. Charles Malik, "Freedom of Thought," May 22, 1944, Folder 4, Box 208, Papers of Charles H. Malik, 51–52.

16. Ibid.

17. Johannes Morsink, *The Universal Declaration of Human Rights: Origins, Drafting, and Intent* (Philadelphia: University of Pennsylvania Press, 1999), 24; Mary Ann Glendon, *A World Made New: Eleanor Roosevelt and the Universal Declaration of Human Rights* (New York: Random House, 2001), 153–55; Vratislav Pechota, "The Development of the Covenant on Civil and Political Rights," in *The International Bill of Rights: The Covenant on Civil and Political Rights*, ed. Louis Henkin (New York: Columbia University Press, 1981), 48–49.

18. Baroody quoted in Morsink, *The Universal Declaration*, 24; Glendon, *A World Made New*, 153–55.

19. GA Third Session, 890. Zafrulla Khan was himself a convert to the small, evangelical Muslim Ahmadiyya sect, and would eventually find himself persecuted by his less tolerant countryman. Whether or not they agreed with the interpretation of Zafrulla Khan or Baroody, the other delegations from predominantly Muslim nations—Egypt, Iran, Iraq, Syria, and Turkey—all voted for the declaration.

20. "Speech by Charles Malik to the Third Committee of the General Assembly," November 15, 1946, Box 96, Folder 3, Papers of Charles H. Malik.

21. UNGA, "Resolution on the Political Rights of Women," December 11, 1946, E/RES/56(I); UNGA, "Summary Record of the Twenty-Third Meeting. Held at Lake Success, New York, on Friday, 15 November 1946, at 11 a.m. Journal No. 34: Supplement No. 3," A/C.3/80; "Women Hail Motion on World Equality," *New York Times*, December 12, 1946, 3. Elizabeth Thompson has noted that the gendered boundaries of citizenship in Syria and Lebanon were in large part legacies of the kind of colonial citizenship established under the French Mandate. See Elizabeth Thompson, *Colonial Citizens:*

Republican Rights, Paternal Privilege, and Gender in French Syria and Lebanon (New York: Columbia University Press, 2000), 246–70. The establishment of full women's suffrage and right to hold public office in Lebanon would come in 1953 as part of a package of reforms by President Camille Chamoun, designed in part to reduce sectarianism in Lebanese politics. See Attié, *Struggle in the Levant*, 48–52.

22. Copies and or summaries of many of these letters are included in Malik's papers. See "List of Communications Submitted to the Commission on Human Rights," Folder 5, Box 75, Papers of Charles H. Malik.

23. SD/CN.4/2, January 16, 1947, Box 43, Position Papers Maintained by the Executive Director, 1945–1974, Records of the Bureau of International Organization Affairs and Its Predecessors, RG 59, NARA.

24. "The More Important Speeches and Interventions of Dr. Charles Malik, Representative of Lebanon and Rapporteur of the Commission," Verbatim Records, United Nations Human Rights Commission, First Session Jan. 27–Feb. 10, 1947, February 7, 1947, 66, Box 76, Folder 9, Papers of Charles H. Malik.

25. UNCHR, "Summary Record of the Fourth Meeting. Held at Lake Success, New York, on Tuesday, 28 January 1947, at 2.30 p.m.," E/CN.4/SR.4.

26. Ibid.; UNCHR, "Summary Record of the Twenty-Second and Last Meeting. Held at Lake Success, New York, on Monday, 10 February 1947, at 2.30 p.m.," E/CN.4/SR.20.

27. UNCHR, "Report to the Economic and Social Council on the First Session of the Commission, Held at Lake Success, New York, from 27 January to 10 February 1947," E/259; United Nations Economic and Social Council [ECOSOC], "Economic and Social Council resolution on communications concerning human rights," August 5, 1947, E/RES/75(V).

28. UNCHR, "Summary Record of the First Meeting. Held at Lake Success, New York, on Monday, 27 January 1947, at 11 a.m.," E/CN.4/SR.1.

29. Malik, "Lebanon and Human Rights: The Centrality of Freedom," 16–17.

30. UNCHR, Drafting Committee, "Summary Record of the Tenth Meeting. Held at Lake Success, New York, on Wednesday, 18 June 1947, at 3.30 p.m.," E/CN.4/AC.1/SR.10; Undated handwritten note [c.1947], Box 80, Folder 7, Papers of Charles H. Malik.

31. UNCHR, Drafting Committee, "Summary Record of the Fifth Meeting. Held at Lake Success, New York, on Thursday, 12 June 1947, at 2.30 p.m.," E/CN.4/AC.1/5; E/CN.4/AC.1/10.

32. UNCHR, "Summary Record of Thirty-Eighth Meeting. Held at the Palais des Nations, Geneva, on Monday, 15 December 1947, at 9 a.m.," E/CN.4/SR.39.

33. SD/CN.4/2, December 6, 1946, Box 43, Position Papers Maintained by the Executive Director, 1945–1974, Records of the Bureau of International Organization Affairs and Its Predecessors, RG 59, NARA.

34. Morsink, *The Universal Declaration*, 17; Glendon, *A World Made New*, 84–85; A. W. Simpson, *Human Rights and the End of Empire: Britain and the Genesis of the European Conventions* (New York, Oxford University Press, 2001), 431.

35. E/CN.4/AC.1/SR.10; Simpson, *Human Rights and the End of Empire*, 416.

36. UNCHR, "Summary Record of Twenty-Eighth Meeting. Held at the Palais des Nations, Geneva, on Thursday, 4 December 1947, at 10 a.m.," E/CN.4/SR.28; UNCHR; "Summary Record of Twenty-Ninth Meeting. Held at the Palais des Nations, Geneva, on Thursday, 4 December 1947, at 3 p.m.," E/CN.4/SR.29.

37. UNCHR, "Summary Record of Thirty-Second Meeting. Held at the Palais des Nations, Geneva, on Thursday, 11 December 1947, at 10 a.m.," E/CN.4/SR.32; UNCHR, "Summary Record of Thirty-Third Meeting. Held at the Palais des Nations, Geneva, on Thursday, 11 December 1947, at 3 p.m.," E/CN.4/SR.33.

38. UNCHR, "Summary Record of Thirty-Sixth Meeting. Held At The Palais Des Nations, Geneva, On Saturday, 13 December 1947, At 10 a.m.," E/CN.4/SR.36; UNCHR, "Summary Record Of Thirty-Eighth Meeting.

39. UNCHR, "Summary Record of Forty-Second Meeting. Held at the Palais des Nations, Geneva, on Tuesday, 16 December 1947, at 9 a.m.," E/CN.4/SR.42.

40. Hannah Arendt, *The Origins of Totalitarianism*, new ed. with added prefaces (New York: Harcourt Brace, 1979), 290-97.

41. UNCHR, "Summary Record of the 8th Meeting. Held at Lake Success, New York, on Friday 31 January 1947," E/CN.4/SR.8; Morsink, *The Universal Declaration*, 15.

42. Karl Marx, "On the Jewish Question," in *Karl Marx: Selected Writings*, ed. David McLellan (New York: Oxford University Press, 1977), 54.

43. UNCHR, "Summary Record of the 9th Meeting held at Lake Success, New York, on Saturday, 1 February 1947," E/CN.6/SR.9. For a less than flattering account of Dukes's participation in the council, see Simpson, *Human Rights and the End of Empire*, 351.

44. UNCHR, "Summary Record of the Tenth Meeting. Held at Lake Success, New York, on Saturday, 1 February 1947, at 3 p.m.," E/CN.4/SR.14.

45. Ibid.; Charles Malik, "Four Basic Principles," in Habib Malik, *Challenge of Human Rights*, 27–29.

46. E/CN.4/SR.14.

47. Ibid.

48. Ibid.; Charles H. Malik, "An Ontology of Moslem-Arab Existence in Its Relations to the West in General and to the United States in Particular," March 26, 1947, Box 207, Folder 2, Papers of Charles H. Malik.

49. Human rights theorist Jack Donnelly articulates a contemporary Lockean view of rights that encompasses the kinds of social obligations and limitations on private property that Malik would have been sympathetic toward. See Jack Donnelly, *Universal Human Rights in Theory & Practice* (Ithaca, N.Y.: Cornell University Press, 1989), 88–106. Nevertheless, Malik was a self-professed Thomist in his sense of the grounding of rights, an orientation that, according to Donnelly, would place him on the far side of the divide between "high medieval and modern political thought." See Jack Donnelly, "Natural Law and Right in Aquinas' Political Thought," *Western Political Quarterly* 33, 4 (Dec. 1980): 520-35.

50. Charles Malik to Julian Knipp, November 19, 1935, Box 26, Folder 12; Charles

Malik to William Hocking, December 1, 1935, Box 54, Folder 2, both Papers of Charles H. Malik.

51. Charles Malik, "Fourteen Months in Germany," October 29, 1936, Box 207, Folder 5, Papers of Charles H. Malik, 9–11.

52. Charles Malik to Frederick C. Lawrence, November 26, 1935, Box 30, Folder 1, Papers of Charles H. Malik.

53. Charles Malik to Afif Tannous, July 31, 1931, Box 48, Folder 2, Papers of Charles H. Malik.

54. Malik, "Fourteen Months in Germany," 11.

55. UNCHR, Drafting Committee, "Twenty-First Meeting, Held at Lake Success, 4 May 1948 at 10:30 a.m.," E/CN.4/AC.1/SR.21.

56. Charles Malik, "Required: National Moral Leadership," in Habib Malik, *Challenge of Human Rights*, 95.

57. Morsink, *The Universal Declaration*, 272–75.

58. UNCHR, "Summary Record of the Seventy-Third Meeting. Held at Lake Success, New York on Tuesday, 15 June 1948, at 10:45 a.m.," E/CN.4/SR.73.

59. Ibid. The evolution of the Indian position may have reflected the fact that the explosion of communal violence and subsequent mass migrations after the August 1947 India-Pakistan partition made the question of minority rights far more politically sensitive on the subcontinent.

60. Simpson, *Human Rights and the End of Empire*, 444; E/CN.4/AC.2/SR.6; Mitoma, "Charles H. Malik and Human Rights," 225–32.

61. UNCHR, Drafting Committee, "Thirty-Eighth Meeting."

62. UNCHR, Drafting Committee, "Twenty-Ninth Meeting." The bifurcation of the single covenant into the International Covenant on Civil and Political Rights and the International Covenant on Economic, Social and Cultural Rights would come later as, Daniel J. Whelan has argued, a symbol of the clash between the First and Third World: *Indivisible Human Rights: A History* (Philadelphia: University of Pennsylvania Press, 2010), 114.

63. Philosopher Thomas Pogge has argued that Article 28 may be "the most surprising and potentially most consequential sentence of the entire *Universal Declaration*," as it provides the ground for demanding moral responsibility from "the institutional order of any comprehensive social system." See Thomas Pogge, "Human Rights and Human Responsibilities," in *Global Justice and Transnational Politics*, ed. Pablo De Greiff and Ciaran Cronin (Cambridge, Mass.: MIT Press, 2002), 65–68.

64. UNCHR, "Summary Record of the Sixty-Fourth Meeting, Held at Lake Success, New York on Tuesday, 8 June 1948, at 3:00 p.m.," E/CN.4/SR.64.

65. UNCHR, "Summary Record of the Sixty-Fifth Meeting, Held at Lake Success, New York on Tuesday, 9 June 1948, at 10:00 a.m.," E/CN.4/SR.65.

66. UNCHR, "Summary Record of the Seventy-First Meeting, Held at Lake Success, New York on Tuesday, 14 June 1948, at 10:45 a.m.," E/CN.4/SR.71.

67. E/CN.4/SR.73.

68. Glendon, *A World Made New*, 123–71; Michael Hoffman, "U.S. Labor Position Is Cited to Russians," *New York Times*, August 19, 1948, 6.

69. John P. Humphrey, *On the Edge of Greatness: The Diaries of John Humphrey, First Director of the United Nations Division of Human Rights*, vol. 1, *1948–1949*, ed. A. J. Hobbins (Montreal: McGill University Libraries, 1994), 24; Michael Hoffman, "U.N. Social Council Closes at Geneva," *New York Times*, August 29, 1948, 16.

70. "Discord Held Bar to U.N. Social Task," *New York Times*, September 28, 1948, 10; "Dr. Malik's View: A Summation," in Habib Malik, *Challenge of Human Rights*, 115; Glendon, *A World Made New*, 161–63. While none voted against it, seven abstentions were recorded from the six Soviet bloc countries and, oddly enough, Canada, which had some lingering concerns regarding federalism. Neither Saudi Arabia nor South Africa recorded a vote.

71. "Speech of Thursday 9 December 1948," in Habib Malik, *Challenge of Human Rights*, 117–25.

72. GA Third Session, *Part 1, Plenary Meetings of the General Assembly, Summary Records of Meetings 21 September–12 December 1948* (New York: UN, 1949), 910-11, 923, 929, 933.

73. Charles Malik, "Spiritual Implications of the Human Rights Covenant," in *Christian Responsibility in World Affairs: A Symposium* (New York: Commission of the Churches in International Affairs, 1949), 7–8. On the opposition of the ABA, see Chapter 5.

74. United Nations, *Yearbook on Human Rights, 1949* (New York: UN Publications, 1951), 330-32. Peng-Chun Chang certainly had reason to be distracted as mainland Nationalist forces were in their final stages of collapse during the spring of 1949, with Mao's armies taking Nanking, Han-k'ou, Shanghai, and Sian as Chang chaired the fifth session.

75. Hobbins, *Diaries of John Humphrey*, 178.

76. Charles Malik, *War and Peace* (Stamford, Conn.: Overbrook, 1950), 31–33; "West Wins in U.N. on Peace Project," *New York Times*, 26 November 1949, 1.

77. Malik, *War and Peace*, 23–26, 34.

78. Albert Hourani, quoted in Derek Hopwood, "Albert Hourani: Islam, Christianity, and Orientalism," *British Journal of Middle Eastern Studies* 30, 2 (2003): 128; Albert Hourani, *Arabic Thought in the Liberal Age: 1789–1939* (New York: Oxford University Press, 1962), 351–52.

79. Charles Malik to James K. Quay, April 14, 1937, Box 38, Folder 9, Papers of Charles H. Malik.

80. NSC-68, "United States Objectives and Programs for National Security," *FRUS 1950*, vol. 1, 238.

81. Steven Casey, "Selling NSC-68: The Truman Administration, Public Opinion, and the Politics of Mobilization, 1950-51," *Diplomatic History* 29, 4 (September 2005): 667.

82. NSC-68, 241.

83. John Lewis Gaddis, "NSC 68 and the Problem of Ends and Means," *International Security* 4, 4 (Spring 1980): 167.

84. Gary B. Ostrower, *The United Nations and the United States* (New York: Twayne, 1998), 59–65.

85. L. H. Woolsey, "The 'Uniting for Peace' Resolution of the United Nations," *American Journal of International Law*, 45, 1 (January 1951): 129–31.

86. Rowland M. Brucken, "A Most Uncertain Crusade: The United States, Human Rights and the United Nations, 1941–1954" (Ph.D. dissertation, Ohio State University, 1999), 231; Pechota, "The Development of the Covenant on Civil and Political Rights," 47–48; Humphrey, *On the Edge of Greatness*, 107–8.

87. Charles Malik to George Hakim, June 20, 1950, Box 20, Folder 1, Papers of Charles H. Malik.

88. Charles Malik, "Sixth Session of the Commission on Human Rights" in Habib Malik, *Challenge of Human Rights*, 182–92.

89. Charles Malik, "America in the World," November 16, 1950, 17, Folder 4, Box 86, Papers of Charles H. Malik.

90. Charles Malik, "The Prospect of Freedom," February 19, 1951, Box 86, Folder 4, Papers of Charles H. Malik.

91. Charles Malik, "For a Policy of True Humanism," *Commonweal*, October 12, 1951, 8.

92. Charles Malik, "The Problem of Asia," December 11, 1950, Folder 4, Box 86, Papers of Charles H. Malik. Ranging over topics as diverse as the nature of science, the necessity of reason, and the essence of the democratic way of life, in this speech, Malik argued that Asia, if it was to assume its rightful place in the world, needed to adopt a conception of humans that acknowledged the individual as "an end in himself" and the supreme importance of freedom of thought and conscience. His analysis managed to attract the attention of John Dewey who, still sharp at ninety-one, wrote to congratulate Malik on his description of the nature of science and democracy. "I could only wish there were more people in the West," Dewey wrote, "who understand as clearly as you do the paramount need of extending and deepening scientific culture if we are ever to solve our problems as rational human beings and not as blind creatures, inflamed with passions, bent on destroying one another." John Dewey to Charles Malik, December 15, 1950, Box 86, Folder 4, Papers of Charles H. Malik.

93. "Position of United States Concerning Draft Covenant on Human Rights in ECOSOC and General Assembly," memorandum of conversation, May 29, 1951, Box 8, Folder: "Human Rights, Miscellaneous, Jan. 1, 1950 to Oct. 18, 1951," Subject Files of Durward V. Sandifer, Deputy Assistant Secretary of State for United Nations Affairs, 1944–1954, RG 59, NARA.

94. Quoted in Glendon, *A World Made New*, 199.

95. United Nations, *Yearbook on Human Rights, 1951* (New York: UN, 1953), 524–36.

96. Whelan, *Indivisible Human Rights*, 134.

97. In addition to lauding Malik's stewardship, Humphrey credited the fact that the

commission was meeting in Geneva away from the distractions of New York, and that the Soviet Union was, at least in the early going, "extremely cooperative." Humphrey, *On the Edge of Greatness*, 144–46; Charles Malik, "Progress on Covenant of Human Rights," Habib Malik, *Challenge of Human Rights*, 204.

98. *Humphrey Diaries*, 133–36; SD/E/CN.4/56, 57, 58: all three 1951, Box 44, Position Papers Maintained by the Executive Director, 1945–1974, Records of the Bureau of International Organization Affairs and Its Predecessors, RG 56, NARA.

99. Charles Malik, "Progress on Covenant of Human Rights," in Habib Malik, *Challenge of Human Rights*, 204.

100. Charles Malik, "Statement to the Bureau de Presse français," June 15, 1952, in ibid., 211–12.

101. Malik, "More Human Rights in the United Nations," 219–20. The notable exception to these voting patterns was on the issue of communications, which had been swept under the rug during the first 1947 session. When the Indian delegate proposed that the rules be modified to allow the commission to bring to the attention of the Economic and Social Council serious human rights violations alleged in certain communications, the U.S., UK, France, and China joined with the Soviet Union, Ukraine, and Poland to block it. Evidently, ideological posturing only went so far. See Humphrey, *On the Edge of Greatness*, 189.

102. Malik, "More Human Rights in the United Nations," 223–25.

103. Ibid., 231–32; Charles Malik, "Reflections on the United Nations," *Christian Century*, 18 March 1953, 314–317, Folder 5, Box 232, Papers of Charles H. Malik.

104. Pechota, "The Development of the Covenant on Civil and Political Rights," 54–64; Charles Malik, "From Dr. Malik's Diaries," December 9, 1954, in Habib Malik, *Challenge of Human Rights*, 234–35. In his despair over the state of things at the UN, Malik had come full circle—not only to his original appraisal of the value of the international organization, but also to his sense that politics in general was a corrupt and worldly realm from which little of value could be expected. Instead it was "the living institutions of the mind and the spirit"—the church and the university—which would eventually stem the tide of "the materialistic revolution" and reaffirm mankind's faith in "truth, justice, and order."

105. Beth A. Simmons, *Mobilizing for Human Rights: International Law in Domestic Politics* (New York: Cambridge University Press, 2009), 49–55.

106. George Middleton quoted in Attié, *Struggle in the Levant*, 107.

107. Ibid., 117.

108. Gordon, *Lebanon*, 227–28. Like Carlos Romulo's service to the Marcos regime, Malik's association with the Lebanese Forces—whose military wing facilitated the massacres at the Sabra and Shatila refugee camps—undermines any effort to depict him as a human rights hero. Indeed, the paradox of Malik's efforts on behalf of human rights in the 1940s and '50s and his militant support of the Lebanese Forces cause in the 1970s and '80s indicates the distance between the human rights project of the immediate postwar period and that of the Cold War.

109. R. D. McLaurin, "Lebanon and the United States," in *Lebanon and the World in the 1980s* (College Park: Center for International Development and Conflict Resolution, University of Maryland, 1983), 106–10.

110. Charles H. Malik, "Will the Future Redeem the Past?" November 6, 1960, Box 220, Folder 5, Papers of Charles H. Malik.

Chapter 5. The NAACP, the ABA, and the Logic of Containment

1. X [George Kennan], "The Sources of Soviet Conduct," *Foreign Affairs* 25 (July 1947): 575–76.

2. George F. Kennan to Carlisle Humelsine, July 8, 1948, Box 8, Folder "Human Rights, General, 1948," Subject Files of Durward V. Sandifer, Deputy Assistant Secretary of State for United Nations Affairs, 1944–1954, RG 59, NARALL.

3. Ibid.

4. W. E. B. Du Bois to Walter White, n.d. [August 1946], Box A634, Folder "General Office Files, United Nations, General, 1945–46," Papers of the NAACP, Group II, Manuscripts Division, Library of Congress.

5. Carol Anderson, *Eyes Off the Prize: The United Nations and the African American Struggle for Human Rights, 1944–1955* (New York: Cambridge University Press, 2003). While it is true, as Anderson maintains, that the Cold War had a "devastating" effect on the possibility of establishing an African American discourse of human rights, it should also be remembered that the Cold War provided a critical opening for transforming a political and cultural dynamic that, since at least the 1880s, had worked against federal intervention on behalf of African Americans. See Mary L. Dudziak, *Cold War Civil Rights: Race and the Image of American Democracy* (Princeton, N.J.: Princeton University Press, 2000); and Thomas Borstlemann, *The Cold War and the Color Line: American Race Relations in the Global Arena* (Cambridge, Mass.: Harvard University Press, 2001).

6. Prior to the legal campaign to end segregation that culminated in the *Brown v. Board of Education* decision, the attempt to secure federal antilynching legislation was the NAACP's signature issue. See Robert Zangrando, *The NAACP Crusade Against Lynching, 1909–1950* (Philadelphia: Temple University Press, 1980).

7. Anderson, *Eyes Off the Prize*, 20–22; David H. Anthony, III, "Max Yergan in South Africa: From Evangelical Pan-Africanist to Revolutionary Socialist," *African Studies Review* 34, 2 (Sep. 1991): 27–55.

8. Anderson, 20–22, *Eyes Off the Prize*; George Streator, "Negro Congress Appeals to U.N.," *New York Times*, 2 June 1946, 33; "U.N. Gets Negroes' Plea," *New York Times*, 7 June 1946, 9.

9. "Summary Record of the Presentation of a Petition by Dr. Max Yergan, President, National Negro Congress," June 6, 1946, Box A637, Folder "United Nations, Petition, 1946," Papers of the NAACP, Group II.

10. Anderson, *Eyes Off the Prize*, 84–87; Roland W. Brucken, "A Most Uncertain Crusade: The United States, Human Rights and the United Nations, 1941–1954" (Ph.D. dissertation, Ohio State University, 1999),143–46. Over the next 18 months, Yergan and

the NNC worked valiantly to publicize the petition, but to no avail. Riven by organizational dysfunction and economic insolvency, the NNC collapsed with a whimper in November 1947.

11. E/CN.4/SR.4; SD/CN.4/2, January 16, 1947, Box 43, Position Papers Maintained by the Executive Director, 1945–1974, Records of the Bureau of International Organization Affairs and Its Predecessors, RG 59, NARA.

12. W. E. B. Du Bois to the American Delegation, May 16, 1945, Box A639, Folder "United Nations, the United Nations Conference on International Organization, 1945 May 11–June," Papers of the NAACP, Group II.

13. Du Bois to Walter White, 26 March 1946; Du Bois to White, 1 August 1946: both Box A634, Folder "General Office Files, United Nations, General, 1945–46," Papers of the NAACP, Group II; Anderson, *Eyes Off the Prize*, 50-55; David Levering Lewis, *W. E. B. Du Bois: The Fight for Equality and the American Century, 1919–1963* (New York: Holt, 2000), 504–10.

14. Du Bois to Walter White, memo, March 26, 1946; White to Du Bois, memo, March 28, 1946, both Box A634, Folder "General Office Files, United Nations, General, 1945–46," Papers of the NAACP, Group II.

15. Walter White, *A Rising Wind* (Garden City, N.Y.: Doubleday, 1945), 144. Generally on White, see his autobiography, *A Man Called White: The Autobiography of Walter White* (New York: Viking, 1948); and Kenneth Robert Janken, *White: A Biography of Walter White, Mr. NAACP* (New York: New Press, 2003). On the rise of African American anticolonialism, see Penny M. Von Eschen, *Race Against Empire: Black Americans and Anticolonialism, 1937–1957* (Ithaca, N.Y.: Cornell University Press, 1997).

16. Anderson, *Eyes Off the Prize*, 94–95; Levering Lewis, *W. E. B. Du Bois*, 521–22.

17. Kenneth Robert Janken, *Rayford W. Logan and the Dilemma of the African-American Intellectual* (Amherst: University of Massachusetts Press, 1993), 111, 180. Logan was no lawyer, let alone an international lawyer, but the arguments he advanced in the NAACP petition have steadily, if still only slightly, gained ground in international law circles. Prominent Columbia Law School Professor Oscar Schachter wrote in 1991 that while "only a few legal scholars" claim the UN Charter creates a binding obligation to promote and defend specific human rights standards, "it is not inconceivable that in time they will carry the day." Oscar Schachter, "International Law in Theory and Practice," in *International Human Rights in Context: Law, Politics, Morals*, 2nd ed., ed. Henry J. Steiner and Philip Alston (New York: Oxford University Press, 2000), 229.

18. Du Bois to White, 29 January 1947; Du Bois, "Chronology of NAACP U.N. Petition," June 1948: both Box A637, Folder "United Nations, Petition, 1948–49," Papers of the NAACP, Group II; Anderson, *Eyes Off the Prize*, 101.

19. Anderson, *Eyes Off the Prize*, 102; Du Bois to White, 24 November 1947, Box A634, Folder "General Office Files, United Nations, General, 1947," Papers of the NAACP, Group II.

20. Du Bois to V. L. Pandit, 18 September 1947, Box A637, Folder "United Nations,

Petition, 1947, Jan-Sept."; Pandit to Du Bois, 25 September 25, 1947, both Papers of the NAACP, Group II.

21. Du Bois to John Humphrey, October 16, 1947, Papers of the NAACP, Group II.

22. George Streator, "Negroes to Bring Cause to U.N.," *New York Times*, October 12, 1947.

23. Walter White, "Introductory Statement by Walter White, Executive Director of the NAACP," 23 October 1947, Box A637, Folder "United Nations, Petition, 1947, Oct.," Papers of the NAACP, Group II.

24. Du Bois, "Statement of W. E. B. Du Bois to the Representatives of the Human Rights Commission and Its Parent Bodies, the Economic and Social Council and the General Assembly," October 23, 1947, Papers of the NAACP, Group II.

25. George Streator, "U.N. Gets Charges of Wide Bias in U.S.," *New York Times*, October 24, 1947; Anderson, *Eyes Off the Prize*, 104–5.

26. Walter White to Du Bois, 12 November 1947, Box A635, Folder "General Office Files, United Nations, General Assembly, 1946–Aug, 1948," Papers of the NAACP, Group II.

27. Du Bois to White, 24 November 1947, Papers of the NAACP, Group II.

28. White to Du Bois, 18 November 1947, Box A637, Folder "United Nations, Petition, 1947, Nov.–Dec.," Papers of the NAACP, Group II.

29. Anderson, *Eyes Off the Prize*, 130-65.

30. John Maktos to Ernest A. Gross, Memo, October 2, 1947, Box 89, Folder: "Human Rights-General," Office of the Legal Advisor, Division of United Nations Affairs, 1945–1959, Miscellaneous Lot Files, 1944–1959, RG 59, NARA.

31. Ernest A. Gross to Tom Clark, 4 November 1947, Box 89, Folder: "Human Rights-General," Office of the Legal Advisor, Division of United Nations Affairs. The Truman administration did, in fact, file an amicus brief on behalf of the plaintiffs in *Shelley v. Kraemer*—a landmark event—and the practice would continue in civil rights cases through *Brown v. Board of Education*. See Mark V. Tushnet, *Making Civil Rights Law: Thurgood Marshall and the Supreme Court, 1936–1961* (New York: Oxford University Press, 1994), 81–98. Mary Dudziak has argued that this novel participation on the part of the Truman administration was spurred in large part by the growing recognition that gross racial injustice at home was a liability abroad. See Mary L. Dudziak, *Cold War Civil Rights: Race and the Image of American Democracy* (Princeton, N.J.: Princeton University Press, 2000), 90-114.

32. Maktos to Gross, October 2, 1947.

33. Gross to Clark, November 4, 1947.

34. Anderson, *Eyes Off the Prize*, 109-11; Eleanor Roosevelt to Walter White, January 20, 1948, Box A635, Folder "General Office Files, United Nations, General Assembly, 1946–Aug, 1948," Papers of the NAACP, Group II.

35. Norbert C. Brockman, "The History of the American Bar Association: A Bibliographic Essay," *American Journal of Legal History* 6, 3 (July 1962): 272–74.

36. R. E. L. Saner, "How Bar Can Promote Better Citizenship," *American Bar Association Journal* 9 (1923): 113–14.

37. Rome G. Brown, "The Socialist Menace to Constitutional Government," *American Bar Association Journal* 4 (1918): 54–56. The conservative bent of ABA policies eventually produced a split in the organization resulting in the formation of the National Lawyers Guild as a decidedly more progressive alternative in 1937.

38. "Part III. Committee Reports," American Bar Association Section of International and Comparative Law Proceedings 1942–1943, 40–65.

39. "House of Delegates Begins Action as to Post-War Problems for Lawyers," *American Bar Association Journal* 29, 4 (1943): 245–51.

40. "House of Delegates Mid-Year Meeting—Third Session," *American Bar Association Journal* 30, 4 (1944): 233–37.

41. The original name was the Committee on the Proposals for the Organization of Nations for Peace, Justice, and Law (it should be noted that "justice" was removed in the renaming). "New Special Committee on Post-War Organization of the Nations," *American Bar Association Journal* 30, 4 (1944): 274. The Comparative and International Law Section continued to press for a more progressive stance and was responsible for a 1946 ABA resolution opposing the so-called Connally Amendment to the U.S. declaration of adherence to the compulsory jurisdiction of the International Court of Justice. Written by Senator Tom Connally (D-Tex.), who had served as a delegate to the San Francisco conference, the amendment adopted and extended the language of UN Charter Article 2(7) to state that compulsory jurisdiction would not apply to matters "essentially within the domestic jurisdiction of the United States *as determined by the United States*" (emphasis added). The ABA resolution urged reconsideration, calling the amendment "a serious backward step" for the court. Michla Pomerance, *The United States and the World Court as a "Supreme Court of the Nations": Dreams, Illusions and Disillusion* (The Hague: Kluwer Law, 1996), 222–37; "The Law: Chance to Go Forward," *Time*, September 5, 1960.

42. "Covenant on Human Rights: House Acts as to Measures for Implementation," *American Bar Association Journal* 34 3 (1948): 277–78; "UN Rights Court Opposed by Bar," *New York Times*, February 26, 1948, 4.

43. "Declaration on Human Rights: Canadian, American Bars Ask Delay of Action," *American Bar Association Journal* 34 10 (1948): 881–82.

44. Despite his wide-ranging experience, the invariably crew-cut Holman cultivated a decidedly provincial image; see Frank E. Holman, *The Life and Career of a Western Lawyer, 1886–1961* (Baltimore: Port City Press, 1963); Charles W. Harris, "Alien Enemy Hearing Board as a Judicial Device in the United States During World War II," *International and Comparative Law Quarterly* 14, 4 (Oct. 1965): 1360-63; "Alien Cases to go to Hearing Board," *New York Times*, December 16, 1941, 29.

45. Frank E. Holman, "World Government No Answer to America's Desire for Peace," *American Bar Association Journal* 32, 10 (1946): 719–20.

46. Lawrence E. Davies, "Liberty Whittled, Head of Bar Warns," *New York Times*, September 10, 1948, 21.

47. "Bar Warned on U.N. 'State Socialism,'" *Los Angeles Times*, September 18, 1948, 4; Gladwin Hill, "U.N. Rights Drafts Held Socialistic," *New York Times*, September 18, 1948, 4.

48. Frank E. Holman, "Human Rights on Pink Paper," *American Affairs* 11 (January 1949): 18–24. See also Natalie Hevener Kaufman, *Human Rights Treaties and the Senate: A History of Opposition* (Chapel Hill: University of North Carolina Press, 1990), 16–36.

49. Durward Sandifer to James Simsarian, February 18, 1949, Box 8, Folder: "Human Rights, 1949," Subject Files of Durward V. Sandifer, Deputy Assistant Secretary of State for United Nations Affairs, 1944–1954, RG 59, NARA.

50. James Simsarian to Durward Sandifer, February 21, 1949, Sandifer Subject Files.

51. James Simsarian, "Three Regional Meetings of the American Bar Association on Human Rights," 22 March 1949, Box 8, Folder: "Human Rights, 1949," Sandifer Subject Files.

52. Frank F. Chuman, *The Bamboo People: The Law and Japanese-Americans* (Delmar, Calif.: Publisher's Inc., 1976), 76–80.

53. Ibid., 218–19.

54. "Sei Fujii v. State of California," *American Journal of International Law* 44, 2 (1950): 590-91.

55. "UN Charter Invalidates Alien Land Law," *Stanford Law Review* 2, 4 (1950): 797–809.

56. Manly O. Hudson, "Charter Provisions on Human Rights in American Law," *American Journal of International Law* 44, 3 (1950): 543–48. Quincy Wright was among those who supported the original California decision but his response to Hudson's article fell, at least within the legal community, on deaf ears. Quincy Wright, "National Courts and Human Rights—The Fujii Case," *American Journal of International Law* 45, 1 (1951): 62–82.

57. "Genocide Treaty Urged in Senate," *New York Times*, January 24, 1950, 5.

58. "Bar Leaders Score Genocide Compact," *New York Times*, January 25, 1950, 9.

59. Kaufman, *Human Rights Treaties and the Senate*, 16–36; Lawrence J. LeBlanc, *The United States and the Genocide Convention* (Durham, N.C.: Duke University Press, 1991), 103.

60. "Genocide Action Put Off," *New York Times*, September 1, 1950, 7. In preparing the convention for a full Senate vote, members of the Foreign Relations Committee had been careful to attach a series of "understandings" that protected states rights generally and ensured that the convention would not function as an "international anti-lynching law" in particular.

61. Frank E. Holman, "The Greatest Threat to American Freedom," *Wyoming Law Journal* 8 (1963): 26; *Sei Fujii v. State of California* (1952), 38 C2d 718.

62. Judith Resnik, "Law's Migration: American Exceptionalism, Silent Dialogues, and Federalism's Multiple Ports of Entry," *Yale Journal of Law* 115, 7 (May 2006): 598–1609.

63. Frank E. Holman, "Treaty Law-Making: A Blank Check for Writing a New Constitution," *American Bar Association Journal* 36, 9 (1950): 393, 397.

64. Kaufman, *Human Rights Treaties and the Senate,* 23–24.

65. W. H. Lawrence, "Stevenson Terms G.O.P Isolationism Aid to Communists," *New York Times,* October 23, 1952, 1.

66. Kaufman, *Human Rights Treaties and the Senate,* 94–116. On Senator Bricker, see Richard O. Davies, *Defender of the Old Guard: John Bricker and American Politics* (Columbus: Ohio State University Press, 1993).

67. John Foster Dulles to Jefferson Davis, February 2, 1949, Box 8, Folder: "Human Rights, 1949"; Durward Sandifer to John Foster Dulles, February 4, 1949, both Sandifer Subject Files.

68. "Dulles Issues Plea for Stronger U.N.," *New York Times,* December 12, 1952, 1.

69. Herman Phleger and John D. Hickerson to John Foster Dulles, February 18, 1953, Sandifer Subject Files.

70. "Text of Dulles Statement Opposing Curb on Treaty-Making Power," *New York Times,* April 7, 1953, 14.

71. "Mrs. O. B. Lord Gets Mrs. Roosevelt's Post," *New York Times,* January 17, 1953, 1; "Dulles Bars Pacts of U.N. on Rights," *New York Times,* April 7, 1953, 1.

72. E/CN.4/SR.339; SD/A/C.3/169/Rev. 1, September 8, 1953, Box 28, Position Papers Maintained by the Executive Director, 1945–1974, Bureau of International Organization Affairs Records, RG59, NARA. On the eve of the ninth session, John Humphrey wrote to Malik lamenting his absence and expressing doubts about the commission's future prospects. "There are nine new members of the Commission some of whom know very little indeed about our work." John Humphrey to Charles Malik, April 9, 1953, Box 80, Folder 4, Papers of Charles H. Malik, Manuscripts Division, Library of Congress.

73. "Summary of Meeting," September 24, 1951, Sandifer Subject Files.

74. SD/A/C.1/206/Rev.1, n.d. [1949], Position Papers Maintained by the Executive Director, 1945–1974, Bureau of International Organization Affairs Records, RG59, NARA.

75. John Lewis Gaddis, *We Now Know: Rethinking Cold War History* (New York: Oxford University Press, 1997), 26–53; Tony Judt, *Postwar: A History of Europe Since 1945* (New York: Penguin, 2005), 129–53.

76. Peter Kenez, "The Hungarian Communist Party and the Catholic Church," *Journal of Modern History* 75, 4 (2003): 885–88. Cardinal Mindszenty's account of the episode appears in his *Memoirs* (New York: Macmillan, 1974).

77. Camille M. Cianfarra, "Pope Pius Is Shocked and Grieved by Arrest of Primate of Hungary," *New York Times,* December 28, 1948, 8.

78. SD/A/C.1/206/Rev.1; Secretary of State to U.S. Mission at the UN, March 22, 1949, Telegram 181, *FRUS* 1949, 5: 239–40.

79. SD/A/C.1/221, n.d. [1950], Position Papers Maintained by the Executive Director, 1945–1974, Bureau of International Organization Affairs Records.

80. Ibid.

81. SD/A/C.1/206/Rev.1.; SD/A/C.1/258, September 4, 1949, Position Papers Maintained by the Executive Director, 1945–1974, Bureau of International Organization Affairs Records, RG59, NARA.

82. Stephen D. Kertesz, "Human Rights in the Peace Treaties," *Law and Contemporary Problems* 14, 4 (Autumn 1949): 631, 633.

83. Joseph S. Roucek, "The Bulgarian, Rumanian, and Hungarian Peace Treaties," *Annals of the American Academy of Political and Social Sciences* 257 (May 1948): 97; "Treaty of Peace with Hungary, 1947," *Journal of International Law* 42, 4 (1948): 225–51.

84. Most of the Minorities Treaties and clauses followed the precedent set by the Polish treaty. See "Treaty with Poland," June 28, 1919, reprinted in Jacob Robinson et al., *Were the Minorities Treaties a Failure?* (New York: Institute of Jewish Affairs of the American Jewish Congress, 1943), 313–17.

85. Carole Fink, *Defending the Rights of Others: The Great Powers, The Jews, and International Minority Protection, 1878–1938* (New York: Cambridge University Press, 2004), 363.

86. Ibid., 364.

87. SD/A/C.1/206/Rev.1.

88. Secretary of State to U.S. Mission to the UN, 10 March 1949, *FRUS*, 1949, 5: 237–38.

89. SD/A/C.1/221.

90. SD/A/C.1/206/Rev.1; Secretary of State to U.S. Mission to the UN, 10 March 1949, 238.

91. Yuen-Li Liang, "Observance in Bulgaria, Hungary and Rumania of Human Rights and Fundamental Freedoms: Request for an Advisory Opinion on Certain Questions," *American Journal of International Law* 44, 1 (January 1950): 101; Secretary of State to the Embassy in the United Kingdom, April 27, 1949, *FRUS* 1949, 5: 242; State Dept. Press Release No. 150, March 16, 1949, Box 32, Folder "Satellite Violations of Human Rights and Fundamental Freedoms (2 of 2)," Bureau of International Affairs, United Nations Delegation Position Papers and Background Books, 1945–1962, RG 59, NARA.

92. Both Australia and Cuba had originally submitted alternative draft resolutions, which were subsequently withdrawn in favor of a joint amendment to the Bolivian resolution. Colombia and Costa Rica also proposed an amendment that would have blocked the three Eastern European states from joining the UN, but withdrew it on a technicality. Secretary of State to the Embassy in the United Kingdom, 10 March 10, 1949, *FRUS* 1949, 5: 236; Liang, "Observance in Bulgaria, Hungary and Rumania," 102; SD/A/C.1/221.

93. Dean Acheson, "Abuse of Human Rights in Satellite States," *Department of State Bulletin* 23, 578 (July 31, 1950): 190-91; Liang, "Observance in Bulgaria, Hungary and Rumania," 109–10; see also *FRUS* 1949, 5: 246–66.

94. Liang, "Observance in Bulgaria, Hungary and Rumania," 112–17.

95. SD/A/C.1/258.

96. Liang, "Observance in Bulgaria, Hungary and Rumania," 113–14; Secretary of State to the Embassy in the United Kingdom, July 8, 1949, *FRUS* 1949, 5: 256–57.

97. "International Court Opens Hearings in Human-Rights Case," *Department of State Bulletin* 23, 579 (August 7, 1950): 234–35. The strained U.S. relationship with the ICJ is outlined in Denna Frank Fleming, *The United States and the World Court, 1920–1966* (New York: Russell & Russell, 1968).

98. "International Court Opens Hearings in Human-Rights Case," 234–25; Dean Acheson, "Abuse of Human Rights in Satellite States," *Department of State Bulletin* 23, 578 (July 31, 1950): 190-91.

99. Secretary of State to Embassy in the United Kingdom, August 28, 1950, *FRUS* 1950, 4: 54–55; SD/A/C.1/333, September 2, 1950, Box 22, Position Paper, Maintained by the Executive Director, 1945–1974, Records of the Bureau of International Organization Affairs and Its Predecessors, RG59, NARA. Although the 1975 Helsinki Accords were not a legally binding treaty, the inclusion of human rights provisions in the Accords—the so-called "Basket Three"—were critical to the collapse of Communist regimes in Eastern Europe and the Soviet Union. See Andrzej Rzeplinski, Wiktor Osiatynski, and Jiri Grusa, "The Internationalization of Human Rights," in *Human Rights in the Democracy Movement Twenty Years Ago—Human Rights Today*, ed. David Robert Evans and Ference Koszeg (Budapest: Hungarian Helsinki Committee, 2006), 102–16. Beth Simmons argues that between the 1950s and the 1970s increased democratization, greater accountability in international law, and expansion of transnational civil society led to greater effectiveness in enforcing human rights through international treaties. Beth A. Simmons, *Mobilizing for Human Rights: International Law in Domestic Politics* (New York: Cambridge University Press, 2009), 24.

100. U.S. Department of State, "Editorial Note," *FRUS* 1950, 4: 59.

101. Margaret E. Galey, "Congress, Foreign Policy and Human Rights Ten Years After Helsinki," *Human Rights Quarterly* 7, 3 (August 1985): 343; Kenneth Cmiel, "The Emergence of Human Rights Politics in the United States," *Journal of American History* 86, 3 (December 1999): 1235.

102. Jimmy Carter, "Inaugural Address," January 20, 1977, http://www.presidency. ucsb.edu/ws/index.php?pid=6575#axzz1RuNYgl1A, accessed 12 July 2011. On Carter and human rights, see generally David F. Schmitz and Venessa Walker, "Jimmy Carter and the Foreign Policy of Human Rights: The Development of a Post-Cold War Foreign Policy," *Diplomatic History* 28, 1 (January 2004): 113–44.

103. Quoted in John Richard Schmidhauser and Larry L. Berg, *The Supreme Court and Congress: Conflict and Interaction* (New York: Free Press, 1972), 99.

Conclusion: Toward Universal Rights

Epigraph: Charles Malik, "Will the Future Redeem the Past?" (address at Williamsburg, Va.: Colonial Virginia, Williamsburg, June 11, 1960), 7.

1. "U.N. Elects Malik Assembly Head," *New York Times*, September 17, 1958, 1; William Fulton, "Elect Malik U.N. Assembly Chief: Arab-Russian Bloc Beaten in 45–31 Vote," *Chicago Daily Tribune*, September 17, 1958, 1; "Lebanon's Malik Named to Head U.N. Assembly: Election of Prowestern Arab Leader over Soviet Bloc Objections Victory for U.S.," *Los Angeles Times*, September 17, 1958, 2; "New U.N. Assembly Head Strongly Pro-American," *Hartford Courant*, September 17, 1958, 6.

2. This reflection came in 1985 from former *Richmond New Leader* editor James J. Kilpatrick in *The Writer's Art* (Kansas City: Andrews McMeel, 1985). Robert J. Whalen, biographer of Joseph Kennedy and Republican political advisor, called the speech "one of the truly great addresses of the time," and M. Carl Andrews, editor of the *Roanoke World News*, compared Malik to Churchill and called the speech "one of the half-dozen greatest public addresses of our times." Robert J. Whalen, *Taking Sides: A Personal View of America from Kennedy to Nixon to Kennedy* (New York: Houghton Mifflin, 1974), 31; M. Carl Andrews, "A Statesman Shocks America with Challenge over Reds," *Roanoke World News*, June 14, 1960.

3. Anders Greenspan, *Creating Colonial Williamsburg* (Washington, D.C.: Smithsonian Institution Press, 2002), 95–100.

4. Andrews, "A Statesman Shocks America."

5. Malik, "Will the Future Redeem the Past?" 15.

6. Ibid. (emphasis original).

7. Ibid., 8.

8. "Oppression of Tibet: Communist China Charged with Use of Force and Terror," *New York Times*, November 8, 1960, 28; "Ecuador Asks U.N. Bid South Africa End Racial Curbs," *New York Times*, April 1, 1960, 1; "Text of Hammarskjold's Report to the U.N. on Lumumba's Arrest in the Congo," *New York Times*, December 6, 1960, 22.

9. Samuel Moyn, *The Last Utopia: Human Rights in History* (Cambridge, Mass.: Belknap Press of Harvard University Press, 2010), 81–83.

10. Ibid., 5, 80–81.

11. Malik, "Will the Future Redeem the Past?" 21. A few months after his speech, Malik received a letter from a Mrs. Marjorie T. Henry of San Jose, California, insisting that "freedom, justice, democratic government and advanced technology" all evolved over hundreds of years in the West and could not be simply transplanted elsewhere, particularly to Asia and Africa where they had proven incapable of achieving these things themselves. Perhaps only Communist dictatorships, she said, could sort out "the human ant heap" of China. Malik's response, polite to a fault, assured her that he, too, thought the West had incubated these ideals over a long history. "However," he continued, "I believe the Asians and Africans are human beings." Malik to Marjorie T. Henry, November 18, 1960, Folder 4, Box 23, Papers of Charles H. Malik.

12. "Johnson Assures Saigon of Aid in Army Build-Up," *New York Times*, May 12, 1961, 1.

13. Malik, "Will the Future Redeem the Past?" 21.

14. Judith Butler, "Restaging the Universal," in *Contingency, Hegemony, Universality:*

Contemporary Dialogues on the Left, ed. Judith Butler, Ernesto Laclau, and Slavoj Žižek (New York: Verso, 2000), 15.

15. Ibid.

16. Ernesto Laclau, "Constructing Universality," in Butler, Laclau, and Žižek, *Contingency, Hegemony, Universality*, 303–4.

17. Malik, "Will the Future Redeem the Past?" 22.

18. This process is, in fact, reflected in the growing UN human rights treaties series, which, in addition to the International Covenants, includes the Convention on the Political Rights of Women (1952), International Convention on the Elimination of All Forms of Racial Discrimination (1965), Convention on the Elimination of All Forms of Discrimination against Women (1979), Convention Against Torture and Other Cruel, Inhuman and Degrading Treatment or Punishment (1984), Convention on the Rights of the Child (1989), International Convention on the Protection of the Rights of All Migrant Workers and Members of Their Families (1990), Convention for the Protection of All Persons from Enforced Disappearances (2006), and Convention on the Rights of Persons with Disabilities (2006).

19. Writing to historian Stephen Hay in 1963 in an effort to arrange a meeting with Buber, Malik noted with uncharacteristic idolization, "It has been my desire ever since I read his *Ich und Du* before the Second World War to seek a meeting with Dr. Buber in order to sit at his feet." Malik to Stephen Hay, 8 August 1963, Box 23, Folder 1, Papers of Charles H. Malik. Tragically, just before their scheduled meeting at the end of June 1965, Buber died at his home in Jerusalem. Malik to Stephen Hay, July 2, 1965, Folder 1, Box 23.

20. See Martin Buber, *I and Thou*, trans. Ronald Gregor Smith (New York: Scribner, 2000).

Index

Acknowledgments

This book is the result of an embarrassment of riches. I have enjoyed the generous support of colleagues, friends, and family through the many years it has taken to bring this book to publication. I owe much and more to my colleagues at the University of Connecticut's Human Rights Institute for providing an unparalleled intellectual and institutional environment in which this work could flourish. In particular, I thank Alexis Dudden and Kerry Bystrom for bringing me to UConn as a fellow with the Foundations of Humanitarianism Program, and Richard Wilson, Eleni Coundouriotis, and Emma Gilligan for their ongoing support of my scholarship. I am particularly indebted to Brendan Kane for his sharp wit, keen sense of argument, and rigorous dedication to the craft of history.

At Claremont, I had the privilege of working closely with Henry Krips and John Seery, both of whom enriched and deepened my work. I also had the good fortune to have colleagues such as Sara Patterson, Karen Linkletter, Dan Cady, and Fay Botham, all of whom were tremendously inspiring as I worked to get this study off the ground. Most important, my time at Claremont was spent under the mentorship of Elazar Barkan, who not only provided a clear and consistent voice of reason, but also helped set me on the path to studying the history of human rights as one of the most compelling intellectual, political, and moral issues of our time.

My research was facilitated by the librarians and archivists at the Claremont Colleges Library, UCLA Young Research Library, University Library at the University of the Philippines, the Manuscripts Division of the Library of Congress, the National Archives and Records Administration, the New York Public Library, and the Roosevelt Presidential Library. Special thanks go to Habib C. Malik for permitting access to his father's papers at the Library of Congress.

I would like to thank Bert Lockwood, Pennsylvania Studies in Human

Rights series editor, for his early and loyal interest, and University of Pennsylvania Press Editor-in-Chief Peter Agree for his patient guidance through the long process of turning the manuscript into a book. Thanks as well to the anonymous readers of my early manuscript—their comments and criticisms were extraordinarily helpful and are, I hope, reflected in the final text.

Finally and most critically, I thank my friends and family, without whom no research would have been conducted and no book would have been written. My parents Marcia Corning Landsman and Michael Mitoma have been unfailingly enthusiastic about my late blooming academic avocation and I am grateful to them and my stepparents Rick Landsman and Anne Mitoma for their support. My sister Molly Mitoma has long been an invigorating intellectual presence in my life. I was particularly luck to have her as my copy editor as well. My dear friend Joel Schoening has, since age five, provided me with the most lucid, most productive, and most challenging conversations, which have informed in numerous ways my work as a scholar. My sons, Miles and Porter, have kept me grounded and hopeful from California to Connecticut. My incommensurable debt of gratitude to them and, at last and most of all, to Mia—for whom this book is dedicated—goes without saying.